The
COMPLETE
BOOK OF
Cheese

All photographs reproduced in this book are by Catherine Madani,
with the exception of the following:
p. 8 © Ventdusud/Shutterstock
p. 14 © Mazur Travel/Shutterstock
p. 21 © Choksawatdikorn/Shutterstock
p. 22 © Elina Litovkina/Shutterstock
p. 32 © Stockfour/Shutterstock
p. 171 © Elena Medoks/Shutterstock

Editorial Manager: Clelia Ozier-Lafontaine
Design and Typesetting: Alice Leroy

English Edition
Editorial Director: Kate Mascaro
Editor: Helen Adedotun
Translation from the French: Ansley Evans
Cover Design: Audrey Sednaoui
Copyediting: Wendy Sweetser
Proofreading: Nicole Foster
Indexing: Chris Bell
Production: Manon Pouch and Louisa Hanifi-Morard
Color Separation: IGS-CP, L'Isle d'Espagnac
Printed in Slovenia by DZS Grafik

Originally published in French as *Le Grand livre des fromages:
Histoire, techniques, recettes, conseils*
© Éditions Flammarion, Paris, 2023

English-language edition
© Éditions Flammarion, Paris, 2024

editions.flammarion.com
@flammarioninternational

24 25 26 3 2 1

ISBN: 978-2-08-044748-7

Legal Deposit: 10/2024

Anne-Laure Pham · Mathieu Plantive
Photography by Catherine Madani

The
COMPLETE
BOOK OF
Cheese

History, Techniques, Recipes, Tips

Flammarion

Contents

Introduction 7

A Brief History of Cheese 9

Cheeses from Around the World 15

Practical Guide
Ingredients 19
The Cheesemaking Process 33

Families of Cheese
Classifying Cheeses 41

Fresh Cheeses 43
Fromage Blanc & Co. 45
Feta & Co. 47
Mozzarella & Co. 51
Ricotta & Co. 57

Soft Cheeses 63
Chèvres & Co. 65
Chaource & Co. 69
Époisses & Co. 73
Brie & Co. 76
Munster & Co. 83
Vacherin & Co. 87
Gorgonzola & Co. 91
Roquefort & Co. 95
Cancoillotte & Co. 101

Semi-Soft & Semi-Hard Cheeses 105
Tomme de Savoie & Co. 107
Morbier & Co. 111
Gouda & Co. 115
Cantal & Co. 119
Cheddar & Co. 123
Stilton & Co. 127

Hard Cheeses 133
Gruyère & Co. 135
Abondance & Co. 141
Emmental & Co. 143
Grana & Co. 147
Pecorino & Co. 153
Provola & Co. 159

Tips

How to Buy Cheese with Confidence **164**
Cutting with Confidence **165**
Composing a Harmonious Cheese Board **166**
Tasting with All the Senses **168**
Choosing the Right Bread **170**
Pairing Cheese with Drinks **172**
Storing Cheese Correctly **175**
Cheese and Health: The Facts **175**

Recipes

Basic Recipes with Cheese **183**
Lyon-Style Herbed Cheese Spread **185**
Fresh Sheep's Milk Cheese Balls **187**
Baked Camembert **189**
Cheddar Crackers **190**
Smoked Mackerel and Fresh Cheese Dip **193**
Marinated Goat Cheese **195**
Fresh Cheese with Chili-Tahini Sauce **196**
Baked Mont d'Or **198**

Savory Recipes with Cheese **201**
Cheesy Mashed Potatoes **203**
Cheese-Filled Ravioli in Broth **204**
Spaghetti Carbonara **207**
Veal Cordon Bleu **209**
Maroilles Tart **210**
Smoked Scamorza Frittata **213**
Grilled Cheese Sandwich **215**
Georgian Cheese-Filled Bread **216**
Georgian Cheese and Herb-Stuffed
   Dumplings **218**
Mac and Cheese **221**
Breaded Fresh Goat Cheese with Spiced
   Quince Paste **223**
Brazilian Cheese Bread **224**
Spinach and Bell Pepper Pastilla **227**
Pesto **228**
Four-Cheese Pizza **231**
Quesadillas **233**
Brocciu-Stuffed Sardines **234**
Cheese Sauce **237**
Parmesan Soufflé **238**
Tartiflette **241**
Parmesan Tuiles **243**
Welsh Rarebit **244**
Fondue **247**
Raclette **249**
Red Kuri Squash Stuffed with Spelt
   and Cantal **250**
Puff Pastry Cheese Straws **253**

Sweet Recipes with Cheese **255**
Cheesecake **257**
Corsican Cheesecake **258**
Bengali Cheese Sweets **261**
Cheese Blintzes **262**
Tiramisu **265**
Gouda Nougat **266**
Turkish Sweet Cheese Pastry **269**
Fresh Tome Brioche **271**
Beaufort, Pear, and Ginger Crumble **272**
Ricotta Pancakes **275**
Crémet d'Anjou **276**
Swiss Chard Tart **279**

Appendixes

Glossary **281**
Bibliography **283**
Index **286**
Acknowledgments **288**

Introduction

What makes a really good cheese? We have set out to answer this question in the following pages, providing a range of clear, uncomplicated, and often amusing explanations.

Far from a convoluted, pretentious tale filled with folklore and chauvinism, this is a living, breathing, and realistic account of cheese.

In France, we revere cheese as a treasured part of our national heritage. As with wine, we feel we should all be connoisseurs, but cheesemaking is an ever-evolving craft. While based on ancient and time-honored know-how, cheesemaking is continually evolving around the world.

Many cheese lovers feel slightly guilty that they don't have an exhaustive knowledge of the beloved product. We witness this daily in our interactions with customers (coauthor Mathieu owns a cheese shop in the city of Nantes) and through our research or discussions (Anne-Laure, the other coauthor, has worked as a food journalist).

We love hearing the questions that we are asked by people of all backgrounds and generations. This is what spurred us to write this book, which is designed to provide readers with a solid grounding, particularly on the technical aspects of the subject—the key to a better understanding of the world of cheese. While it does not aim to be exhaustive, this book offers a practical and nuanced overview.

Enjoy this dairy-rich journey, friends!

Anne-Laure Pham and Mathieu Plantive

The official definition

What is cheese?
According to a French decree published on November 12, 2013, cheese is "a product that may or may not be fermented or aged, made with the following ingredients of dairy origin only, either alone or combined: whole, low-fat, or nonfat milk; cream; fat; and buttermilk. [These ingredients] may be fully or partially coagulated, either before being drained or after partially eliminating the whey.... There must be a minimum of 23 g of dry matter per 100 g of cheese."

In light of this very formal and precise description, this book is more indispensable than ever!

A Brief History of Cheese

Cheesemaking began with the domestication of certain animal species. After dogs, small ruminants, including goats and sheep, were domesticated from 10,000 BCE. These animals enabled humans to benefit from vegetation that they could not consume themselves, such as grasses and shrubs. While humans provided protection, the animals supplied milk, meat, wool, hide, and bones. Eight thousand years ago, having gained experience with goats and sheep, humans domesticated the cow's wild ancestor, the aurochs, in Mesopotamia (modern-day Iraq). Since then, each generation has selected and bred the most docile, fastest-growing animals with females that produce the most milk.

As milk sours naturally, fermented milk was likely the first dairy product that humans learned to make and consume. Fermenting was a way to keep milk for longer and make it digestible for adult humans, who did not yet produce lactase and were thus lactose intolerant. Horses, camels, and yaks were also domesticated in many areas of the Middle East, India, and China for their milking and, later, cheesemaking potential.

The earliest traces of cheesemaking, found in Poland, date from the Neolithic era (5000 BCE). Traces of fermented dairy products have also been found at several sites in northern Europe, dating from 6000 BCE, and in Egypt and Mesopotamia, dating from 3000 BCE. Some experts believe that our ancestors accidentally discovered the coagulating properties of animal rennet while transporting milk in bags made of dried calves' or lambs' stomachs. However, contrary to conventional wisdom, this was not the only way early humans made the first cheeses, as specialists have found traces of ruminant milk fermented not with rennet but with kefir on a Chinese mummy dating from 2000 BCE. This starter culture of bacteria, yeasts, and carbohydrates launches the fermentation process in milk or sweetened water. Cheesemaking techniques were subsequently perfected and spread due to invasions and other forms of migration. This was particularly true in Europe during the Roman Empire between 27 BCE and 476 CE.

During the Middle Ages, European monastic orders—particularly the Benedictines—had a significant influence on agriculture. To reclaim land for farming, they undertook major works to drain wetlands in rural areas. The monks made cheeses to conserve the milk they received as tithes and these are mentioned in abbey records.

A vital way to preserve milk

Cheesemaking also developed on farms, where it was an important food source for families. In fact, for a long time cheese was only consumed in rural households. Little by little, farmers began to collaborate and set up communal facilities, such as early *fruitières*—cooperative cheesemaking houses that first appeared in Jura villages in the thirteenth century.

The same occurred in the medieval Middle East, where cattle, sheep, and goats, as well as donkeys and camels, were used for milk. Dairy products were an essential staple in rural areas, especially those near grazing lands. Textual sources from the period attest to a wide variety of milk-based foods.

In both Europe and the Middle East, cheese was mainly made on farms up until the nineteenth century. As geographer Claire Delfosse explains in her book *La France fromagère (1850–1990)*, cheese was the fruit of domestic labor, intended for the family's own consumption and a way for them to exploit the resources at hand to achieve self-sufficiency.

Milk microbiology

In the late nineteenth century, advances in science and technology enriched the art of cheesemaking. In a crucial discovery, the French scientist Louis Pasteur and one of his students, Émile Duclaux, came to understand the role of cultures and the fermentation process. Pierre Mazé, a student of Duclaux, developed cultures for soft cheeses such as Brie and Camembert. Other significant inventions of the time include the characteristic Camembert box; parchment paper for packaging; mechanized brushes and needles for Roquefort; and a machine for molding *bondons*—small fresh cheeses which were the forerunners of today's Petit Suisse, created by Étienne Pommel and Charles Gervais. In 1874, the Danish pharmacist Christian D. A. Hansen extracted and stabilized rennet for the cheesemaking industry that kept well and had uniform strength (see Rennet, p. 27). This made it possible for producers to obtain reliably consistent results.

THE BIRTH OF PASTEURIZATION

In the early nineteenth century, the French inventor Nicolas Appert discovered how to extend the shelf life of perishable liquids by filling bottles to the brim, sealing them hermetically, and heating them in a hot-water bath. Later, Louis Pasteur and his team studied Appert's technique and in 1865 filed the first patent for the process, called pasteurization. Among the benefits, this improved milk storage time and helped to eradicate two milk-borne bacterial diseases: brucellosis and tuberculosis. Today, these diseases are regularly monitored in domestic animals in many countries including France, the UK, and the US; while brucellosis has been mostly eliminated in these countries, tuberculosis is still present, although cases are extremely rare.

Cheesemaking industries emerged, linking production areas with consumers elsewhere. This was especially the case for Camembert (made with milk from Normande cows) and Brie (made with milk from Flemish and Dutch cows), which became popular among Parisians. *Fruitières*—cooperative cheesemaking houses—opened in the Jura and Savoie regions to produce cooked pressed Alpine cheeses with Pie Rouge cow's milk—a savoir faire shared among cheesemakers in France and Switzerland. Roquefort developed in the Les Causses region, with its famed natural caves and milk from the local Lacaune sheep, although milk from Pyrenees and Corsica sheep was later permitted as well, to satisfy popular demand for the cheese.

"Safe" cheeses

During this period, the first herdbooks were published, first in England and then throughout Europe. These official records of breed pedigrees were initially intended for the sale of breeding stock, but the idea of improving breeds to make them more productive soon arose. The dairy industry expanded after World War I, while small-scale local cheese production on family farms declined and many cheeses disappeared. Langres, Livarot, and Pont-l'Évêque were essentially supplanted by Camembert. Other cheeses appeared that were considered reliable, consistent, and "safe" to eat, and these new products benefitted from innovations in marketing, including consumer advertising. In the early 1900s, for instance, "Fromage moderne" hit the shelves, and this popular processed cheese was later renamed La Vache qui Rit (The Laughing Cow). Repeating a similar pattern, the industrially produced Saint Paulin was inspired by the original monastic recipe for Port Salut. Some cheeses were now made just about everywhere, with no regard for terroir. As cheese production increased, and national and international trade grew, so did the number of imitations and competitor takeovers. In 1925, Roquefort became the first cheese protected by law.

Protecting cheesemaking traditions at home and abroad

At the end of World War II, much of Europe was left hungry. To address food shortages, the Common Agricultural Policy (CAP) was introduced in Europe in 1962. At the same time, the so-called "Green Revolution" was underway, transforming farming systems worldwide with new methods (the use of fertilizers, pesticides, and machinery); new science (genetic improvements); and new health and safety measures. Meanwhile, cheese-producing countries continued efforts to protect their products and expertise from being copied within and beyond their borders. A first international agreement was reached at the Stresa Convention in 1951 on the shores of Lake Maggiore in northern Italy. Signed by just eight European countries, this agreement restricted the use of appellations of origin and cheese denominations. Participating countries agreed to protect a number of cheeses, including Roquefort, Camembert, Brie, and Saint Paulin in France; Pecorino Romano, Fontina, Fiore Sardo, and provolone in Italy; and Emmental and Sbrinz in Switzerland.

After 1960, larger amounts of milk could be processed using increasingly efficient production methods. A process used by Eastern European manufacturer Stein-Hutin made it possible to produce a steady supply of soft cheeses and to transport milk from increasingly distant collection points. At the same time in France, milk collection rates increased 200 percent in twenty-five years between the 1960s and 1980s.

Resistance from farmstead and artisan producers

The growth of large-scale dairy companies continued to put a strain on traditional cheesemaking areas in France. Large companies bought up smaller, family-run operations, and cheese production shifted to western France, which was a more productive and competitive region. The big dairy group Entremont, for instance, opened a factory in the Morbihan region in 1966 to produce Emmental, which had traditionally been made in Switzerland. Farmstead and artisan producers resisted the trend, particularly in mountainous areas, and sought to protect their unique traditions:

- Beaufort producers formed a cooperative and obtained recognition for their cheesemaking expertise and the local breed, the Tarine cow, via an AOC in 1968.
- Producers in Aubrac also formed a cooperative, Jeune Montagne, and obtained an AOC for Laguiole cheese in 1961 that also safeguarded the Aubrac cattle breed.
- The producers of picodon—a seasonal goat cheese made around the Rhône Valley in southern France—did the same, obtaining an AOC in 1983. Specifications allow the curds to be frozen for year-round production.

The advent of the European Free Trade Association (EFTA) in the 1960s opened up a new market for the French dairy industry. In the early 1980s, Germany became the second largest exporter of dairy products, after France.

Cheese produced anywhere using standardized milk

The introduction of European milk quotas in 1984 forced major dairy companies to focus on high-value-added products like cheese. After this, large-scale producers—private companies and cooperatives—opened factories all over France and abroad. In the 1980s, cheese with a long shelf life and little or no odor took over supermarket shelves. It could be produced anywhere using standardized milk and eaten anywhere, too. Among the industrially produced cheeses, fresh cheese was the most popular category in France in 1991.

The European Union sought to protect consumers with strict health and safety regulations, but it also recognized regional specificities, including the use of raw milk. After all, in 1991, French raw-milk cheeses accounted for a quarter of total cheese sales in the country. In 1992, the European Union harmonized the appellation system and created the Appellation d'Origine Protégée (AOP) label in French (PDO in English, DOP in Spanish and Italian, and so on), which replaced the France-based Appellation d'Origine Contrôlée (AOC).

Revival and standardization

At the same time, consumers once again took an interest in the concepts of local, traditional, and terroir. They discovered—or rediscovered—local farmstead and artisanal cheeses, which experienced a renaissance:
- Producers revived certain cheeses that had all but disappeared, including Banon, from the Alpes-de-Haute-Provence region.
- The production of other cheeses was "re-localized." This was the case for Époisses, for instance, as many imitations were being made outside its birthplace, the Pays d'Auxois in Burgundy.
- Regions began to see cheese as a means to promote themselves, such as Poitou with its AOP cheese, Chabichou du Poitou.

ORGANIZATIONS DEFENDING APPELLATIONS AROUND THE GLOBE
The appellation, or designation of origin, system is important for producers to stake their claim amid international trade regulations and protect their intellectual property rights worldwide. Several organizations champion the system, including:
• Organization for an International Geographical Indications Network (oriGIn), a global alliance of Geographical Indications (GI) producers that advocates for GI protection worldwide and promotes GI recognition in developing countries, to leverage the value of local resources and fight poverty.
• Slow Food, a global movement in support of Geographical Indications that was created to counter fast-food culture and the standardization of taste worldwide, and to promote the benefits of eating locally. Preserving local culinary traditions and diversity around the globe are critical components of the Slow Food mission. Through initiatives like the global Terra Madre network of small-scale farmers, the biennial Cheese event, and the Presidia program, Slow Food has bolstered many AOC and raw-milk cheeses as well as products without official labels.

Despite this revival, cheese production remains highly standardized due to multiple factors, from the codification of production processes, to the use of commercial cultures, to the numerous imitations of well-known cheeses. The cheesemaking landscape has become more complex and nuanced as industrial manufacturers make their own versions of "traditional" cheeses, and farmstead cheesemakers reappropriate heritage breeds and ancient savoir faire. Major dairy companies continue to have a stranglehold on the market, pressuring regulatory agencies to allow more flexible production methods within the AOPs. In response, AOP specifications became even more restrictive in the 2000s.

Today, the new AOPs are increasingly so-called "niche" products that reflect the philosophy of the Slow Food movement's Presidia: foods produced on a small scale that protect "traditional and artisanal products at risk of disappearing." Established in the 1980s in Italy, Slow Food aims to preserve local culinary traditions and reduce the environmental impact of food production (see Organizations Defending Appellations Around the Globe, p. 12). Several time-honored European cheesemaking techniques have been revived to create new cheeses, such as:
- The use of indigenous cultures by a handful of producers in France, Italy, and elsewhere.
- The use of plant-based rennet to transform the milk of local Girgentana goats into cheese by producers in Sicily.
- The preservation of breeds that have faced or could face extinction, through emblematic dairy products including Salers Tradition AOP cheese, made with milk from Salers cows; sheep's milk tommes "*d'estive*," made in summer with milk from pastured Manech Tête Noire sheep in the Basque Country; Brousse du Rove AOP, made with milk from Rove goats; and Gwell, fermented milk sourced from Bretonne Pie Noir cows.

FERMIER, ARTISANAL, AND INDUSTRIAL: CHEESE PRODUCTION IN FRANCE
• The use of the term *fermier* to refer to cheese is regulated by French law and means the cheese has been made by the farmer on the farm where the milk is produced. "Farmstead" and "farmhouse" are English equivalents.
• *Artisanal* refers to cheeses made from the milk of one or more herds, usually raised close to the processing site. Artisans, rather than the farmers themselves, process the milk and produce the cheese on a small scale.
• Industrial describes cheeses produced on a large scale, often using pasteurized milk. The production chain is automated.

Cheeses from Around the World

Cheese is made all over the globe, offering a wealth of aromas, flavors, and textures. France is famed for its stunning array of *fromages* and its variety of cheesemaking techniques, but the product is far from being a uniquely French specialty. There is much to discover and taste beyond the country's borders, so let's take a world tour around this delectable universe.

France boasts an incredible variety of different climates—from oceanic and continental to alpine and Mediterranean—as well as landscapes, including wooded plains, high-mountain pastures, and arid scrubland. Around the country, farmers raise many different types of livestock that are best suited to each terrain. As a result, the country has a great diversity of milk-producing breeds, cheesemaking practices, and cheeses, from mass-produced to micro-batch varieties. Some producers maintain traditional techniques, while others have revived them, either crafting time-honored cheeses—such as Brousse du Rove, Beaufort Chalet d'Alpage, and sheep's milk tommes in the Basque Country—or creating new ones.

Italy is another fabled cheese country with an ancient pedigree and a wide range of terroirs, from the high Alps and the rich Po Valley in the north to the lower-lying Apennines and the Mediterranean south. There is not a strong tradition for producing soft-type or blue cheeses (except for Gorgonzola), but rather thousands of variations of hard cheeses, *pasta filata* (stretched-curd) cheeses, and ricottas. Italy produces many excellent cheeses following well-preserved traditions.

On the **Iberian Peninsula**, Spanish cheesemakers transform milk from cows in the northwest and from sheep and goats just about everywhere else into a diverse range of cheeses. Beyond the famed Manchego and other well-known types, there are also many lesser-known gems. Portugal produces many soft, creamy cheeses that are still made with vegetable rennet.

In the **Netherlands**, one of Europe's biggest milk producers, Gouda dominates the cheesemaking landscape. Whether produced on a large or artisanal scale, a significant proportion of this well-known cheese is exported.

Germany is Europe's largest milk producer and exports more milk and cheese than any other European nation. In Bavaria, the main cheese-producing and exporting region, pressed cheeses are the main specialty.

The tradition of cheesemaking virtually disappeared in the **British Isles** when the production of Cheddar was industrialized after World War II. More recently, however, an artisanal and farmstead cheese renaissance has gained momentum once again.

In **Scandinavia**, producers reduce whey to make the dense, slightly sweet "brown cheese," or brunost, as it is called in Norway. The Iranian qaraqurut is made similarly.

← Sulguni, a Georgian cheese

Cheesemakers in the **Balkans, Greece, Turkey, Cyprus, and Malta** transform primarily sheep and goat's milk into highly prized fermented milks and cheeses, including a significant number of stretched-curd and brined varieties. "Eastern Europe has centuries of gastronomic traditions," recalled Piero Sardo, president of the Slow Food Foundation for Biodiversity, during a Milk Workshop at the foundation's 2013 Cheese event. Today, southeastern Europe faces a number of challenges, including badly damaged roads and limited access to running water and electricity in rural areas. Soviet occupation also left a traumatic mark on the population, and many cheesemakers still refuse to collectivize their production tools. As a result, cheese consumption remains very much a local, family affair.

A few of the local specialties that have been mapped by the Slow Food Foundation are:
- Albanian Mishavin: crumbled, salted, and fermented curds made in the fall.
- Bulgarian Tulum: cheese made with milk from the native Karakachan sheep.
- Macedonian Bieno Sirenje: a salty cheese with an elastic texture.
- Romanian Branza de Burduf: a sheep's milk cheese made in the Bucegi Mountains and aged in fir bark.

In **Morocco, Algeria, and Tunisia,** the following cheeses are particularly popular:
- Jben or killa: fresh cheese made with raw sheep or goat's milk coagulated with thistle flowers.
- Rayeb and lebne: two types of fermented cow's milk served chilled.
Camel's milk is still widely consumed raw in pastoral areas throughout the region, although transforming it into cheese is a relatively recent enterprise. The United Nations Food and Agriculture Organization (FAO) launched the initiative in the 1980s, without much success.

On the rest of the **African continent,** cheese production remains artisanal and highly localized, limited by the extreme climatic conditions and a lack of cheesemaking traditions. Yet shepherds crossing the grazing lands from the Sahel to Kenya's Rift Valley have long used the milk from their herds, either drinking it fresh or turning it into yogurt.

In the **Middle East,** goat's and sheep's milk are most typically consumed in fermented form, either strained (labneh) or diluted and salted (ayran). Fresh cheeses in brine are also popular, as are stretched-curd cheeses.

Here is an overview of the top favorites by country, bearing in mind that many specialties have different variations throughout the region:
- **Lebanon:** Several fermented milks (such as labneh); halloum or halloumi (a cheese made with sheep's and/or goat's milk with a slightly elastic texture, which is often served grilled).
- **Turkey:** Ayran (fermented milk diluted with water); beyaz peynir (a pressed fresh cheese akin to feta).
- **Iraq:** Jameed (very dense salted yogurt shaped into balls and typically dried in the sun); qaraqurut (concentrated fermented buttermilk); rowqan (clarified butter).
- **Saudi Arabia:** Jibneh arabieh (a feta-style cheese); baladi (reminiscent of mozzarella).
- **Iran:** rowqan (clarified butter); panir (a brined feta-style cheese); doogh (a yogurt drink); qaraqurut (concentrated fermented buttermilk).

In **Russia,** the cheesemaking industry is concentrated in the country's center and is mainly dedicated to cooked and uncooked pressed cheeses, including national favorites like Kostromskoy, Uglichsky, and Poshekhonsky. Russians also make Gouda and other cheeses of Dutch (Gollandsky) and Swiss (Shveytsarsky) inspiration.

In **Central and East Asia,** the techniques are simpler. The main dairy products consumed in this part of the world include:
- Butter, which is generally clarified for a longer shelf life.
- Fermented milks and other products made with cow's, yak's, or mare's milk, such as airag (as fermented mare's milk is known in Mongolia) and kefir (the cow's milk equivalent).

Either fermented milk or buttermilk may also be boiled, strained, and dried in the sun to form small, hard balls that can be used in cooking or slowly chewed for hours, such as kurut. A staple of Central Asian herders for centuries, these dried milk balls are reminiscent of the Iraqi jameed. Nomadic peoples in these regions who kept many cows were able to produce cheese from a very early date.

Here is a selection of Central and East Asian specialties:
- **Georgia:** Imeruli (similar to mozzarella); sulguni (made from cow's, goat's or buffalo's milk and also similar to mozzarella).
- **Armenia:** Tan (a drink similar to ayran); feta- and halloumi-style cheeses.
- **India** (the world's leading milk producer) and **Pakistan:** Ghee (clarified butter); paneer (a fresh curd cheese); lassi (a fermented milk drink).
- **The Himalayas:** Yak butter; dried cheeses made of skimmed or fermented milk and shaped like small pebbles.
- **China:** Fermented milk, but also, in the Yunnan province, near Mongolia, rubing (a cheese made with cow's or goat's milk that is boiled and acidified with dried vine stems and leaves); rushan (a fan-shaped cheese made with cow's milk curds that are stretched and pulled from a wok with chopsticks).
- **Indonesia:** Dangke (a buffalo's milk cheese coagulated with papaya sap and wrapped in banana leaves).

- In Australasia, there are few long-standing cheesemaking traditions. **Australia** produces large amounts of Cheddar, in particular for export to Asia. In **New Zealand,** the world's leading dairy exporter, most milk is transformed into powder, although Cheddar is also very popular.

In the **United States**—a huge milk producer and the world's largest cheese exporter—Cheddar (once again) is the leading cheese produced, and hard cheeses are generally the most popular. Among the exceptions is Monterey Jack, a soft, creamy cow's milk cheese that, when aged, is reminiscent of Parmesan. However, in the last fifteen years or so, there has been a boom in high-quality, artisanal cheesemaking and there are many gems to discover, from copies of classic European cheeses to unique varieties.

In **South America,** cheese production remains highly localized. Minas, a cow's milk cheese made in the Brazilian state of Minas Gerais, is one such hyperlocal product. Recently, interest has grown in the use of raw milk, which was previously prohibited.

Practical Guide

Ingredients

Milk, the source of (almost) everything

What is milk?

Beyond containing about 80 percent water, milk is also composed of dry matter or solids, including protein (casein), minerals, sugar (lactose), fat, and vitamins. By law in France, the word "*lait*" (milk) can only be used to describe a product that is "secreted from mammary glands and obtained by one or more milkings, with nothing added or removed." If the product has "undergone treatment that has not changed its composition" or "its fat content has been standardized," it may still be called *lait*. In the US and UK, however, there have been rulings allowing the use of the term "milk" for plant-based milks.

When the word "milk" is used alone, with no indication of the animal species, it designates cow's milk. Otherwise, the animal must be specified, whether it be a goat, sheep, donkey, or another dairy-producing species. Cow's milk is the most commonly consumed type in the Western world, whereas other countries and regions have different dairy traditions based on the livestock most suited to their climate and terrain, from goats or sheep to buffalo, camels, yaks, mares, elk, reindeer, and even zebu.

What is milk made of?

Milk composition varies from animal species to species. The following figures are averages, as the numbers differ according to—among other things—the season and the animal's diet, its breed, age, and parity (the number of times it has given birth). The fat content shows the most variation. The milks below contain the following components in addition to water.

Cow's milk

Cow's milk contains about 3.5 percent protein, 4 percent fat, and 5 percent lactose, but this varies from breed to breed. Often consumed in liquid form—either fresh or fermented—cow's milk is also used to make cheese, butter, and cream.

Goat's milk

Goat's milk is similar to cow's, with 3 percent protein, 4.2 percent fat, and 4 percent lactose. The milk is always white because goats do not accumulate the carotene in the grass, so it does not take on a yellow hue in spring as cow's and sheep's milk do. In Africa and South Asia, goat's milk is usually consumed raw or fermented. Elsewhere, it is typically made into cheese.

Sheep's (ewe's) milk

Sheep's milk is richer in fat than cow's and goat's milk. It is also packed with lactose and protein, making it a perfect candidate for making yogurt and cheese.

Buffalo's milk

Containing 9 percent fat, buffalo's milk is twice as rich as cow's milk. It also has an abundance of casein and calcium. This is a perfect combination for making cheese, such as the renowned mozzarella di bufala. Like goat's milk, buffalo's milk remains pure white.

Yak's milk

An essential food in the Central Asian highlands, yak's milk, like buffalo's milk, is rich in fat and protein. Sweet in taste, it is often consumed raw, mainly in tea, but it is also fermented and transformed into cheese and butter. The latter is used to make the famous Tibetan butter tea, *po cha*, that is served throughout the day.

Camel's milk

Camel's milk is saltier and richer in vitamin C than other milks. It can be consumed raw or fermented.

Horse (mare's) and donkey's milk

Horse and donkey's milk are similar in composition to human milk, with little fat and protein. They contain even less casein but are still rich in lactose. They are generally consumed in fermented form and are not suitable for cheesemaking.

> **WHY IS MILK WHITE?**
> If milk contains about 80 percent water, what gives it its characteristic white color? The fat and protein in milk refract light, making the liquid opaque. Milks with less protein, such as human milk, are nearly transparent, while fat-rich milks have a yellow hue. A milk's color also depends on the animal's ability to convert the beta-carotene—a red-orange pigment found in fresh grass—into colorless vitamin A. Goats and buffaloes process nearly all the beta-carotene, hence their pure white milk. In contrast, some pastured cattle breeds process little, producing milk that is ivory-colored.

Why is the milk from some animals used for cheesemaking, and not from others?

Milk only comes from mammals, a large animal group encompassing a wide range of creatures from moles, dogs, hares, and bats, to rats, pangolins, elephants, and sperm whales. All mammals feed their young with milk produced by the female's mammary glands. Before the notion of milk-collecting or cheesemaking came about, certain species had to be domesticated. Early humans selected the most docile animals that were best suited to their lifestyles, whether nomadic or sedentary, and their terrains, from prairies to cultivated fields. Eventually, humans began to select individual varieties according to criteria specific to each region and breeder. Much later, in the late nineteenth century, this concern for selection and pedigree led to the creation of the first herdbooks: official records of recognized cattle breeds and their descendants. After World War II, the modernization of agriculture and technical progress in the dairy industry pushed many farmers to replace local breeds with more productive and economically viable ones.

Cattle breeds

Today, a small number of cattle breeds dominate the market, and many have disappeared. Yet numerous breeders worldwide are working to preserve or revive traditional breeds. On an international scale, Holsteins (Fresians) are omnipresent—they can be found on every continent, either purebred or crossed with local breeds. Holsteins are the highest-yielding breed in France, producing over 2,000 gallons (9,000 liters) of

milk per year; they are mainly found in the western part of the country. A Holstein's life expectancy is generally short on intensive farms, averaging no more than three lactation periods. Seemingly omnipresent, Holsteins are raised in different farming systems and their milk used to make a wide variety of world-famous cheeses, including Brie de Meaux, Parmigiano Reggiano, Swiss Gruyère, and Cheddar.

Other cattle breeds are better adapted to specific environments. Although they may produce less milk, it is of higher quality and particularly suitable for cheesemaking. Here are some examples:

- In France, Montbéliarde cows produce over 1,800 gallons (7,000 liters) of milk annually. Primarily found in mountainous areas, the breed is used to make cheeses including Comté, Morbier, Mont d'Or, Saint-Nectaire, Cantal, reblochon, Abondance, Munster, and Langres. This is the top breed among French AOP cheeses.
- Normande cattle come in a close second in terms of sheer numbers and performance. The breed is particularly suited to landscapes with hedgerows, orchards, woodlands, and heath, such as those found in western France. Normande milk is used to make Camembert, Pont-l'Évêque, Livarot, and Neufchâtel.
- Milk from Brune cattle is used to make Époisses in France and Parmesan and Gorgonzola in Italy. In their native Switzerland, Brunes are raised to make several renowned cheeses.
- Other dairy breeds are strongly linked to specific terroirs or cheeses, including Abondance and Tarinem (or Tarentaise) cows, which are emblematic in Savoie; Brunes, indissociable from Époisses; Simmentals, which are used for Laguiole and Langres; and Vosgiennes, used for Munster.
- Finally, some breeds have been saved from extinction and continue to be raised for cheesemaking purposes. These include the Salers cow, whose milk is used to make the AOP cheese Salers Tradition, and several Breton breeds—Bretonne Pie Noir, Froment du Leon, Ferrandaise, and Flamande—which are maintained by a handful of passionate breeder-cheesemakers. Other such breeds include Bianca Modenese, used for Parmigiano Reggiano; Podolica, for burrata; and Gloucester, whose milk goes into Stinking Bishop cheese, a soft cheese with a very strong aroma, as its name implies. These breeds produce little milk (less than 800 gallons/3,000 liters per year—three to four times less than a Holstein), but the quality is extraordinary.

Sheep breeds

Important milking breeds include Lacaune sheep in France, which are used to make Roquefort; Manchega sheep in Spain, which are used for Manchego; and Sarda in Italy, whose milk goes into Pecorino Romano. Through selective breeding, Lacaune ewes now produce up to about 100 gallons (350 liters) of milk annually. The results have been far more modest with the Corsican and Manech Tête Noire sheep, which are both well suited to their respective territories. These produce between 40–50 gallons (150–180 liters) of milk annually. Other examples among the many breeds found throughout the Mediterranean include Entrefina and Merina sheep, whose milk is used to make Torta del Casar in Extremadura, Spain, and the Bordaleira sheep in the Serra da Estrela mountains in Portugal, used for Serra da Estrela cheese.

Goat breeds

Alpine and Saanen goats, originally from the Alps, are the main goat breeds in France, and their milk can be found in most French AOP goat cheeses. Quite similar, they both produce around 300 gallons (1,000 liters) of milk per year. The few other goat breeds in France include Poitevine goats, found in western France; Rove goats, used to make Brousse du Rove, which recently obtained AOP certification; and Pyrenean goats, which graze in summer pastures after the sheep have moved on. Breeds found elsewhere in Europe include Murciano-Granadina in Murcia and Andalusia, Spain; Toggenburg in Switzerland; Skopelos in Greece; and the remarkable, yet endangered Girgentana in Sicily. Like sheep, goats can be found in many parts of the Mediterranean, but the breed standards are not always clearly defined.

No milk without calves, kid goats, or lambs

Milk (or cheese) cannot be produced unless female milk producers give birth. The gestation periods for common dairy animals are as follows:
- Buffalo: about ten months
- Cows: about nine months
- Sheep (ewe): about five months
- Goats: about five months

Cows and buffaloes are capable of breeding throughout the year. On farms, births are staggered to obtain milk at the right times, either to maintain a more or less constant volume throughout the year, or according to the market or grass availability. With goats and sheep, it's a little more complicated. They are seasonal breeders, meaning the females reach peak fertility at a particular time of year, usually in the fall when a decrease in daylight makes them go into heat. Does or ewes bred in September or October will kid or lamb in February or March, corresponding to the end of winter and the time when new vegetation appears. While this is true in France, daylight hours vary less with the seasons nearer the Equator. In the Mediterranean region, the seasonal effect is less marked, with natural births occurring in the fall and others in the spring. Breeders adjust the reproduction cycles of their animals according to different parameters, including the amount of milk needed and forage availability.

WHAT IS OUT-OF-SEASON BREEDING?

This entails breeding female goats and sheep (ewes) outside their natural heat period. Some goat breeders do this to have kid goats in the fall and milk in winter. Several out-of-season breeding techniques exist, including hormone (prohibited in organic farming) and light treatments. The latter technique tricks goats by exposing them to artificial light in late winter and then gradually reducing their exposure to light, so they think it's fall in the spring. Females then naturally go into heat. For sheep, the "buck effect" is more commonly used: after isolating males and females for a period of time, breeders place ewes in contact with bucks, triggering the heat cycle.

Good feed equals good milk

The food that animals eat is crucial to the quality of their milk. Most dairy comes from ruminants: animals that can draw nourishment from plants that humans cannot digest. Cows and sheep are grazers and essentially eat grass, while goats are browsers. Although they will eat grass, goats prefer leaves from trees and shrubs, as well as herbs, which they select as they go. In the past, dairy cows were exclusively grass-fed, eating fresh grass in pastures during the warmer months and hay in winter. However, intensive methods pushed dairy farmers to produce more and more milk, and feeding with silage—green forage preserved by fermentation and stored in silos—became more widespread. Cows enjoy eating this type of feed, which is also more energy-dense than grass.

More than just grass

In their search for the optimal feed, some dairy farmers began to use corn silage, too, which has an even greater concentration of sugars than other types. In such intensive production systems, the cows' diet is unbalanced, so farmers also give them pellets made with soy or other ingredients for protein. This practice is not limited to cows alone as, today, the vast majority of dairy goats do not leave the barn and are fed hay, pellets, and even silage. As for sheep, silage is authorized in certain appellations, including Ossau-Iraty and Roquefort. The main concern with silage-based diets is that they are generally too nutrient-dense, which ends up tiring the animals out. As a result, the animals do not live as long, so herds must be renewed more frequently. These diets also impact cheesemaking, especially if the milk is used raw. For example, the potential presence of butyric acid bacteria spores in the milk can cause problems in the cheesemaking process, which is why using silage as feedstock is prohibited in many PDO cheese regulations. For industrial dairy production, milk is sourced from many farms. Some farmers very likely work with small herds of pasture-fed local breeds, while others keep their Holsteins in confined lots (no grazing), feeding them a silage-based diet. Between the two extremes, there are countless variations in practices.

Cultures

Most cheeses begin with fermented milk that is transformed in myriad ways through other types of fermentation. To make all the different kinds of cheeses, cheesemakers use different starter and ripening cultures.

Typically the first step in cheesemaking, known as lactic acid fermentation, occurs when voracious bacteria present in the milk—native and/or added—consume the sugar (lactose), and transform it into lactic acid. This acidifies the milk and causes the protein—casein—to coagulate. These microbes perform invaluable work that influences the flavor and texture of the final cheese. Later, the yeast family will also come into play during salting and the early ripening stage.

> **FERMENTATION-FREE**
> Certain cheeses that are eaten fresh do not need to be inoculated with starter cultures. This is the case for brousse, mascarpone, and some industrial cheeses, such as the mozzarella family, which may be acidified with citric acid or vinegar. So, these cheeses do not undergo fermentation.

Discovering bacteria and fungi

What causes this acidification? The friendly genera of lactic acid bacteria, including *Streptococcus*, *Lactobacillus*, *Enterococcus*, and *Leuconostoc*. All temperature-dependent, some of these bacteria thrive at temperatures between 68°F and 104°F (20°C–40°C) and "naturally contaminate" the milk and curds. Others prefer to get to work when the temperature is over 104°F (40°C).

> **RICH RAW MILK**
> Raw milk contains up to 400 different species of microorganisms, providing a greater variety than those found in pasteurized milk. That's quite a family!

Other types of microorganisms are involved throughout the cheesemaking process. These include:

Bacteria responsible for the holes in some cheeses

Certain *Leuconostocs* create the holes—technically known as "eyes"—in some cheeses and allow for the development of blue veins in Roquefort and its cousins.

Dairy propionibacteria

Used as ripening cultures in the production of Emmental cheese, they degrade lactic acid, contributing to "eye" or hole formation and giving such cheeses their characteristic flavor.

Flavor- and aroma-boosting bacteria

Lactobacilli are responsible for the characteristic flavors of Cheddar and Gruyère cheeses, while *Brevibacterium linens* impart an earthy aroma and red-orange hue to many soft cheeses, including Livarot, Époisses, and Brie, as well as hard cheeses like Abondance and L'Étivaz.

Yeasts and molds

Mainly found on the surface of cheeses, yeasts and molds digest lactic acid and make cheese less acidic, particularly during the salting and ripening phases.

A star in this category, the fungi species *Geotrichum candidum* is responsible for the wrinkled rind of goat cheeses and many other soft, surface-ripened varieties. Other noteworthy types are:
- *Penicillium camemberti*, which produces the powdery white surfaces of bloomy-rind cheeses such as Camembert.
- *Penicillium roqueforti*, responsible for the blue veins in many blue cheeses.
- *Penicillium glaucum*, used to produce the blue veins in Gorgonzola and Bleu de Gex.
- *Penicillium album*, used on the surface of certain bloomy-rind goat cheeses, including Pouligny-Saint-Pierre, Rigotte de Condrieu, and Charolais.
- *Mucor*, a fungi found on Saint-Nectaire, which is also known as "*poil-de-chat*" (cat's fur) in French for the light gray fuzz it produces on the rind.

100% natural cheesemaking

Up until modern times, milk was cultured via microbes naturally present in the milk and environment, such as on the animals' udders, on the milkers' hands, in the air, and so on. The equipment used can also naturally inoculate the milk. This is true of *gerles*, the wooden vats used to make Salers Tradition. To preserve the beneficial microbes in the wood, the *gerles* are simply washed in cold water between batches. Depending on the bacterial species and its vigor, fermentation will occur more or less rapidly—or not at all, if unwanted bacteria take over, or if the desirable microbes get wiped out by the dreaded bacteria-eating viruses.

Today, few cheesemakers work exclusively with ambient flora, which requires impeccable hygiene and technical skills in addition to considerable flexibility. A round of applause goes to the rare producers still working without commercial cultures, often with a view to maintaining the typicity and aromatic complexity of their cheeses. That being said, there is an increased interest in such "natural cheeses"—as the Slow Food Foundation calls them—following the example of natural wine. This has drawn attention to the exceptional cheeses made today with native microbes. Producers are working to preserve and even promote microbial diversity as a key component of overall biodiversity.

Commercial cultures

Since the twentieth century, an increased focus on hygiene in the dairy industry has severely depleted the microbial diversity of milk. The solution to this has been commercial starter cultures composed of selected microorganisms that make it possible to obtain more consistent results. In most cases—such as in industrial, artisanal, and farmstead production—cheesemakers use bacterial cultures in liquid, frozen, or freeze-dried form made in laboratories known as culture houses. This has significantly reduced the microbial diversity in the world's cheeses, so some cheesemakers prefer to use richer, more diverse "homegrown starters," including whey from a previous batch (often used for goat cheeses and mozzarella) or fermented milk that they've produced themselves.

Rennet

Rennet is an enzyme that coagulates milk. It is an essential ingredient in cheesemaking and is derived from several sources.

Animal rennet

When was rennet discovered?
The coagulating properties of animal rennet were discovered by our ancestors, who first domesticated cattle, goats, and sheep and used containers made of dried calves' or lambs' stomachs to store their animals' milk. These early breeders were lactose intolerant and may well have discovered cheesemaking as a means to make the milk digestible and obtain nourishment from it. Nomadic tribes in Anatolia, for instance, would transport milk in such containers, helping to separate the curds from the whey. The Romans observed, appropriated, and mastered these cheesemaking techniques and exported them throughout the Empire in the early Common Era.

What exactly happens in these animals' stomachs?
The stomachs of unweaned ruminants contain chymosin, a milk-clotting enzyme secreted by the mucous membrane of the abomasum—a fourth stomach. When liquid milk reaches the abomasum, the rennet separates it into curds and whey. The chymosin and native bacteria naturally acidify and coagulate the milk, making a cheese of sorts in the animals' stomachs.

How is animal rennet obtained?
The abomasa of calves, kids, or lambs freshly slaughtered for meat are left to soak to recover the enzymes. Traditionally, the stomachs were filled with air to dry them out and then cut into strips and soaked. For some cheeses, such as Gruyère, the abomasa were soaked in whey from previous batches, which provided starter cultures for the next round of milk. Today, cheesemakers almost exclusively use rennet that has been sterilized after soaking and thus provides no starter cultures. Interestingly, cheesemakers in Italy's Abbruzzo region use pig rennet to make the unique Pecorino di Farindola.

Vegetarian rennet

Other cheesemaking traditions use plant-based coagulants. Fig leaves were used in Greece, for instance. However, *Cynara* or thistle flowers were most commonly used, especially in North Africa and the Iberian Peninsula. *Cynara* flower pistils contain cyprosin, an enzyme with coagulating properties. As they impart a bitter taste to cow's milk cheeses, they were more prevalent in sheep's or goat's milk products. Still today, *Cynara*-derived rennets are the only types authorized in some Portuguese appellations, including Queijo de Azeitão and Serra da Estrela. In England, the yellow bedstraw plant was used to make Gloucester, before being replaced by animal rennet in the late eighteenth century. In addition to coagulating the milk, the flowers also gave the cheese its yellow color, which is now obtained with annatto—a natural pigment obtained from the seeds of the achiote (*Bixa orellana*), a tropical plant native to South America and the Caribbean. In western France, *chardonnette*—a type of thistle—was commonly used until the twentieth century to prepare fresh cheeses including caillebotte and jonchée.

Commercial rennet

In 1874, the Danish pharmacist Christian D. A. Hansen discovered how to extract and stabilize animal rennet. His economical, timesaving method produced rennet with consistent coagulating power that inhibited the production of potentially undesirable microorganisms. Standardized rennet was a resounding success, and the vast majority of traditional cheesemakers gradually adopted it. In the second half of the twentieth century, strong growth in cheese production prompted manufacturers to look for new substitutes. In the 1960s, fungal enzymes were developed, which behave differently from animal rennet. In the 1990s, a new generation of pure coagulating enzymes derived from genetically modified organisms (*Aspergillus niger*) appeared on the scene. Highly prized by industrial producers for their low cost and high yield, they are prohibited for use in France's AOP and organic cheeses.

Salt

Salt plays many valuable roles in the cheesemaking process. Although insufficient on its own, it significantly slows the growth of microbes that can harm the quality of a cheese and cause spoilage. It also influences the activities of the different beneficial cultures and enzymes that play a part in the ripening process, affecting moisture levels, texture, and, of course, flavor. Finally, salt dehydrates the surface of the cheese and contributes to rind formation.

Salt is added in different ways during the cheesemaking process.
- **Before pressing:** Drained and cut curds are mixed with dry salt, which is gradually absorbed.
- **After pressing:** Dry salt is applied to the surface of a cheese that has already been molded.
- **Via brining:** Molded cheese curd is submerged in a solution with a high salt content.
- **During ripening:** Some cheeses are washed with a brine solution during aging. The *affineur* first brushes or wipes the older cheeses with the solution, followed by the younger ones. This loads the solution with surface cultures, encouraging beneficial bacteria growth on the younger cheeses. This solution is called *morge*.

The salt content in different cheese families

Cheese families	Salt content (mg of sodium per 3½ oz./100 g cheese)
Fresh cheeses	200–700 mg
Bloomy-rind cheeses	600–800 mg
Washed-rind cheeses	500–1000 mg
Blue cheeses	400–1000 mg
Uncooked pressed cheeses	300–500 mg
Cooked pressed cheeses	700–900 mg

Processing aids

During the cheesemaking process, several so-called "processing aids" may also be used, but they are by no means mandatory.

Calcium chloride
Relatively common in industrial cheese production, calcium chloride is mainly used for milk that has lost mineral content, either through pasteurization or because it has been kept in cold-storage for too long—and all too often for both reasons. It produces firmer curds.

Citric acid
Citric acid quickly acidifies milk and is often used to produce fresh cheeses, including mozzarella and ricotta. Vinegar is another alternative used for other fresh cheeses such as Brousse du Rove.

Lysozyme

An abundant protein in animals and plants, lysozyme is particularly plentiful in hen egg whites. It can be used to produce pressed cheeses that have relatively long aging times. Lysozyme destroys *Clostridia*—bacteria that produce unpleasant tastes as well as gases that cause cracks and fissures known as "late blowing"—in the aforementioned cheeses. Incidentally, *Clostridia* are also found in the silage used to feed dairy herds on intensive farms. Lysozyme accelerates cheese ripening, which appeals to certain manufacturers who do not want to store their cheeses for too long.

Potassium chloride

Used as a salt substitute to produce lower-sodium cheeses, potassium chloride is forbidden in organic cheese production in France.

Calcium carbonate and acetic acid

These two substances act as acidity regulators.

Colorings and flavorings

After the natural shades of white and creamy yellow, orange is the most predominant cheese color. Cheeses such as mimolette and certain Goudas and Cheddars are orange throughout, while others, like reblochon and Langres, may have orange-hued rinds. This orange shade is often produced by annatto: a natural pigment obtained from the seeds of the achiote (*Bixa orellana*), a tropical plant native to South America and the Caribbean. Beta-carotene also makes cheese orange and is often added as a food coloring (E160). It may be of natural origin, but is most often produced synthetically. *Brevibacterium linens* are cultures that naturally produce beta-carotene and are responsible for the red hue on several washed-rind cheeses. Also known as "red mold," *Brevibacterium linens* give cheeses such as Époisses, Munster, and Abondance their characteristic (and natural) orange rinds.

As for flavorings, those that produce a "smoked" taste are among the most prevalent. Some producers still smoke their cheeses over natural materials, including myrtle wood in Corsica and Sardinia, beechwood in the Jura and Savoie regions, and wheat straw in Italy, which is used for the best scamorza di bufala. But most producers today either "cold smoke" their cheese or submerge it in liquid smoke—a flavoring made of condensed natural smoke from burning wood. The flavorings used in cheese are as varied as their makers' imaginations. While there are some traditional flavored cheeses, such as caraway-seasoned Munster and saffron-scented Piacentinu Ennense—a Sicilian pecorino—many cheese flavorings are purely commercial ideas dreamed up with a view to selling products that are, on the whole, of average quality.

Coatings

Fresh tommes are coated at the beginning of the ripening process to prevent rind formation and retain moisture in the cheese. In the past, cheesemakers used wax, but today, for efficiency, many use plastic coatings made of vinyl acetate or microcrystalline waxes, which are resistant and breathable. For instance, paraffin wax and vinyl acetate are authorized in the Tomme des Pyrenées IGP regulations.

Preservatives

Some producers use natamycin or E235 to prevent spoilage, as this preservative inhibits the growth of fungi, such as yeasts and molds, during the ripening phase and beyond. It is prohibited in organic cheeses in France and elsewhere. Nisin (E234) protects against microbial growth and significantly increases the shelf life of mini-mally ripened cheeses, but it, too, is prohibited in organic cheese production. Anti-clumping agents—including rice, corn, potato starch or flour, and even cellulose or silica—are often added to shredded or grated cheese packages to prevent the individual shreds from sticking together.

This list is far from exhaustive, as most additives are prohibited in organic cheeses and in the majority of French AOPs. They are hardly ever used in raw milk cheeses made on a small scale—one more reason to buy from farmstead and artisan producers whenever possible.

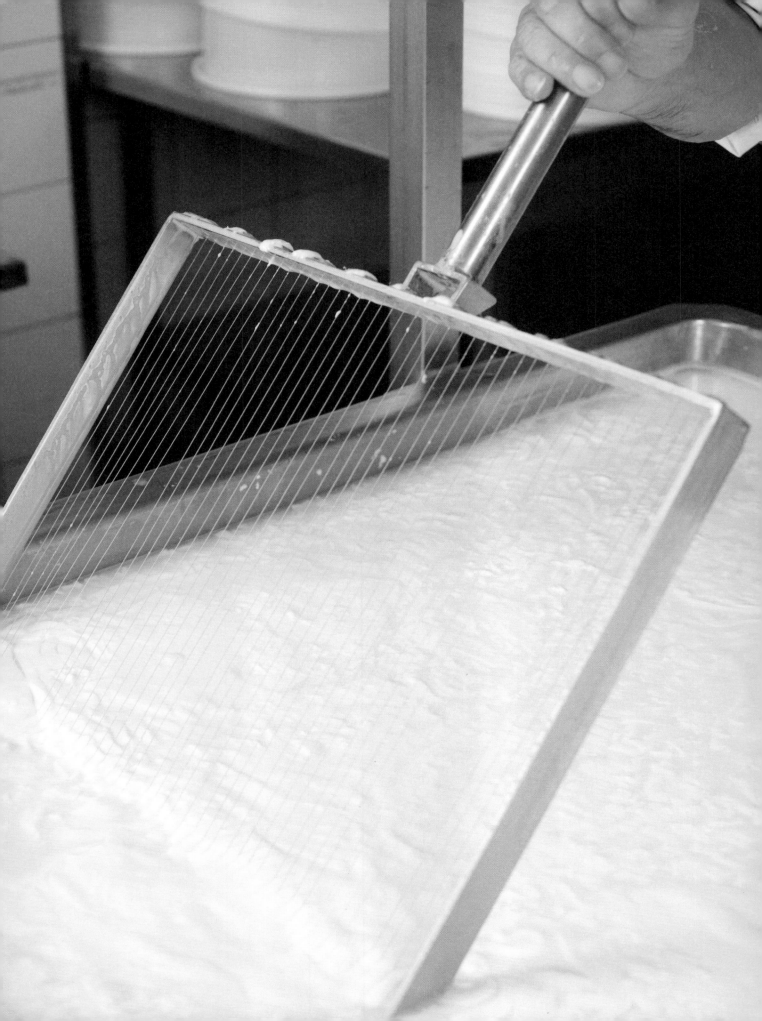

The Cheesemaking Process

Preparing milk for cheesemaking

Cheesemaking begins with milk, which is transformed in countless ways to make all of the world's diverse cheeses. From the moment it is extracted from the animal, this essential base ingredient is handled in different ways depending on the type of cheese.

Removing impurities

Straw, dust, animal hairs, and other impurities that may have accumulated during milking or transportation, must first be filtered out, although advances in mechanical milking have made such impurities rare. In the past, farmers used plants, such as ferns and nettles, to perform this task—a technique still used today by a few select cheesemakers.

Storing milk

Depending on the recipe, cheesemakers may store milk until there is enough from one or more additional milkings to make an entire batch. Artisanal and industrial cheesemakers may mix in milk from other herds, although *fermier* (farmstead) producers must use milk from their own animals and make their cheeses on the farm. To safely store milk, it needs to be cooled to avoid excessive bacterial growth. In the mountains, some dairy farmers keep just-collected milk cool in containers submerged in cold running water. Most industrial producers use tanks that quickly lower the milk's temperature to 39°F (4°C) to limit microbial growth. For some raw-milk cheeses, such as Comté, milk is stored at 50°F–64°F (10°C–18°C) to allow for controlled growth of the native microbes that make the cheese unique.

The right amount of fat

Different cheeses require different levels of fat. The milk is often standardized to obtain exactly the right amount for each one. In other words, the fat content is adjusted to the desired level. Part of the cream is removed and then recombined with whole or skim milk, depending on the cheese.

Cheesemakers use different techniques to standardize their milk:
•**Gravitational skimming:** Some cheesemakers let the milk sit overnight (or longer in some cases) to allow the cream—which is less dense than water—to rise to the surface naturally, and then skim part of it off. This technique is used to make authentic Camembert de Normandie.
•**Centrifugal skimming:** Some producers use separators: mechanical centrifuges that quickly separate cream from milk.
•**Adding fat:** Fat must be added to make some cheeses, such as Brillat-Savarin and Saint-Félicien (both triple-cream). Most of the fat used in the cheesemaking industry is pasteurized or sterilized.

Heating the milk and adding starter cultures

At this point, cheesemakers heat the milk to within a specific temperature range, depending on the cheese.

• **Pasteurization** is the primary heat treatment used in industrial cheese production, and the vast majority of cheeses today are made with pasteurized milk. This process involves heating milk to a temperature of over 160°F (72°C) for at least 15 seconds to eliminate potentially harmful bacteria, including the particularly resistant *Salmonella*. Initially, pasteurization was developed for this very purpose, but it has additional advantages as well, not least of which is improved cheese yield. It also ensures a consistent, uniform flavor along with the subsequent addition of "defined" or selected bacterial strains.

• **Thermization** is an intermediate technique that involves heating the milk to a lower temperature than that used for pasteurization, typically between 145°F and 162°F (63°C–72°C), for a minimum of 15 seconds. This eliminates most bacteria, so some beneficial cultures must be added back in later.

• Cheesemakers who use **raw milk** may heat it to 93°F–99°F (34°C–37°C), if necessary, to jump-start the fermentation process. This method preserves a greater microbial diversity in the milk than pasteurization or thermization. In this case, cheesemakers must use other measures to prevent the growth of harmful pathogens before and during the production process. The flavor complexity of raw milk cheeses is unparalleled.

• Next, cheesemakers add **starter cultures.** Pasteurized or thermized milks no longer contain the flora needed for fermentation, and raw milks are often too "clean"—meaning they have too few microorganisms. Cultures—either commercially produced (in liquid or powder form) or artisanal (including fermented milk or whey from previous batches)—must be added to transform the milk into cheese.

Acidification and coagulation: Different paths for different cheeses

Depending on the cheese they produce, cheesemakers use different methods to turn liquid milk into solid curds. The extent to which acidification predominates over coagulation will determine whether the resulting curds are delicate or firm.

A glass of raw milk left to stand for a few days will curdle on its own due to the growth of native bacteria, which transform the lactose (sugar) into lactic acid. The longer the milk is left out, the more it acidifies and curdles. This occurs naturally, but over the centuries cheesemakers have developed different ways to harness the process to produce a seemingly infinite variety of cheeses.

• **Acidification**—a drop in the milk's pH (acidity) level—occurs when lactic acid bacteria in the milk digest the lactose and transform it, through fermentation, into lactic acid. These bacteria may be naturally present or added by the cheesemaker in the form of starter cultures. Acidification starts at temperatures of at least 68°F (20°C) and can last for up to forty-eight hours. During this stage, the milk begins to solidify into a fragile gel made of casein—the milk protein essential to cheesemaking. Vinegar or a citric acid (such as lemon juice) can also be added to acidify milk. This technique, known as direct acidification, is used to make many fresh cheeses, including some ricotta-type cheeses and industrially produced varieties.

• **Coagulation, also known as curdling**, is produced by enzymes found in rennet: chymosin and pepsin. Active at around 104°F (40°C), these enzymes allow the casein proteins to bind together and form a dense matrix. Unlike the coagulum formed by lactic acidification, this one has a custard-like texture and is less fragile. The tight casein matrix traps the other milk components: water, fat, sugar, vitamins, and minerals. Cheesemakers use different methods to coagulate milk, depending on the desired results.

> **COAGULUM AND CURDS ARE ONE AND THE SAME**
> Or not quite! The terms "coagulum" (or "gel") and "curds" both refer to the mass of solid matter produced when milk is acidified and coagulated. But there is one slight nuance: technically speaking, coagulum and gel refer to curd that has not yet been cut. However, the terms are often used interchangeably.

In cheeses made using **acid-rennet** or **lactic coagulation**, acidification predominates, followed by coagulation. Cheesemakers add just a small amount of rennet in addition to starter cultures, and coagulation is slow—it can take up to forty-eight hours for the milk to curdle. The resulting coagulum is fragile, and the next step in the cheesemaking process must be carried out with care.

Examples of acid-rennet (or lactic) coagulated cheeses: fromage blanc, Selles-sur-Cher, Saint-Marcellin, Rocamadour, pélardon, Mothais sur Feuille, Valençay, Maconnais, Sainte Maure de Touraine, faisselle, Robiola di Roccaverano.

Other cheeses are made using **rennet coagulation**. In this case, coagulation occurs quickly, at a relatively high pH, followed by acidification afterward. It generally takes less than an hour for the milk to curdle, and the resulting coagulant is much more solid and resilient, with the custard-like texture mentioned above. It can be manipulated in a wider variety of ways to produce an incredible diversity of cheeses.

Examples of rennet coagulated cheeses: Laguiole, Tomme Sartenaise, Livarot, Beaufort, Morbier, Comté, Salers, Ossau-Iraty, Manchego, Cheddar, Parmesan, feta, paneer.

In some cases, acidification and coagulation occur simultaneously, although one may predominate slightly over the other, depending on the cheese. This is sometimes referred to as **mixed coagulation**, known as "*caillé mixte*" in French.

Examples of "*mixte*" cheeses: Camembert, Brie de Meaux, Langres, Roquefort.

In extremely rare cases, no rennet is added. Cheesemakers start with fermented milk, which is drained delicately because the coagulum is extremely fragile. Once the texture is firm enough, the cheese is left to ripen. This is one variant of **acid coagulation**, produced exclusively by lactic acid bacteria.
<u>Examples of such acid-coagulated cheeses:</u> kurut (Kyrgyzstan) and kashk (Iran).

In some manufacturing processes, particularly in industrial settings, milk is acidified using citric acid, which means it does not undergo fermentation. Although this makes it easier to control the production process and the results are more constant, the final product lacks the complex flavor that fermentation can impart.

Draining or "the great whey escape"

How do cheesemakers separate the curds from the whey? This depends on the acidification and coagulation processes used (see pp. 34–35), as the resulting coagula differ.

Passive draining for lactic curds
The coagulum produced by acid-rennet (or lactic) coagulation is fragile and must be handled with care. In most cases, molding and draining are carried out simultaneously. Using a ladle, cheesemakers gently transfer the curds to perforated forms or molds. As the curds settle and fuse together, pressure from their own weight and gravity naturally expels the liquid. Known as whey, this liquid is composed of water, lactic acid, proteins, a little fat, vitamins, and minerals. In the production of some cheeses, the curd is pre-drained in fine-weave bags and then transferred to a mold when it reaches the desired consistency.

Hands-on draining for rennet curds
The coagulum produced by rennet coagulation is supple, solid, and impermeable. If cheesemakers proceeded as above, the whey would remain trapped inside, so they need to help it drain out. This begins with *décaillage*, which involves cutting the curd into small pieces using a manual or mechanized cutter. In the early nineteenth century, the traditional manual cutters used were made from tree branches.

Cutting the curd
Cutting the curd into pieces encourages the casein network to contract and expel the whey—a process known in the language of cheesemaking as syneresis. The curd acts somewhat like a magic sponge: squeezing it removes the liquid, but it does not reabsorb moisture, even if it remains in water.

The smaller the cut, the more readily the curds contract, releasing more whey. In other words, the firmer and drier the cheese, the finer the cut needs to be. To make the soft Mont d'Or, cheesemakers cut the curd into walnut-size pieces, while Parmesan makers cut the curd into pieces the size of rice grains. In the case of rennet-coagulated curd, cheesemakers use a range of different methods to facilitate curd contraction and whey expulsion, including the following:
• **Stirring** the curds in the whey, which encourages them to expel the liquid more quickly.
• **Heating** the curds gradually to temperatures above 131°F (55°C), which accelerates syneresis, i.e., whey expulsion.

Both methods have their risks. If curds are heated too quickly or stirred for too long, a fine skin will form on the surface, known in French as "*coiffage.*" This will prevent the curds from knitting together properly later on, resulting in an uneven texture. In some cases, however, this is precisely what cheesemakers are looking for. In the case of Roquefort, for instance, this unevenness, with spaces between the curds, is what allows the blue mold to develop.

In short, rennet curds expel most of their whey during the cutting and stirring process, even if they are still floating in liquid. In many cases, cheesemakers then stop stirring and allow the curds to settle on the bottom of the vat, where they form a compact mass.

•**Pressing:** The curds are then pressed to expel the final amount of whey. This is achieved in different ways, depending on the cheese. For Cheddar, blocks of curd are stacked and rotated (known as "cheddaring"), while for other cheeses, like Cantal, cheesemakers place the curds in molds and apply varying amounts of external pressure. For example, reblochon makers apply light pressure using a weight, while makers of hard cheeses such as Gruyère apply greater pressure using a cheese press. Pressing not only removes excess whey but also helps the curds to knit together.

Molding: Giving cheese its shape

Molding is another crucial step in the cheesemaking process. Once placed in molds, the curds finish draining and fuse together into the desired shape. In the past, molds were made of earthenware, wood, or even braided rush, but today the majority are in plastic or stainless steel.

Molding lactic curds
As seen on the previous pages, the fragile curd produced by acid-rennet (or lactic) coagulation is carefully transferred to molds, where it drains passively. The molds are taller than the final cheese as the curd takes up more space when saturated with whey. The shape and size of the mold, as well as the number and position of the holes in it, influence the draining and, thus, the final consistency of the cheese. In most cases, the cheese is turned over at some point and placed back in the mold to ensure even draining.

Molding rennet curds
Rennet curds expel most of their whey before they are transferred to molds, the size and shape of which depend on the cheese. If the cheese will be stored for several months, then a large mold is needed—the largest are those used for Parmesan, Grana Padano, Emmental, and Gruyère. A smaller mold can be used for cheeses that will be conserved for shorter periods, such as Munster, Camembert, and reblochon. Molds are generally cylindrical, similar to cake pans, as this is by far the most practical shape for unmolding. Wheels of cheese are also easier to handle afterward. However, there are also square molds, generally for smaller cheeses. Some molds have unique features: they may be made of wood and adjustable according to the amount of milk available or with concave sides like those used for Beaufort. Two molds are used together to make Fiore Sardo, giving the cheese its rounded sides.

Salting

Another essential step is salting, which draws moisture from the cheese. This completes the draining process and encourages rind formation. Salt also has antibacterial properties and allows cheesemakers to control microbial growth during ripening. It is also, of course, a notable flavor enhancer. Dry salting is typically used for small, moist cheeses, which are more fragile than larger varieties. This typically entails applying salt to the surface of the cheese after it is formed. In the case of pre-drained cheeses, such as Rocamadour and Neufchâtel, dry salt is mixed directly into the curds before they are molded and pressed. This technique is also used to make Cantal and Cheddar, but most cheeses, especially rennet-coagulated ones, tend to be salted using brine. This entails immersing the shaped cheeses in brine—a salt-water bath—for several hours. This technique is generally followed by a surface wash with a brine composed of salted water and ripening cultures, encouraging rind formation and the growth of desired microbes. A reblochon-type cheese stays in the brine for one to two hours, while Grana Padano is left to soak for fourteen to thirty days.

Affinage

Also known as ripening, maturing, or aging, affinage is the final phase in cheese-making. This is the art and science of making cheeses better through time and care, with the exception of fresh cheeses, which do not require aging. This time-consuming stage is often entrusted to specialized *affineurs*, or cheese maturers, to make certain cheeses, such as Comté, reblochon, and Saint-Nectaire. Each type of cheese requires specific techniques, lengths of time, and ambient conditions including temperature, humidity level, and airflow. During affinage, cheese matures to its fullest potential, expressing its optimal texture and flavor. This cannot be done just anywhere, and especially not in a refrigerator. So, what conditions need to be considered?

Temperature
Temperature significantly influences microbial activity, so it is a crucial parameter in the ripening process. While 95°F–113°F (35°C–45°C) is the optimal range for cultures, cheeses are generally aged at temperatures of between 45°F and 55°F (7°C–13°C), which allows for greater control of the microbial activity. Some cheeses are placed in warm caves or aging/ripening/curing rooms (at a temperature of 68°F–77°F/20°C–25°C) to facilitate the growth of propionibacteria, responsible for the holes in Emmental, or to make them "sweat" and form a protective rind, as for Parmesan. Other cheeses, such as Roquefort, may be stored below freezing, at a temperature as low as 23°F (-5°C), to keep microbial activity to a minimum and ensure slower ripening.

Humidity
Humid conditions favor microbial growth, which is why soft cheeses with a higher moisture content ripen quickly. Different cheeses prefer different conditions. Some, such as Saint-Nectaire, must be aged in caves with a high relative humidity to encourage the growth of *Mucor* fungi (see Cultures, p. 25). Others, such as Livarot or Époisses, must be washed regularly to allow *Brevibacterium linens* (also known as "red mold") to flourish on the rind. Other cheeses are aged in relatively dry conditions, as often occurs in the Netherlands. In this famously flat country, there are no naturally humid caves, which is why Gouda and Edam are covered with a layer of wax to retain as much moisture as possible inside the cheese. No matter the ambient humidity level,

all cheeses lose some weight during affinage due to water loss—a well-known phenomenon known as "*freinte*" (shrinkage) in French.

Airflow

Cheese caves must have proper ventilation to eliminate the gases that cheeses emit as they ripen. Ammonia, for instance, can saturate the air and limit access to oxygen, inhibiting microbial growth on the cheese surface. Blue cheeses must be pierced to allow for airflow inside and foster the development of *Penicillium*. Stronger airflow is often needed in the early stages of affinage to dry the surface of the moistest cheeses. Known as "*ressuyage*" in French, this active drying process is used for lactic chèvres and soft cheeses like Camembert.

Other affinage techniques

Small, high-moisture cheeses are placed on racks to allow air to circulate freely around them. They must be turned frequently and may be aged anywhere from a few days to a few weeks. Others are placed on rough-cut spruce boards, which regulate the humidity on the cheese surface and create a favorable environment for beneficial ripening cultures. The cheeses are regularly turned and brushed or washed with brine. In different regions and for different cheeses, the rind may also be washed with alcohol (such as the grape spirit Marc de Bourgogne in the case of Époisses); vinegar (used on some Mediterranean sheep's milk tommes); or oil. Depending on the cheese, *affineurs* use other techniques, including smoking (to protect the cheese from mites and draw out new flavors) or coating the cheese with any number of materials, including grape pomace (*marc de raisin*), spices, hay, or clay. The sky's the limit!

Three main biochemical reactions take place in cheese during affinage:
- Lactic acid is further metabolized.
- The casein matrix breaks down in a process known as proteolysis. This modifies texture, making moist cheeses like Camembert and Munster creamier and dry cheeses like pecorino and Parmesan more crumbly.
- The fats break down, imparting a range of flavors to the cheese.

> **"CHEESE CRYSTALS" IN AGED CHEESES**
> Some aged cheeses, including Gruyère and Parmesan, have tiny white specks that crunch when bitten into. Often mistaken for salt, these "cheese crystals" are, in fact, calcium lactate or amino acids (particularly tyrosine) that crystallize as the proteins in the cheese break down.

The *affineur*'s job is a daily one. The cheeses must be turned regularly so that all sides are well aerated and the rind is uniform, and they must be brushed and washed with brine. *Affineurs* closely watch their cheeses to see how they are evolving. The *affineur* decides when a cheese is ready to be sold or, au contraire, requires further aging.

> **MITE-FUELED AFFINAGE**
> Some cheesemakers encourage cheese mites (*cirons, cérons,* or *artisous* in French) in the ripening process. These tiny insects devour the rind, creating cracks and specific flavors. Their handiwork can be witnessed in long-aged mimolettes and some aged tommes, known as "*ceronnées,*" such as the tomme "*aux artisous*" produced in the Haute-Loire.
> But more often than not, cheeses are regularly brushed to prevent the proliferation of mites, which quickly make themselves at home.

Families
of Cheese

Classifying Cheeses

Depending on the desired end results, cheesemakers and *affineurs* make different decisions at each stage in the cheesemaking process. The multitude of possible approaches to fermentation, coagulation, draining, and ripening (see pp. 33–39) help to explain the stunning diversity of cheeses around the world today. Although there is no single way to classify this impressive array, here are some of the most commonly used classifications.

→ One common way to categorize cheese, especially among non-experts, is by simply differentiating between **fresh** and **aged** cheeses.

→ Another classification system proposed by Maurice Beau and Charles Bourgain in their book *Industrie fromagère* (1926) categorizes cheese based on the **cheesemaking technique** and the **aging time**.

→ In his 1947 work, *Technologie du lait*, Roger Veisseyre described even more technical distinctions between types of **coagulation, draining, and ripening methods and times,** for a total of twenty-three categories.

→ Today's prevailing cheese classification system, found in official French texts, is based on the following categories:
- Fresh cheese (*fromages frais*)
- Bloomy-rind cheese (*pâtes molles à croûte fleurie*)
- Washed-rind cheese (*pâtes molles à croûte lavée*)
- Uncooked pressed cheese (*pâtes pressées non cuites*)
- Cooked pressed cheese (*pâtes pressées cuites*)
- Blue cheese (*pâtes persillées*)
- Goat cheese (*chèvres*: a mix of all types of cheese, from fresh to ripened, as long as they are made with goat's milk)
- Processed cheese (*fromages fondus*)
- *Pasta filata* (stretched-curd) cheese (*pâtes filées*)
- Whey cheese (*les recuites*)

In the following pages, we examine the "families" we feel are most evocative, from the softest, freshest cheeses to the ripest, driest varieties, and a little of everything in between, including blue cheeses and gooey, smelly, washed-rind types. Unfortunately, it would be impossible to include all the cheeses found worldwide in this book; besides the sheer number that exist, cheeses regularly disappear, while at the same time even more are being created, dreamed up by the fertile imaginations of today's cheesemakers. We sincerely apologize for all of the cheeses that do not appear in this book.

Our goal is to explain how the main types of cheese are made and help readers to understand this magical world of milk-loving microbes!

Fresh Cheeses

Fromage Blanc & Co. 45

Feta & Co. 47

Mozzarella & Co. 51

Ricotta & Co. 57

Some family members

- *Fromage blanc*
- *Faisselle*
- *Petit Suisse*
- *Cream cheese*
- *Fromage à la pie*
- *Caillebotte*
- *Fresh chèvre (goat cheese)*
- *Flavored fresh cheeses*

Fromage Blanc & Co.

Characteristics

APPEARANCE Containing up to 70 percent water, fromage blanc family members are glistening and moist. They range from pure white to ivory, partly because they do not have rinds. If they appear to have one, it means molds and yeasts have begun to grow, which is not a good sign! These cheeses are sold pre-packed or loose, and sometimes fresh out of their molds.

TASTE Decidedly tangy, fromage blanc and its kin have a fresh, milky taste. In some varieties, added cream rounds out the flavor with sweet notes.

Origins

These unripened lactic cheeses are the simplest to prepare, whether made with cow's, goat's, or sheep's milk. Among the typical homemade cheeses, they require the least mastery, which has made them staples in rural areas.

A selection of the many variants:
- **Caillebotte:** Made in several western French regions, this rennet-curdled milk ("*cailler*" means to curdle in French) is typically served chilled and sprinkled with sugar (see p. 28). In Poitou, the milk was traditionally coagulated with a plant-based rennet: *chardonnette* thistles (a wild artichoke). The same specialty was prepared in the Balearic Islands by stirring boiled milk with a young fig branch with an X-shape cut at the base to release the fig sap, which acted as a coagulant.

← Fromage blanc

- **Jonchée:** In Charente, cheesemakers drain and shape caillebotte in woven rush mats to make this specialty.
- **Petit Suisse:** This creamy blend of cow's milk and cream originated in Switzerland (hence the name), before producers in Normandy adopted the recipe in the early nineteenth century. The original *bondons*—small cylinders of cheese, about 1¼ in. (3 cm) in diameter—were eventually wrapped in wax paper to retain moisture, improve shelf life, and facilitate transport and handling.
- **Cream cheese:** This stirred, drained fresh cheese with added cream is soft and spreadable. It's the key ingredient in a classic baked cheesecake.
- **Fromage blanc:** Literally "white cheese," this lightly fermented fresh cheese has many variants in France, from smooth versions to the more rustic fromage blanc "de campagne" or "*à la pie*." Another type, **faisselle**—named after the eponymous cheese strainer—is typically packaged in perforated tubs surrounded by its own whey.

How they're made

Fresh cheese results from the first two stages in the cheesemaking process: preparing and coagulating the milk. Adding rennet to milk is all it takes, whether the latter is skimmed or whole, raw, thermized, or pasteurized—anything goes. After a coagulation period of twelve to twenty-four hours, the curd is then drained and shaped in a mold (or not). *Et voilà!*—the cheese is ready as, by definition, fresh cheeses are not aged.

Peak season

These types of fresh cheese are traditionally eaten year-round, whenever fresh milk is available.

Food and drink pairings

Typically mild, fresh cheeses go well with both savory and sweet flavors, such as:
• Fresh fruit, honey, or jam. Classic desserts such as the English fruit fool or the French Fontainebleau—also known as crémet—make the most of this affinity, combining fresh cheese with cream and sugar, along with seasonal fruit. This idea isn't new—references to crémet d'Anjou (see recipe p. 276) appeared in documents as early as 1702.
• Fresh herbs. Chives, mint, and parsley take top honors here. Adding a little fresh garlic and shallot and a drizzle of olive oil takes this combination to the next level. Lyon's herbed cheese spread, *cervelle de canut*, is a classic of the genre (see recipe p. 185).
• Crisp, fresh vegetables. Raw carrots, zucchini, fresh peas, and more are delicious with fresh cheese—either on its own or in dips and spreads.
• Spices, including smoked paprika, freshly ground pepper, and ras el hanout, are wonderful seasonings for fresh cheeses.
• In terms of beverages, fresh cheese pairs particularly well with fruit or honey beers or hefeweizens (white beers brewed with wheat and barley originally from Bavaria).

Some family members

- *Feta (Greece)*
- *Beyaz peynir (Turkey)*
- *Bijeni sir (Macedonia)*
- *Sirene (Bulgaria)*
- *Domiati (Egypt)*

Feta & Co.

Characteristics

APPEARANCE The members of this group are pure white. They are often sold sliced or cubed and preserved in brine.

TASTE These salty, firm cheeses have powerful notes of milk and aromatic scrubland. They are typically used in salads and appear in a variety of Mediterranean dishes, including many cooked ones.

Origins

Mediterranean and Balkan countries produce 80 percent and 50 percent of the world's sheep's and goat's milk, respectively.

In the mountainous areas of the Balkans (including Greece), the hot, dry summers and mild, rainy winters nourish a stunning array of plant species. Around six thousand different varieties of plants thrive here, among which 15 to 20 percent are endemic. These figures are especially remarkable when compared to those of the large neighboring regions (Western and Central Europe and the Maghreb and Middle East). However, there are few fertile valleys suitable for cattle raising. Sheep and goat farming have flourished, with indigenous breeds well adapted to the rugged conditions.

Remarkably rich in protein and fat, goat's and sheep's milk are perfect for making cheese. Archaeologists have found evidence of cheesemaking in ancient times on

terra-cotta tablets discovered in Mycenae and Pylos, and there are even references to the craft in Homer's *Odyssey*.

In these parts of the world, brined white cheeses form one of the foundations of the famous Mediterranean diet. Each region has developed its own variations, using goat's or sheep's milk, or a blend of the two. Still, the results are broadly similar: fresh, rindless cheeses preserved in brine for up to several months, if necessary, and often eaten daily. The average Greek, for instance, consumes over 40 lb. (20 kg) of feta per year.

In the twentieth century, massive waves of Greek emigration to North America, Australia, the UK, and Germany popularized feta cheese around the globe. Today, France is the world's second largest consumer of feta, coming in just behind Greece.

Faced with ever-increasing demand, many ersatz feta cheeses were born, primarily produced industrially. Although the original recipe was sometimes respected, other manufacturers used cow's milk and whitening agents. From the 1970s, a large part of the world's feta was produced outside Greece—in Western Europe and beyond. After many years of fighting, Greece finally obtained Protected Designation of Origin (PDO) status for feta in 2002. Today, genuine Greek feta must be additive-free and made with sheep's milk only or a mixture with up to 30 percent goat's milk, whether pasteurized or raw.

PDO feta can be produced throughout the whole of Greece, with the exception of all the islands apart from Lesbos. Such an extensive geographical area is rare among PDO products. Today, feta accounts for around 10 percent of Greek food exports, reflecting its international reach.

The sector has expanded in Greece, driven by large international dairy companies. As more intensive practices take hold, much of the country's goat and sheep farming has moved from mountain pastures to the plains. Yet, agriculture in Greece remains largely small-scale, and locally available ingredients, including artisanal cheeses, still shape the diet in many parts of the country. In the Balkans and Turkey, production remains largely traditional.

How they're made

The PDO for Greek feta prohibits the use of cow's milk and allows only up to 30 percent goat's milk in the recipe. The rest, of course, must be sheep's milk, but other fresh brined cheeses can be made using different milk combinations. For example, the Egyptian Domiati is a blend of cow's and buffalo's milk.

Whether raw or pasteurized, the milk is then coagulated with rennet. Traditionally, the rennet came from kid-goat's or lamb's stomachs and was prepared by the cheesemakers themselves. Nowadays, producers mainly use commercial rennet.

← Feta

After the milk has coagulated, it is placed in square or round molds for draining. The cheese is then dry-salted on the surface before being placed in containers filled with brine or salt water to age. Feta makers use wooden barrels or stainless-steel tanks.

Feta is typically left to age for two months before being sold, but if stored in the right conditions, it will keep for over a year without any problems.

Peak season

In the Balkans and around the Mediterranean, the production season is well defined. Goats and ewes usually give birth in the fall, just before the rainy season. They generally dry up (stop producing milk) in early summer when the temperatures become too high for the vegetation and the animals. Dairies operate for no more than eight months a year. However, cheeses preserved in brine are available all year round.

Food and drink pairings

•The famous Greek salad (*horiatiki*), made with feta, cucumbers, tomatoes, and Kalamata olives, is always a hit and, although not part of the traditional recipe, can have small wedges or slices of watermelon added for a refreshing summery version.
•Feta and its kin are also used to stuff *boreks* and other savory pastries.
•We particularly like feta roasted in the oven, wrapped in fig leaves, and seasoned with ground pepper and a few pieces of preserved lemon.
•Other ingredients that pair beautifully with feta et al. include fresh herbs, honey, finely chopped or sliced red onion, fava beans, and dried spices such as sumac and za'atar.
•As for beverages, try a feta martini—a cocktail that's not for the faint-hearted, but nevertheless irresistible! To make 1 cocktail, stuff 2–3 green olives with feta and spear them with a toothpick. Pour 4 teaspoons (20 ml) vodka into a shaker filled with ice cubes and add 2 teaspoons (10 ml) dry vermouth and 1 tablespoon plus ½ teaspoon (17.5 ml) of the brine strained from the feta. Shake for 15 seconds and strain into a martini glass. Taste and adjust the quantities, if necessary. Serve garnished with the stuffed olives.

Some family members

- *Mozzarella di bufala*
- *Burrata*
- *Halloumi*
- *Fior di latte*
- *Scamorza*

Mozzarella & Co.

Characteristics

APPEARANCE When fresh, members of this family are rindless and range in color from porcelain white to ivory. Many are sold in bags or sealed pots containing lightly tangy, salty water, while others come vacuum-packed. When drained and sliced, a little white liquid may ooze out—this is the sign of a good buffalo milk mozzarella. They come in all sizes and shapes, including small balls (*bocconcini*), knotted (*nodini*), braided, folded in half (halloumi), or pear-shaped and tied with raffia (scamorza).

TASTE These cheeses are creamy and milky in flavor and elastic in texture when fresh, becoming more meltingly soft over time. Low-moisture mozzarellas, packaged as "cucina (cooking) mozzarella" are highly popular for baked dishes, especially pizzas.

Origins

The *pasta filata* (stretched-curd) technique (literally "spun paste" in Italian) has been used to make cheeses with cow's or buffalo's milk in southern Italy since the eleventh century. Native to Asia, buffalo were brought to Campania during the Arab invasions in the tenth century. *Pasta filata* cheeses were probably first consumed ripened, more akin to the provola family (see pp. 158–62). Cooking the curds made the cheeses storable and safe to eat. Over the centuries, the cheese spread to central and northern Italy and then beyond the peninsula. In the early twentieth century, more and more dairies sprang up in small towns, supplying residents with fresh mozzarella and milk.

As a result of mass Italian emigration and the global success of pizza, mozzarella is one of the most widely produced and consumed cheeses in the world today.

To counter the widespread use of the generic term "mozzarella" for pale imitations around the world, a DOP now protects Mozzarella di bufala Campana. This "true" mozzarella must be made with 100 percent water-buffalo milk exclusively produced and transformed in Campania, around Naples. Since 2018, a DOP has also protected Mozzarella di Gioia del Colle—a traditional cow's milk mozzarella made in Puglia.

SHOW THE REAL MOZZARELLA YOU CARE
In 2021, 450,000 metric tons of mozzarella were sold worldwide, of which 54,000 were DOP certified. In the same year, 37 percent of the certified mozzarella produced in Italy was exported. In the mozzarella family, a DOP (or IGP in the case of burrata) guarantees that the cheese is made using a specific type of milk. The vast majority of mozzarella sold today is produced on an industrial scale all over the world, including in New Zealand, the US, and even in Brittany. Look for DOP-certified mozzarella, and check the information-packed label for the milk origin. You can also ask the seller for more details, if you have any questions.

Burrata, which literally means "buttery" in Italian, is thought to have originated in the 1920s in the south of Murgia, in Puglia. Zero-waste before the catchphrase existed, burrata was born as a means of taking advantage of leftovers from the mozzarella-making process. According to popular lore, one particular Puglian cheesemaker, Lorenzo Bianchino Chieppa, was the first to mix the cream that formed on the surface of the milk with leftover pieces of mozzarella curd he'd shredded by hand, called *stracciatella* ("little rag" or "shred" in Italian). However, there is no written evidence of this, and other local producers have also laid claim to the invention. This stracciatella-cream mixture is then enclosed within a mozzarella pouch tied with a knot. In the past, cheesemakers wrapped the resulting burrata pouch in asphodel leaves, a native Mediterranean plant, to protect it from the scorching sun. Although refrigeration protects the cheese today, some burrata makers still use the leaves in a nod to tradition.

Puglian producers currently export burrata worldwide. Since there is not enough milk from the cows in the Murgia valleys, milk and cream are imported from other parts of Italy and other European countries, including Germany. In 2016, eight dairies fought to obtain a Protected Geographical Indication (PGI) for Burrata di Andria—a guarantee that the milk and cream come exclusively from Puglia. While this is undoubtedly progress, the PGI specifications do not prohibit industrial production: cheesemakers can still use citric acid to coagulate the milk instead of true fermentation, and the use of UHT cream is permitted.

← Mozzarella

How they're made

Traditional makers of mozzarella family cheeses combine fresh milk with whey from the previous day to acidify the milk, and then add calf's rennet as a coagulant. To guarantee consistency, industrial producers typically use either commercial starter cultures or citric acid to acidify the milk and lab-grown microbial rennet.

The resulting curd is drained and cut into small pieces, which are heated in water at 175°F–195°F (80°C–90°C). This softens the curds, which cheesemakers then stretch and pull, often using a stick. Small balls are cut by hand—*mozzare* means "to cut" in Italian—and then either submerged in cold water so they hold their shape or in hot water for stretching and braiding.

Several *pasta filata* cheeses are smoked. Those made the artisanal way, such as scamorza and burrata, are smoked over wheat straw, while industrial cheeses tend to get their smoky taste and appearance from added flavorings and colorings.

Peak season

Due to its global popularity, mozzarella is available year-round. Mozzarella di bufala Campana is considered best in winter when the buffalo mainly eat fresh grass, but this is true for all cheeses produced in southern Italy.

Food pairings

• The pairing possibilities are seemingly endless with this family of cheeses. Fans of bold flavors can go for potent combinations: fresh chili peppers, chili oil, freshly ground pepper, and anchovies all pair beautifully with fresh *pasta filata* cheeses.
• For a more refreshing pairing, try fruit. Roasted apricots or fresh watermelon are delicious with halloumi, for example.

Halloumi

Halloumi might seem like the odd one out in this group of cheeses. So, what is a grillable cheese doing in the mozzarella family?

Characteristics

Available around the world, halloumi is a salty cheese with an off-white hue and a rubbery texture when raw. It is typically sprinkled with mint, folded in half, and sold vacuum-packed. Like mozzarella, halloumi is a *pasta filata* (stretched-curd) cheese. Cheesemakers stretch the curd in very hot water and then press it. As a result, halloumi can withstand high temperatures without melting and can be fried or grilled without dripping through the grates.

PDO

Halloumi was granted PDO status in October 2022, although this relatively new appellation is still contested. While originally from Cyprus, halloumi is now produced in Turkey, the UK (the largest importer of Cypriot halloumi), Finland (yes, really), the US, Australia, and New Zealand. As with mozzarella, producers worldwide are challenging the notion of protecting a name that they deem generic.

Interesting facts

Made with milk from sheep and Damascus (Shami) goats using the *pasta filata* technique, halloumi gradually evolved in its own way over the centuries in Cyprus.

Considered part of the world-renowned Mediterranean diet, this traditionally made cheese has grown in popularity over time. It can be grilled, fried, or cut into chunks and threaded onto skewers for tasty vegetarian kebabs, making it a popular choice for barbecues. It has all the ingredients to make it an international success.

Some family members

- *Ricotta (Italy)*
- *Brocciu AOP (Corsica)*
- *Greuil and Breuil (Pyrenees)*
- *Sérac (Alps)*
- *Manouri (Greece)*
- *Urdă (Romania)*
- *Brousse du Rove AOP (Provence)*
- *Cacioricotta (Italy)*
- *Geitost (Norway)*

Ricotta & Co.

Characteristics

APPEARANCE Shiny and ranging in color from porcelain to off-white, the members of this family are soft, creamy, and sometimes grainy. They are typically sold freshly made in tubs or perforated molds of different shapes. The size and shape of the molds used to make the highly select Brousse du Rove, which has been protected by an AOP since 2020, are strictly regulated. They must be conical, measuring 3½ in. (85 mm) in height and 1¼ in. (32 mm) in diameter at the top, and have three holes for draining at the base. This shape makes it impossible to mistake Brousse du Rove for any other cheese.

TASTE These cheeses typically have a mild, subtle flavor (not bland, as some detractors might say!). Depending on the local vegetation, they may reveal grassy or herbaceous notes. In texture, they are soft and firm at the same time. Certain types made with added milk, such as Corsica's AOP Brocciu, can have a more assertive taste.

Take note: these cheeses do not keep for long and must be eaten fresh.

Origins

Humans have made ricotta-type whey cheeses since at least ancient times and traces have been found in Sumerian and Egyptian civilizations. These were probably among the first dairy products that people learned to prepare, alongside fresh, soft cheeses. Later, they were produced mainly in Italy before spreading to the Alps and Pyrenees.

← Ricotta

Long considered "poor man's food," due to them being made from a by-product of cheesemaking (see below), they were a staple of shepherds' diets, along with bread or polenta.

How they're made

Whey is the star ingredient in this group of cheeses. A by-product of cheesemaking, whey is the liquid that separates from the curd when milk is coagulated. It is composed primarily of water, but it also contains a portion of the milk's dry matter, including protein (albumin and globulin), sugar, and minerals. For every 26 gallons (100 liters) of milk used to make cheese, around 24 gallons (90 liters) of whey are produced. This family of cheeses was born as a means to get the very most out of the raw material, milk.

All the members of this group have one thing in common: they are made using sweet whey—a by-product of rennet-coagulated cheeses (see p. 35). This differs from the whey expelled during the pressing stage of the same cheeses and from the acid whey expelled from acid-coagulated or lactic cheeses. The latter two types would be too acidic for ricotta-type cheeses and prevent the curd from forming. Ricotta-type cheeses are obtained through a physicochemical reaction known as flocculation. In this process, whey proteins cluster and form curd "flakes" or "flocs" on the surface. To initiate this reaction, cheesemakers first stir and heat the sweet whey. This explains the name "ricotta," which means "re-cooked" or "cooked twice" in Italian (this is the second time this component of the original milk has been heated). The French term for this category of cheeses, "*recuites*," means the same thing. They then add an acidulant, such as vinegar, lemon juice, fig sap, or even sour whey from the previous day, as in Sicily. The resulting flocculated curd—composed of proteins and fats—is scooped out using a skimmer and drained in perforated molds.

When fresh, whey cheeses should be consumed within five or six days due to their low acidity. They can also be salted, dried, aged, or smoked for a longer shelf life. Here are some of the many different types of whey cheese made around the world:
- Bearnese greuil and Basque breuil, both by-products of sheep's milk tommes.
- Recuite, made in France's Aveyron region with whey left over from pérail cheesemaking.
- Sérac, a secondary product of Swiss Gruyères, French Comtés, and other similar hard cheeses.
- Manouri, made with whey from feta production.
- Romanian Urdă, made with sheep's milk whey.
- Belgian maquée (makêye in Walloon), traditionally made with buttermilk and whey (although today the term is generally used in Belgium for fromage blanc).

The following whey cheeses are made with added whole milk, producing creamier, smoother, and more flavorful results:
- Greek Mizithra, made with about 2 gallons (7 liters) of milk per ¾ gallon (3 liters) of whey.

- Tunisian rigouta, originally made with sheep's milk but now with cow's milk, at a ratio of about ¼ gallon (1 liter) of milk per 2½ gallons (9 liters) of whey.
- Corsican AOP Brocciu, made with a maximum of 20 percent sheep's milk.
- Ricotta di bufala Campana DOP, made with buffalo's milk whey and up to 6 percent added whole milk.
- Ricotta Romana DOP, made with sheep's milk whey and up to 15 percent fresh sheep's milk, then drained for up to 24 hours to add texture and make the cheese denser.

> **MASCARPONE, BUT INCOGNITO**
> A close relative of this family is mascarpone, the emblem of the Italian region of Lombardy and star of tiramisu. It is prepared the same way as ricotta, but with one key difference: it is made with fresh cream rather than whey.

Peak season

The availability of whey from other cheesemaking processes determines the season for the different whey cheeses. For example, high-mountain cheeses are made during the summer and last throughout the winter, but their by-products made with fresh whey are produced and consumed during the same season. In the Mediterranean region, Corsica's brocciu is available from December to July, but the best is made in spring when the maquis (the dense vegetation covering the island's lower slopes) is in full bloom.

Food pairings

Ricotta and other similar cheeses can add a creamy texture to dry foods and balance out strong, bold flavors. This is particularly true for ricotta, which has a slight sweet taste. Feel free to experiment with the fresh whey cheeses available in your area in the following combinations.

• We are especially fond of Sicilian *cassatta*: a dessert cake made with ricotta, genoise sponge, marzipan, and candied fruit.
• Spice-roasted peaches with honey and brocciu make for an equally exquisite combination.
• On the savory side, a simple white bean salad with lemon and herbs is delicious heaped on toasted bread with garlic and sérac.
• All sorts of fruits, vegetables, herbs, and meats pair beautifully with fresh whey cheeses: bell peppers, kale, asparagus, peas, parsley, mint, tomatoes, berries, anchovies, sausage, bacon, smoked meats, to name but a few.

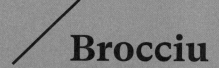

Brocciu

Although technically a by-product of cheesemaking, brocciu (or brousse) is a national treasure in its own right in Corsica and a culinary emblem on the island. The exceptional flavors of this distinctive cheese capture the very essence of its terrain.

Characteristics

APPEARANCE Pure white, brocciu has all the qualities of a lightly salted fresh cheese with a delicate, moist texture.

TASTE Rich and thick on the palate, brocciu has a fresh flavor with subtle notes of leather and the Corsican maquis. It is sold in a plastic strainer basket that leaves an imprint reminiscent of the traditional woven rush strainers used in the past.

Interesting facts

To make brocciu, it is first necessary to make other cheeses, including niulincu, calinzana, and venachese in northern and eastern Corsica; Tomme Sartenaise in the south; and bastellicacciu in the Ajaccio region. The leftover whey is recovered, mixed with fresh milk, and heated to 172°F (78°C). At this temperature and above, the whey proteins bind together and trap the other components present, including fat, other proteins, water, vitamins, and minerals. A sort of foam forms on the surface and is delicately transferred to molds to become brocciu.

A symbol of Corsican identity, brocciu can be found on every table on the island, even though this delicacy is generally more expensive than the cheeses themselves.

Brocciu features in a number of traditional Corsican recipes. It may be used in omelets with fresh mint; mashed with a fork to add to a filling for cannelloni tubes; or mixed with eggs, lemon, eau de vie, and sugar to make *fiadone* (Corsican cheesecake, see p. 258). It is also served on its own or drizzled with chestnut honey and myrtle liqueur.

Soft Cheeses

Chèvres & Co. 65

Chaource & Co. 69

Époisses & Co. 73

Brie & Co. 76

Munster & Co. 83

Vacherin & Co. 87

Gorgonzola & Co. 91

Roquefort & Co. 95

Cancoillotte & Co. 101

Some family members

-*Pélardon*
-*Picodon*
-*Charolais*
-*Macônnais*
-*Rigotte de Condrieu*
-*Saint-Marcellin*
-*Sainte Maure de Touraine*
-*Selles-sur-Cher*
- *Chabichou du Poitou*
- *Valençay*
- *Pouligny-Saint-Pierre*
- *Chavignol*
- *Rocamadour*
- *Pérail*

Chèvres & Co.

Characteristics

APPEARANCE Chèvres, or French goat's milk cheeses, range in size from the mini Boutons de Culotte, often weighing less than an ounce or a few grams each, to more imposing tommes. The fruit of cheesemakers' ingenuity over the years, they come in an incredible variety of shapes. They can be eaten at all stages of the ripening spectrum, from fresh, pure white, and rindless to ultra-dry and brittle with diverse surface molds ranging from blue-gray to reddish in hue. The rinds are typically rough—they have been compared to a stormy sea!—and are covered with ivory-hued wrinkles. This is caused by the mold *Geotrichum candidum*, which is widely used as a ripening culture. They are sometimes coated with ash or even herbs or spices. Others, ripened with *Penicillium glaucum*—another edible mold—have a downy white bloomy rind.

TASTE Principally made with goat's milk, as the name implies (chèvre means "goat" in French), these cheeses often have tangy, lactic flavors with notes of grass, herbs, nuts, and the occasional animal tones. They can be strong and peppery, and occasionally may have a slightly soapy taste, which some people find unpleasant. The texture can be soft and even runny, like Rocamadour or pélardon, or firm, like Charolais or picodon. A smooth, matte, uniform inside is the sign of a good chèvre.

The flavor and texture of these cheeses evolve quickly, so it's essential to ask your cheesemonger for advice to find the ones that best suit your taste.

← Chèvres

Origins

For the purposes of this book, we'll begin in the seventh century CE. By this time, goats had spread throughout southwestern Europe, including central France, due to the Arab conquest. The southeastern region of France, with its Mediterranean climate and hardscrabble soils ill-suited to crop farming, provided an ideal habitat for goats. The animals thrived in the region's characteristic scrubland that was rich in aromatic plants.

In the past, cheese production was organized in a way that allowed farmers to alternate between different tasks. The cheesemaking process was carried out in a building located near the farmhouse, which made it easier to add curds from successive batches to the molds until they were full. Until the mid-twentieth century, typical production sites for these small cheeses were based on either:
- a group of three to four goat-farming families who made cheese for their own consumption, or
- small herds of about a dozen goats used to make cheeses to be sold on a small scale. This was particularly prevalent in regions with large towns that offered plenty of market opportunities.

During the 1950s, the agricultural industry was modernized, and farms became increasingly specialized. In the aftermath of the phylloxera crisis that devastated their vines, many growers gave up their vineyards and wine production. At the same time, goat and cattle farming expanded, particularly in the Poitou region. Over time, large dairy farms emerged, especially in the fertile central western part of the country, and these farms began supplying their milk to industrial cheese producers. Farming practices became more intensive: the animals grazed less, milk (even goat's) was produced in every season, and fresh curds were frozen to allow for year-round cheese production.

Many goat cheeses made in this part of France are produced in a similar manner, although they come in different shapes and sizes. Several have been awarded AOPs to preserve traditional cheesemaking techniques and promote unique local products:
- In the 1970s, AOC status was granted to Pouligny-Saint-Pierre, Selles-sur-Cher, Crottin de Chavignol, and picodon.
- In the 1990s, Chabichou du Poitou, Sainte Maure de Touraine, Valencay, Rocamadour were protected by AOPs.
- In the 2000s, pélardon, Banon, Mâconnais, Rigotte de Condrieu, and Charolais received AOP status.

The specifications for these AOPs are among the strictest in the cheese industry in terms of how the milk must be produced and processed.

A WELL-HONED CRAFT
Today, many goat farmers process their own milk and make some exceptional farmstead cheeses, even without AOP recognition.
Seasonal production and grazing are becoming increasingly common

again, as are local goat breeds, including Poitevines, Rove, Pyrenées, and Massif Central. In terms of their recipes, more cheesemakers are ladling their curds by hand and using their own native starter cultures, resulting in cheeses with greater typicity.

NO GOAT CHEESE WITHOUT KID GOATS
For these dairy breeders, the question remains of what to do with all the kid goats they produce as, today, kid meat is rarely consumed in France. In the best-case scenario, the kids are fattened, slaughtered, and sold in countries with a greater appetite for the meat, such as Italy or Spain. If the sector is to remain both profitable and sustainable over time, and we still wish to eat goat cheese, kid goat meat needs to make a comeback.

How they're made

These small cheeses take their time. The milk coagulates slowly, with very little added rennet, and lactic acid bacteria play a primary role. The curd can take twelve to forty-eight hours to set, but it typically takes eighteen to twenty-four hours.

The "*caillé doux*" (sweet-curd) goat cheeses traditionally made in Provence are an exception. Due to the high summer temperatures in the region, cheesemakers add large amounts of rennet to make the curd form more quickly, in under two hours.

The resulting curd is fragile and must be handled with care, which is why these cheeses are generally hand-ladled into molds of different sizes and shapes, including logs, truncated pyramids, cylinders with rounded ends, and puck-like *palets*.

These cheeses drain passively and do not need to be pressed.

Generally ripened for only a few days, the cheeses in this family are high in moisture, so they need sufficient airflow to dry out the surface. Molds, especially the *Geotrichum candidum* mentioned earlier in this chapter, develop rapidly.

Certain chèvres are ripened in a particular way, such as the ultra-rare Banon from the Provence-Alpes-Cote d'Azur region, which is aged neatly wrapped in chestnut leaves. This increases the storage time, makes the cheese creamier, and gives it more complex, powerful flavors.

LOOKIN' GOOD
Some chèvres are coated with ash—charcoal reduced to a fine powder. Although primarily aesthetic, ash also has drying power and contributes to rind formation.

Peak season

The very best time to eat chèvre is in the spring, as goats give birth toward the end of winter. With this boost in milk supply, production shoots up and market stalls overflow with choice from April to May.

Traditionally, chèvre production continues throughout the summer and fall, up until the animals are left to rest at the onset of winter before the next lactation cycle begins. Although a few techniques exist (more or less questionable, see p. 24) to breed goats out of their natural kidding season, the selection of cheeses available is more limited during the end-of-the-year holiday season.

Food and drink pairings

• What could be better than fresh chèvre with the first fresh peas from the garden (or supermarket), the first fava beans, or the first asparagus?
• Fresh chèvres are sublime in salads with toasted hazelnuts or drizzled with hazelnut oil.
• More-ripened chèvres pair beautifully with figs.
• When it comes to wine, chèvres pair well with crisp, fresh whites like a Sauvignon Blanc, Chenin Blanc, fruity Viognier, or sweet Pineau des Charentes fortified wine.
• For a beer pairing, try a light pilsner, wheat beer, or even a pale ale with tropical fruit notes along with a more mature cheese.
• Apricot nectar and green tea are also good options for drinks.

Chaource & Co.

Characteristics

APPEARANCE The cheeses in this group are soft with velvety white "bloomy" rinds, due to the microflora that develop during the ripening stage. They have a smooth, ivory-colored texture. The ripening cultures sometimes break down the proteins in the curd in a process known as proteolysis (see pp. 39 and 282). This weakens the cheese structure and produces a softer, creamier texture.

TASTE These cheeses are markedly sweet, with notes of cream and butter, and also fresh mushrooms. They can become more assertive over time, displaying distinct bitter notes. A quite mature Neufchâtel can have a more intense, animal flavor than its traditional heart shape would suggest, and as it ages the cheese and its rind turn a browner hue.

Origins

The beginnings of Chaource and its kin can be traced to Burgundy and Champagne, specifically the wet, grassy valleys and plains of the Aube, Yonne, and Côte d'Or departments. Cows were the only animals that could be raised there, as they tolerate humidity better than goats and sheep and guarantee milk production on such fertile lands. Lactic cheeses have been made there since the Middle Ages, following a slow and largely hands-off process that was in tune with the daily rhythm of farm life, leaving time for the many other farming tasks.

Milking would typically be done in the morning or evening, and the milk would be left to curdle naturally before moving on to the next phase at the end of the day or the following morning. This explains why the production stages are so long and simple. The resulting small cheeses were mostly consumed domestically, but they were also used for bartering or for paying taxes in kind.

Brillat-Savarin cheese was developed in the 1930s by the legendary Parisian *fromager* Henri Androuët as a tribute to Jean Anthelme Brillat-Savarin. A "foodie influencer" before his time, this well-known judge and writer penned *The Physiology of Taste*—his landmark book on food and eating—in 1830. Brillat-Savarin is known as a "triple-cream" cheese because it is made by adding cream to whole milk to increase the fat content, making it especially rich and creamy. The final cheese contains 35 percent fat—the same amount found in Comté, for example.

On the other side of Paris, in the Pays de Bray, Neufchâtel (not to be confused with the spreadable cheese of the same name) has been produced since the twelfth century. Formerly sold fresh, it now comes in six different shapes, including the famous heart.

How they're made

These cheeses begin in the same way as the lactic goat cheeses mentioned in the previous chapter: with a slow coagulation period. This lasts over twelve hours for Chaource and Brillat-Savarin, and over eighteen hours for Neufchâtel.

The makers of the first two use the same techniques as producers of other lactic cheeses, with passive draining in molds. Neufchâtel cheese, on the other hand, is made using a more specific technique. The curd is drained in a cloth bag, without applying pressure, for four to twelve hours. Following this, it is pressed and mixed with salt before being transferred to molds.

After these cheeses are removed from their molds, they are placed in well-ventilated "*hâloirs*"—drying rooms used for soft cheeses—where *Penicillium candidum* can develop on the surface, covering the cheeses with their characteristic bloomy rinds.

Peak season

These cheeses can be found year-round due to the constant milk supply in the wet areas where they are produced.

← Chaource

Food and drink pairings

• Bread or baguettes with sesame seeds or figs are perfect companions for these cheeses.
• Fresh spinach, sundried tomatoes, shallots, and cured ham all pair well with cheeses from this family.
• Rich in fat, creamy Brillat-Savarin is particularly good at absorbing flavors. Cut it in half horizontally through the center and stuff it with porcini mushrooms, truffles, or even mustard seeds. You could also use rum-soaked raisins for a sweet-savory combination. Chefs love using Brillat-Savarin in sauces and mousses.
• Chaource family members are excellent with a brut Champagne, Crémant de Bourgogne, amber beer, hard apple or pear cider, or a good artisanal apple juice.

Some family members

- *Époisses AOP*
- *Soumaintrain IGP*
- *Langres AOP*

Époisses & Co.

Characteristics

APPEARANCE These cheeses have washed rinds that are wrinkly and display a gamut of reddish-orange hues. Soumaintrain ranges from ivory to ocher, while Langres is more orange, and Époisses may appear brick-red or even brown when aged. They all have a cylindrical shape, and Langres has a sunken top. They have a smooth texture that ranges from ivory to light beige in color and can be chalky or very creamy. Being soft, they are often packaged in wooden boxes to make handling and transport easier.

TASTE The members of this group are often referred to as "stinky cheeses" due to their powerful scent. Depending on how long they've been aged, the aroma can range from vegetal to animal in the case of Soumaintrain and Époisses, while Langres leans more toward herbaceous. The latter is also the lightest of the three on the palate. All of them have a tangy flavor with varying degrees of bitterness. Notes of hay, straw, and humus blend with animal nuances, depending on the season and ripening stage.

Origins

These washed-rind cheeses have the same origins as the bloomy-rind types described in the previous chapter (see pp. 69–71). They were first produced in abbeys, and sixteenth-century Cistercian monks in Burgundy perfected the recipes and ripening techniques before passing their knowledge on to local farmers. We owe those monks our thanks!

How they're made

As with other lactic cheeses mentioned earlier, the coagulation process is more or less slow in the case of Époisses and Soumaintrain: up to sixteen hours for the former and at least eight hours for the latter. Langres, on the other hand, takes two and a half to five and a half hours. The latter is chalky when young because of this relatively quick coagulation process.

The affinage or ripening techniques differ from those used for bloomy-rind cheeses, whose surface molds and yeasts are left to develop naturally. In the case of these washed-rind cheeses, the work takes longer and is more demanding, as the cheese-maker or *affineur* must periodically wash the rinds with a brine solution. This technique is challenging to master, as the cheese can quickly evolve in the wrong direction.
- Époisses AOP is aged for four weeks and hand-washed several times in brine with Marc de Bourgogne mixed in.
- Soumaintrain IGP is aged for at least three weeks and washed four times in brine.
- Small rounds of Langres AOP are aged for at least fifteen days and washed a few times in brine, which may or may not contain annatto (a natural plant-based dye that gives the cheese an orange-red hue).

Keeping the rinds moist during ripening encourages a high level of proteolysis (the decomposition of the cheese proteins), which gives these cheeses their meltingly soft and even gooey textures. This skillfully maintained humidity also favors the growth of *Brevibacterium linens* (aka "red mold")—the bacterium responsible for strong odors, which is also present on human skin and the culprit for stinky feet!

> **SUNKEN TREASURE**
> Identifying a more or less ripened Langres is easy: you just need to look for the sunken top, known as a "*cuvette*" or "*fontaine*" in French. The deeper the divot, the riper the cheese. As Langres is only turned once or twice as it matures, the surface continues to cave in over time.

Peak season

These cheeses are available throughout the year, as the wet areas where they are produced guarantee a continuous milk supply.

Food and drink pairings

• The spicy crunch of black radish goes perfectly with these cheeses.
• Époisses and other family members pair well with wines from the same region, including Blanc de Noirs Champagne, Chablis, or another Burgundy wine.
• A classic way to serve Langres is to pour a little Marc de Champagne or Marc de Bourgogne into the *fontaine*. If the cheese is very ripe, try plum brandy instead.

← Époisses

Brie & Co.

Characteristics

APPEARANCE The cheeses in this group are flat and cylindrical, and range in diameter from 4–16 in. (10–40 cm). Their thin bloomy rinds are downy and white and may have reddish-orange streaks—traces of *Brevibacterium linens*, or "red mold," more often found on washed-rind cheeses (such as Époisses, Munster, and Maroilles, see pp. 73 and 83). Cheeses with these streaks will have a more pronounced flavor.

TASTE Brie family cheeses have a soft, smooth texture. When young, they can be crumbly and have delightful notes of milk and button mushrooms. As they age, bitter undertones become increasingly prominent, and more intense animal flavors, evocative of the farm, emerge.

Origins

Like many other cheeses, Brie also has medieval origins. In the eighth century, Emperor Charlemagne is said to have discovered the cheese while visiting an abbey in the Brie region. Initially put off by the unattractive greenish hue the rind had in those days, he then tasted and praised the monks' cheese. This medieval "influencer" is also thought to have done the same for another unique cheese: Roquefort. Philippe II of France and Louis XVI were also allegedly devoted fans of Brie, the so-called "king of cheeses" or "cheese of kings" made in the Paris basin.

Peak season

These cheeses are produced year-round, although those available in May through June are generally the softest and most balanced in terms of taste.

Food and drink pairings

• Brie and Camembert are all-time favorites on cheese plates, but they are also delicious grilled or coated in breadcrumbs and deep-fried until golden.
• You can also cut them in half and stuff them with walnuts or sautéed porcini mushrooms (or even black truffles) just before serving to make them even more decadent.
• Did you know that Camembert cellars smell strongly of green apples in the early ripening phase? The classic pairing of Camembert with apples is no coincidence after all!
• The bloomy rind on Brie can have bitter notes, so a dry white wine works better than a robust red. But if you prefer to serve a red wine, select a lighter-bodied Pinot Noir with mellow tannins or a Gamay, as both are good matches.
• With a soft, creamy texture, these cheeses also pair beautifully with bubbles. Champagne made with Pinot Meunier grapes is an excellent choice, as are Vouvrays and Crémants. Hard ciders, whether apple or pear, also make excellent companions.

Camembert de Normandie AOP

Characteristics

APPEARANCE A large round weighing at least 9 oz. (250 g), Camembert de Normandie has a downy white rind and is ivory-to-yellow in color, with small holes when it is well made.

TASTE On the nose, Camembert has a pleasant mushroom aroma and occasionally reveals barnyard notes. When young, it is pleasingly sweet and melts smoothly in the mouth. As it ripens, the texture becomes creamier, and the flavor more intense. At all stages, the taste has light salty notes.

Interesting facts

Choosing a Camembert is no easy task. In addition to Camembert de Normandie AOP, there are two other types found on supermarket shelves: one labeled "Camembert fabriqué en Normandie" ("made in Normandy") and another simply called "Camembert," which can be made as far away as Canada or Japan. From the outside, it can be hard to differentiate between a very good Camembert and a mediocre one. Unlike the AOP versions, there are no regulations governing the production of non-AOP Camemberts. The latter may be produced using pasteurized, homogenized, or even ultrafiltered milk, and the curds may be ladled mechanically. Every aspect of the process is optimized. Some brands even vaunt the consistency of their cheese, which is always the same and "*fait à coeur*"—ripened all the way through. Fortunately, there are still a few rare exceptions made the traditional way with raw milk.

Buy Camembert de Normandie AOP whenever possible, as a guarantee of quality. This certification ensures that the cheese has been made with raw milk produced in the original Camembert terroir, from cows that have grazed in pastures for at least six months of the year. Most importantly, the AOP guarantees that the cheesemakers and *affineurs* have followed time-honored methods specific to this very cheese.

In fact, Camembert de Normandie AOP is the only cheese in France—and, dare we say it, in the world—whose curd is hand-ladled into molds in five successive layers, each added forty minutes apart. It is a demanding process, to say the least, and it is well worth seeking out and supporting this unique cheese.

Some family members

- *Munster AOP*
- *Maroilles AOP, Vieux-Lille, or Gris de Lille*
- *Pont-l'Évêque AOP*
- *Livarot AOP*
- *Niolo, Calenzana, and Venachese (Corsica)*
- *Herve AOP (Belgium)*
- *Limburger (Germany, Belgium, and the Netherlands)*
- *Stinking Bishop (southwestern England)*

Munster & Co.

Characteristics

APPEARANCE The cheeses in this family come in different sizes and shapes, including rounds, squares, and rectangular slabs. They have an orange rind that is sticky to the touch in some cases, and the color of the cheeses ranges from ivory to light beige.

TASTE The taste has nothing in common with the smell, which is reminiscent of stinky feet. In fact, the *Brevibacterium linens* bacteria that nestle between our toes are cousins of the ones that grow on the surfaces of these Munster family cheeses (also found in the washed-rind lactic cheese family). On the palate, these cheeses are floral with notes of dry grass, while those on the riper end of the spectrum can have animal notes and a slightly smoky taste. The texture ranges from soft and supple to gooey and almost spoonable.

Origins

Belonging to a sub-family of surface-ripened cheeses, the members of this group are regularly washed and brushed during the ripening period to activate fermentation. These are known as washed-rind or smear-ripened cheeses.

These cheeses have roots in northern France, above a line that stretches from Normandy to Burgundy. In these gently undulating lowland regions, the wet valleys with lush, abundant grass were better suited to cattle farming than grain cultivation. With a constant and reliable year-round milk supply, there was no need to produce

← Munster

long-keeping cheeses, so this is soft, surface-ripened cheese territory. Moderately ripened bloomy-rind cheeses are produced here, in addition to these more labor-intensive washed-rind types. Over the centuries, industrious cheesemakers have perfected techniques for ripening the latter, producing cheeses with a longer shelf life. Many, such as Maroilles and Munster, evolved in monasteries in the sixth and seventh centuries; the latter gets its name from the Alsace town of Munster, where the cheese was conserved and matured in monks' cellars. Farmers near the abbeys learned and built on the techniques, which later spread elsewhere.

Washed-rind cheeses are also produced in northern Corsica. Venachese, Niolo, and Calenzana are made there with raw sheep's or goat's milk according to recipes specific to villages and even individual cheesemakers. They are mainly consumed locally.

Although some washed-rind cheeses, such as Maroilles, Munster, Livarot, and Herve, are well known and recognized as culinary heritage, there are also many lesser-known artisanal versions now produced throughout France and elsewhere.

How they're made

The cheeses in this group begin like many bloomy-rind types. Full-fat or lightly skimmed milk is coagulated quickly, in contrast to washed-rind cheeses with a lactic profile, which require a much longer coagulation period. The curd is barely cut, if at all, and then carefully transferred to molds. This slow, gentle process preserves the curd structure as much as possible and contributes to the cheese's final texture.

To make bloomy-rind cheeses, cheesemakers and *affineurs* only turn the cheeses occasionally, and they allow the *Geotrichum* and *Penicillium* molds to develop on their own. Washed-rind cheeses, on the other hand, require more intervention. The rind needs to be washed or brushed periodically with a salt-water brine, sometimes mixed with annatto, whey, wine, beer, cider, or spirits. This eliminates unwanted microbes and encourages desirable ones to proliferate, influencing the color, texture, and flavor of the final cheese. Washing and brushing may be done by immersion or by hand, using a sponge or brush. This produces the reddish-orange rind and potent smell characteristic of these cheeses, due to the presence of the famous *Brevibacterium linens* bacteria. The surface of the cheese must always be moist, but not too moist. This is a delicate exercise in controlling microbial activity, which, if too intense, can produce a runny cheese.

Previously, the use of annatto was authorized in certain AOPs, including Pont-l'Évêque and Livarot. This is no longer the case. Niolo and Calenzana cheeses are washed by hand and then lined up together, tops and bottoms touching, in wooden troughs or crates for ripening. This gives them their typical square shape with rounded corners. Venachese is ripened on boards, so it retains its round shape. This ripening technique makes it possible to keep the cheeses for longer—typically up to several weeks.

Munster made with Vosgian cow's milk

An iconic Alsatian cheese, Munster often gets a bad rap due to its undeniably distinctive smell. Yet this reputation is highly unjustified, given the impressive finesse of some varieties.

Characteristics

APPEARANCE Munster has a flat round shape and a smooth, glistening, orange-hued rind.

TASTE While the aroma is strong and persistent, the flavor is subtle, with notes of spice, nuts, and hay, drawn out by a soft, creamy finish.

Interesting facts

Munster cheese is made in two places: around Munster in Alsace and around Gérardmer in Lorraine. This explains why the cheese has two different names, Munster and Géromé—a vestige of the local dialect. The two are now grouped together under the Munster-Géromé AOP.

Originally made in the Vosges mountains, Munster is now produced throughout the surrounding plains in seven different French departments. If you can find it, it is well worth trying Munster made exclusively with milk from Vosgian cows (Munster can also be made with milk from the Simmental, Prim'Holstein, and Montbéliarde breeds). Vosgian cows are well suited to harsh mountain conditions as they are not very sensitive to sudden temperature changes. The breed has been recorded since the seventeenth century and is said to have evolved through Scandinavian ancestors mixed with local breeds. It nearly disappeared after the two World Wars, during the Trente Glorieuses—the thirty-year boom period in France following World War II. The farm sector rapidly modernized, and ultra-productive breeds were favored.

Vosgian cattle are listed in the Slow Food Ark of Taste—a catalog of traditional food products and local breeds at risk of extinction. Buying cheese made with Vosgian cow's milk helps to support biodiversity and preserve traditional savoir faire.

Peak season

Most of these cheeses are made with cow's milk in regions that enjoy mild summers, so milk is available throughout the year. The season for the Corsican cheeses is tied to the milk supply from goats and ewes, and lasts from Christmas to July.

Food and drink pairings

• If these washed-rind cheeses are too strong for your taste, sprinkle them with a little ground cumin to mellow them out. You can also cook them to temper the flavor, or serve them with sweet brioche.

• Potatoes, leeks, and shallots all pair well with Munster family cheeses in gratins, soups, or tarts. These cheeses are also excellent in tartiflette (see recipe p. 241).

• Munster and Stinking Bishop have an affinity with fennel seeds, so why not combine them in crackers (see recipe p. 190), as best-selling food writer Niki Segnit suggests in *The Flavor Thesaurus*?

• For a bold combination, try any of these cheeses with spiced black tea over ice.

• Munster and company go well with high-strength, slightly sweet Tripel beers, and demi-sec or sweet white wines with some structure. With its juniper notes, chilled gin is a particularly refreshing option.

Some family members

- *Mont d'Or, or Vacherin du Haut-Doubs, AOP (France)*
- *Vacherin Mont d'Or AOP (Switzerland)*
- *Vacherin des Aravis or "La Manigodine" (France)*
- *Vacherin d'Abondance (France)*
- *Vacherin des Aillons (France)*

Vacherin & Co.

Characteristics

APPEARANCE The members of this group are easy to recognize: like mythical heroes, they wear a belt in the form of a wooden strap, which helps them to maintain their shape despite their soft—even runny—texture. The rinds are typically washed during ripening, giving them an orange hue and, occasionally, a delicate white down develops on the surface, as in the case of Mont d'Or.

TASTE These cheeses have a sweet and creamy taste with animal undertones that vary in intensity based on their production process and ripening stage.

Origins

Originally from the mountainous Jura and Savoie regions, these cheeses get their name from the *vachers* (cowherds).

> **DESSERT OR CHEESE?**
> A note for those with a sweet tooth: there is also a dessert called vacherin, which consists of layers of meringue sandwiched with ice cream and whipped cream. Created in the nineteenth century in Switzerland, it became popular in Germany and then in Lyon, France. The name is said to have been inspired by vacherin cheese.

Official references are scarce, but "*fromage sanglé*"—cheese encircled with a strap—is thought to have first appeared in the twelfth century in the Jura Mountains region. During this period, the Saint-Claude and Montbenoît abbeys cleared large swathes of mountain pasture, making way for cattle herding and dairy production. According to one story, the recipe was developed in 1265 in a (Spanish rather than French!) monastery in Montserrat by a man named Vaccarinus—a cow-herding monk originally from Münchenwiler in Switzerland; however, nothing could be less certain. In any case, it is clear that these cheeses developed in parallel to the *fruitières*— the cooperatives that emerged in the late Middle Ages, collecting milk from several farmers to make large cheeses like Gruyère.

In late autumn, the cows would return from mountain pastures to their barns, as the snow began to fall and the paths to the cooperatives became impassable. The cowherds (*vachers*) would then transform what little milk they got from their animals into a small cheese: vacherin. The Jura versions (both French and Swiss) grew in popularity and were eventually packaged in their distinctive wooden boxes to make them easier to transport. Nowadays, several more or less conventional varieties are available, some of which are produced using sheep's or goat's milk.

How they're made

Whole milk—never skimmed—is the base ingredient in all of these cheeses. The milk is usually used raw, although this depends on the cheese. Thermized milk, for instance, is used to make the Swiss Vacherin Mont d'Or AOP.

Once the milk has coagulated, the curd is cut into large pieces and transferred to molds. Since the milk is high in fat, the whey does not separate easily. As a result, the cheese doesn't hold together well and must be encircled with a strap immediately after it is unmolded to maintain its shape. This strap is usually made of spruce sapwood, which is the part located just below the bark.

These cheeses are ripened in a cool cave at around 59°F (15°C), where intense microbial activity results in a high level of proteolysis—the breakdown of the cheese's proteins. In other words, the amount of water the cheese retains and the ripening temperature make these cheeses so creamy. To maintain this moisture, the cheese is regularly washed, which gives it its lovely orange color.

In some cases, the AOP specifications authorize light pressing for a few hours, such as for the Swiss Vacherin.

> **SMALL MOUNTAINS, BUT A GREAT CHEESE**
> Why does the Mont d'Or rind seem to have folds that resemble the gently rolling Jura Mountains? It's because the cheese is squeezed into a box with a smaller diameter than the wooden strap.

← Mont d'Or

Peak season

Vacherins were originally made in the fall and winter, once the summer dairy season had ended. During this time, the cows were brought down from the mountain pastures and fed on hay instead of fresh grass. As a result, they produced less milk, but it was richer in protein and fat. The AOPs have emphasized this traditional seasonality by imposing a strict range of production dates: from August 15 to March 15 for the French Mont d'Or and from August 15 to March 31 for the Swiss Vacherin Mont d'Or. The Savoyard Vacherins are rare and are only produced toward the end of the year, as the holiday season approaches.

The other more modern creations are not subject to any particular specifications, so they can be found year-round, depending on availability.

Food and drink pairings

• Cow's milk vacherin is delicious eaten warm, straight from the oven, with potatoes or bread for dipping (see recipe p. 198). Garlic, mushrooms, or even a sprinkling of nutmeg are all perfect additions.
• Vacherin can be used in vegetable tarts, to jazz up *crozets* (small, square-shaped pasta from the Savoie region), or to give burgers a twist.
• Artisanal pear or apple juice, or an Arbois Chardonnay offer crisp acidity and fresh notes that partner well with these fat-rich cheeses.
• Wines from Savoie or Muscadet also make excellent companions. If you're taking the red route, a fruity, low-tannin profile is best—a Beaujolais Gamay, Pinot Noir with ultra-smooth tannins, or Loire red are all good choices. Sparkling wines, like Crémant du Jura, also pair beautifully with vacherins.

Close cousins

The following cheeses are special cases that combine several different cheesemaking techniques. In our opinion, they fit best in the vacherin family.
→ **Reblochon AOP:** This is a kind of vacherin without the spruce strap. The curd is lightly pressed with a weight, and the cheese is regularly washed after unmolding. After a few weeks of ripening, it has a meltingly soft texture and flavors that range from herbaceous to fruity, or even animal, depending on the producer and the season.
→ **Chevrotin AOP:** This is the goat's milk version of reblochon. Farmers in Savoie used to keep a few goats to maintain their pastures, as they eat plants that cows won't touch. This appellation is exclusively farmstead.

Some family members

- *Strachitunt*
- *Gorgonzola*
- *Taleggio*
- *Stracchino all'antica delle valli orobiche*

Gorgonzola & Co.

Characteristics

APPEARANCE The non-blue members of this group are generally square in shape, while the blue ones are typically round. The color of the cheeses ranges from white to straw-yellow, while the rinds are thin and naturally pink.

TASTE These cheeses have an array of sweet and tangy notes on the palate that sometimes linger in a truffle finish. The texture can vary from creamy to oozing. The blues in the group are generally mild, and the marbling lends flavors that enhance the overall taste, including the occasional boozy note. Ripened for longer, the "*piccante*" versions of the blues have a firmer texture and—as the name suggests—an intense, spicy flavor.

Origins

Known as stracchino cheeses—from the Italian *straccare*, which means "to tire"—the members of this group were traditionally made when cows returned from the high Alpine pastures at the end of summer. The term *straccare* refers to the cows being worn out from their journey, but although these weary cows produced less milk, it was richer in fat and, therefore, perfect for cheesemaking. The most famous stracchino, Taleggio, gets its name from Val Taleggio, the Italian mountain valley where it originated. It has a washed rind and a soft, oozing texture, and was initially made only in the mountains. From the tenth century onward, the recipe spread throughout the valleys of Lombardy, Piedmont, and Treviso, which is the current production area of the DOP-protected Taleggio.

The origins of strachitunt, a cheese variety from northern Italy, can be traced back to the nineteenth century in Val Taleggio, situated high above Bergamo in the Lombardy region. The name strachitunt is a combination of two words: *stracchino*, the style, and *tunt*, referring to the cheese's round shape (as opposed to *quader*, or square-shaped, like Taleggio). This cheese all but disappeared in the 1970s.

Like Taleggio, strachitunt's blue version originated lower in the valley. Mainly produced around the town of Gorgonzola, near Milan, it was originally called "stracchino di Gorgonzola" or "stracchino verde." The name was later shortened to "Gorgonzola."

After World War II, the large dairies in Lombardy simplified the recipe in order to meet the growing demand. Exported worldwide, Gorgonzola was granted a DOP in 1970. During the twentieth century, pasteurizing the milk became the norm, as it guaranteed more consistent results and improved the cheese's shelf life, making it easier to export. From a technical standpoint, pasteurization favors proteolysis, giving Gorgonzola its creamy and runny texture. Today, Gorgonzola DOP is one of the most widely produced cheeses in Italy, after Parmigiano Reggiano DOP and Grana Padano DOP.

How they're made

As explained above, stracchino cheeses have long been made with autumn milk, when cows graze on the green Lombardy pastures after coming down from the mountains. This milk is rich in fat and was traditionally used whole. Today, Taleggio DOP can be made with raw or pasteurized milk. After a quick coagulation process, the curd is roughly cut and then transferred to molds, producing a soft, fragile, and highly moist cheese. The wheels are first placed in a warm room or cave for several hours to kickstart the microbial activity. Later, they are ripened in cool caves with high relative humidity, where they are regularly turned and washed with brine. The ripening time varies but must last for at least thirty-five days in the case of Taleggio DOP.

Strachitunt cheese is made by combining two batches of curd—one made with evening milk and the other with morning milk. This is known as the "double-curd" technique. The two curds are then layered in molds and left to rest and drain for twelve hours. After a few days, the cheese is pierced with a copper needle, which allows air to enter the spaces between the curds, creating the perfect breeding ground for the molds typical of blue cheeses. In the case of strachitunt, the molds that form the blue veins are completely natural, whereas Gorgonzola DOP is deliberately inoculated with *Penicillium glaucum*.

This double-curd method recalls the one used to make blue cheeses in the neighboring Savoie region, such as the rare Bleu de Termignon, which is made in France's Vanoise National Park by just five producers.

← Gorgonzola

Gorgonzola production, on the other hand, has been simplified. The milk must be pasteurized, and—as mentioned above—the cheese is inoculated with *Penicillium* molds to produce the blue veins, so the double-curd technique is not strictly necessary. The creamy, sweet version (*dolce*) is aged between 50 and 150 days, while the stronger Gorgonzola *piccante* is left to ripen for between 80 and 270 days.

Peak season

Historically, these cheeses—from fresh to long-ripened versions—were available from fall to spring. Today, Taleggio and Gorgonzola are made and sold year-round. The milk is generally standardized in terms of fat content, so the quality is relatively consistent.

Strachitunt remains a niche cheese, with just fifty wheels produced each week, and there are only four artisan dairies in the appellation consortium.

Food and drink pairings

• Stracchino cheeses have a natural affinity with pears, figs, walnuts, and berries.
• For a perfect summer aperitif, top watermelon wedges with Taleggio, chopped pistachios, and thyme, then place them briefly under the broiler to melt.
• Cheese sauce made with Gorgonzola or Taleggio is delicious over pasta with sage and freshly ground pepper.
• Sweet, creamy Gorgonzola *dolce* calls for a white wine, such as a Riesling, demi-sec, or semi-sweet moelleux. A double malt beer or good grape juice are also excellent choices.
• The more assertive Gorgonzola *piccante* pairs nicely with Chianti or another well-structured red with mellow tannins.

Some family members

- *Roquefort AOP*
- *Bleu des Causses AOP*
- *Bleu d'Auvergne AOP*
- *Fourme d'Ambert AOP*
- *Bleu de Laqueuille*

Roquefort & Co.

Characteristics

APPEARANCE These blue cheeses come in round wheels and have a distinctively craggy, mottled look. Ivory in color, the cheese is dotted with small holes lined with mold of varying shades, ranging from light blue to dark blue, and even bluish-green. These cheeses are often wrapped in foil to prevent a rind from forming.

TASTE Known for their bold flavor, these cheeses display fruity, spicy overtones with a metallic tang and a rich mouthfeel.

Origins

We'll spare you the popular myth of Roquefort being the result of a hapless shepherd leaving his bread and cheese behind in a cave. The same goes for the story of Charlemagne, who was supposedly won over by Roquefort (see the Brie chapter, p. 76). We'll also only give a brief mention to Pliny the Elder, who referred to a sheep's milk cheese from the Babales region—present-day Lozère—in his *Natural History*, the monumental encyclopedia he wrote in the first century CE. Finally, we're not going to call it the "king of cheeses," an oft-used title that also crowns other varieties, including Époisses and Brie. However, we will insist on the first historical mention of Roquefort, which was in 1070, in the cartulary of Conques abbey, in the Aveyron region, on a page listing the institution's properties.

GEOGRAPHICAL CONFUSION
Although there is a village in the Landes region of southwestern France called Roquefort, the cheese gets its name from Roquefort-sur-Soulzon—a village with six hundred inhabitants in the Aveyron. Now, that would make a great trivia question!

No matter its exact origins, this ancient cheese is intrinsically linked to the natural limestone caves of Mont Combalou, in Roquefort-sur-Soulzon, southeast of the small city of Rodez. Caused by a collapse a million years ago, these caves are connected to one another, and cracks or faults in the rocks (known as *fleurines*) allow cool, humid air to circulate, favoring mold growth. In other words, the caves provide the ideal conditions for ripening Roquefort.

As occurred with many other cheeses, Roquefort production shot up in the nineteenth century due to technical innovations, industrialization of the caves, and improved storage and transport. Sales expanded throughout France, and then internationally as well. To keep pace with growing demand, production was stepped up on the Larzac plateau and on neighboring limestone plateaus, known as Causses. After World War I, the market remained dynamic but disorganized, and "cheating" was rampant throughout the industry:
- Sheep's milk producers were paid poorly, so it was not unusual for the milk to be cut with water, skimmed, or, most commonly, mixed with cow's milk.
- Some cave owners ripened their Roquefort in so-called "bastard" caves, which were natural but not located in Mont Combalou.
- Many imitations appeared abroad, as well as in France, including the "Roquefort-style" ("*façon Roquefort*") blues made in Auvergne.

A lively debate ensued over which characteristics most defined the cheese. Was it the milk? Should Roquefort be made exclusively with milk from local sheep, instead of the imported milk from North Africa or Corsica that some producers used? Or was it the caves? Some producers even argued that cheese ripened in "bastard" caves could be better than that from Mont Combalou caves.

In response, Roquefort became the very first French cheese to receive an Appellation d'Origine Contrôlée (AOC) in 1925. Since then, it has been made with milk from Lacaune ewes only. A producers' association was created to organize the sector known as La Confédération Générale des Producteurs de Lait de Brebis et des Industriels de Roquefort. The debate was settled. Roquefort had to be ripened in the Combalou caves, and the milk could come from the region, Corsica, or the Pyrenees—but not from North Africa.

In 1842, the Société des Caves et Producteurs Réunis de Roquefort had been founded by a group of fifteen local merchants and *affineurs* who aimed to establish a near-monopoly. By the 1920s, they had largely succeeded, accounting for 71 percent of all Roquefort production. This group later became the well-known brand Société, which is now a subsidiary of dairy giant Lactalis. Instead of trying to keep related cheeses and those produced nearby out of the market, the manufacturers shrewdly invested in them. They created a trade union and, in 1937, obtained a decree that protected Bleu de l'Aveyron, made with cow's milk. This cheese later became Bleu des Causses and is now protected by an AOP.

The Société group also took control of Bleu d'Auvergne in 1920 by acquiring the largest producer, Auvergne Laitière. By the end of the 1970s, Société controlled 80 percent of Roquefort production, but sales were decreasing. Production levels dropped, which made way for newer products to emerge in the French market, such as feta, and for the creation of new appellations, including Ossau-Iraty in the Pyrenees and brocciu in Corsica. By 2021, only seven Roquefort AOP producers-*affineurs* remained, and only one producer and two *affineurs* continued to make Bleu des Causses AOP. While Roquefort production is limited by the ripening process and confined to the Mont Combalou caves, this is not the case for Bleu des Causses, and two farmstead producers have taken up the challenge in the past two years.

In 2017, the Bleu d'Auvergne appellation area was reduced by 40 percent, refocusing production on the region's volcanic mountain terroir. Today, six dairies and eight farmers produce this cheese. Blue cheeses without appellations but very similar to this one include Bleu de Laqueuille and other farmstead blues.

> **WHY IS FOURME D'AMBERT INCLUDED IN THIS FAMILY?**
> After World War II, Fourme d'Ambert producers stopped grinding and salting the curd before transferring it to molds for draining—the same technique used for Cheddar and Cantal. Instead, they drained the curds less and applied salt to the surface of the already-formed cheese, producing something more akin to the other Roquefort family members with their melt-in-the-mouth consistencies. Today, nearly 1,200 producers make Fourme d'Ambert AOP, and 15 percent of the wheels produced each year are made with farmstead raw milk.

How they're made

Each of these blue cheeses from the Massif Central in France has its own unique characteristics. These depend on whether the cheese is made using cow's or sheep's milk and whether the milk is raw or pasteurized, and whole or standardized. Beyond this, the production process is essentially the same:
- The milk is inoculated with a starter culture and *Penicillium roquefortii* mold. In the past, powdered mold from rye bread was used (tasty!), but now nearly all producers use lab-grown strains in liquid form.
- Like Camembert and Brie, these are "*caillé mixte*" cheeses, meaning rennet and starter cultures are added to the milk, and acidification and coagulation occur at the same time (see p. 35). It takes the milk one-and-a-half to two hours to coagulate.
- Next comes a crucial stage: the curd is cut into corn kernel-sized pieces and then stirred. Each piece releases whey, and a fine skin forms on the surface, known as

"*coiffage*" in French. This prevents the curds from fusing together, leaving open spaces in the cheese where *Penicillium* can grow.
- During the ripening phase, the cheese is pierced with needles, which introduces air and allows the mold to bloom. Ripening lasts for a minimum of one to three months, depending on the type of cheese and the desired strength. According to AOP regulations, Roquefort must spend at least twelve days in the famous Mont Combalou caves.

Peak season

Although cow's milk is produced year-round, sheep's milk is seasonal and collected mainly between October and June. These cheeses are ripened in cold rooms or caves (at around 32°F/0°C), so they can be kept for a relatively long period of time before being sold. As a result, end-of-year Roquefort is generally stronger than spring Roquefort.

Food and drink pairings

• You can't go wrong by pairing a soft creamy blue with a date or quince paste.
• These cheeses also marry well with the flavors of grapefruit, broccoli, pear, melon, or watermelon.
• Speculoos cookies and gingerbread emphasize these cheeses' creaminess and strength.
• These characteristically bold blues pair naturally with a sweet companion. Try them with freshly squeezed orange juice with a dash of pomegranate juice, a sweet white wine like Montbazillac or Côteau du Layon, or a *vin doux naturel* (a sweet, fortified wine) like Maury or Rasteau. Sweet-leaning beers such as dark, sweet ales, Baltic porters with their rich roasted notes, and barley wine also make great partners.

Close cousins

→ **Sassenage AOP:** Produced in the Parc Naturel Regional du Vercors, this soft, creamy blue has notes of hazelnuts and undergrowth.
→ **Bleu de Gex AOP:** Made in Franche-Comté, this blue is both crumbly and meltingly soft. It has a drier rind than the other cheeses in this group and looks similar to a tomme from the outside.
→ **Bleu du Queyras:** Made in the Hautes-Alpes department, this cheese has a white to brown rind and is creamy and sweet with delicate woody notes.

Some family members

- *Cancoillotte IGP*
- *La Vache Qui Rit
  (The Laughing Cow)*
- *Crème de fromage
  (cheese spread)*
- *Fromage fort*

Cancoillotte & Co.

Characteristics

APPEARANCE The creamy and spreadable texture of the members of this family ranges from slightly moist to sticky, or even runny. They are generally ivory-white to light yellow, although—logically—Roquefort cheese spread has a bluish hue.

TASTE These cheeses have mild, sweet flavors reminiscent of cream and butter. They are often flavored with more or less natural ingredients (be sure to read the label), from the traditional garlic, *vin jaune* (a deep yellow white wine made in the Jura region), or porcini mushrooms, to tomato, ham, and combinations like eggplant and cashew or salmon with dill. The imagination knows no bounds!

Origins

Welcome to the zero-waste fraternity! A significant amount of cream and butter is produced in the "low country" at the base of the Alps and Jura and Vosges mountains, including the AOP-certified Beurre de Bresse and Crème de Bresse, made between the Auvergne-Rhône-Alpes and Bourgogne-Franche-Comté regions. Rather than letting the leftover skimmed milk go to waste, producers put it to use to make cancoillotte. Although not widely known outside of Franche-Comté, this smooth, creamy cheese gained popularity during World War I when it was included in soldiers' food rations.

In regions that produce Gruyère and other similar cooked pressed cheeses, cheese-makers have long used a process very similar to that for making cancoillotte to turn

← Cancoillotte

imperfect wheels into something they could sell. Industrialization has improved the shelf life, eliminating the need for refrigeration, and some brands, such as La Vache Qui Rit (The Laughing Cow), which was launched in 1921, are exported all over the world, particularly to Asia and Africa, where the cheese is often sold in single-serving portions and used in local dishes.

Throughout France, people have found ways to make the most of cheese scraps, mixing them with wine, eau-de-vie or brandy, and herbs. Known as fromage fort (literally "strong cheese"), this preparation has many regional variations, including bosson maceré in the Bouches-du-Rhône and Ardèche, pourri bressan in Ain, and fort de Bethune in Pas-de-Calais. The Rhône-Alpes region boasts an especially extensive range of variants, including fromage fort de la Croix Rousse in Lyon, pétafine in the Dauphiné area, toupine or tomme fort de Savoie in and around Nice, foudjou in the Drôme, and cachet or fort de Ventoux in the Vaucluse, among others.

The same basic recipe extends the life of old or dried-out bits of cheese, which are stacked in earthenware jars, mixed with alcohol and herbs, and left to ferment for at least a few days. Some are even kept throughout the year with regular "feedings" of alcohol and cheese.

How they're made

A specialty of the Franche-Comté region, cancoillotte is produced by melting ... another cheese. Known as "metton," this cheese is made with skimmed milk left over from cream and butter production. After coagulating the milk, producers cut and dry the curd to make metton: a yellow-hued, slightly rubbery cheese broken into crumb-like clumps. The metton is ripened at 68°F–86°F (20°C–30°C), which causes it to ferment.

To make cancoillotte, the ripened metton is salted, sometimes peppered, and then melted in water heated to 175°F (80°C).

Also made with melted cheese, processed specialties like La Vache Qui Rit (The Laughing Cow) use by-products from the production of different cooked pressed cheeses, including Cheddar, Comté, Emmental, and Gouda. Cheeses with imperfections that prevent them from being sold are shredded and mixed with butter, milk powders, emulsifying or melting salts, and citric acid, and are then cooked and kneaded until they obtain a creamy texture. Once sterilized, they are shelf-stable and do not require refrigeration.

The various fromages forts—spreads made with leftover cheese scraps—are mostly homemade. Ground-up or shredded cheese is combined with wine and eau-de-vie or brandy and left to ferment. Considered somewhat old-fashioned today, fromage fort inspired the legendary imaginary "foune" dish that appeared in the 1979 French comedy film Les Bronzés font du ski (French Fried Vacation 2 in English).

VERY DISCREET AGENTS

For cancoillotte and various *crèmes de fromage* (cheese spreads)—made with cheeses like Gruyère, Roquefort, and Brie—melting salts are added to produce a uniform creamy texture, allowing the milk proteins to emulsify. The additives used vary and may include citric acid (E330), sodium citrate (E331), potassium phosphate (E340), or polyphosphates (E452); each has slightly different characteristics. Polyphosphates are particularly valued in industrial cheese production as they prevent bacterial growth and extend shelf life. Consuming high doses of melting salts, like other food additives, can have an adverse effect on human metabolism. Polyphosphates, for instance, can reduce the absorption of minerals, including calcium, and are banned in organic production in France.

Peak season

As these cheeses have a long shelf life, they are available throughout the year.

Food and drink pairings

• Spread any of these cheeses on toast for a simple yet delicious snack.
• To make Franche-Comté-style fondue, serve cancoillotte warm with potatoes, bacon, and Morteau or Montbéliard sausage.
• *Poulet à la cancoillotte* (chicken in a sauce of cancoillotte, *vin jaune*, and crème fraîche) is another famous dish in the Franche-Comté region.
• Make squash or zucchini soup deliciously creamy by adding any of these cheeses into the mix. Well, maybe not fromage fort (we're not suggesting you be quite that daring).
• As a mellow counterpoint to bold fromage fort, try a sweet (*moelleux*) or syrupy (*liquoreux*) white wine, a Tripel beer, or a slightly tannic cider. To add an extra kick, an eau-de-vie, brandy, or a good whisky will hold its own alongside this assertive cheese.

Semi-Soft & Semi-Hard Cheeses

Tomme de Savoie & Co. **107**

Morbier & Co. **111**

Gouda & Co. **115**

Cantal & Co. **119**

Cheddar & Co. **123**

Stilton & Co. **127**

Some family members

- *Saint-Nectaire AOP*
- *Tomme de Savoie IGP*
- *Tome des Bauges AOP*
- *Ossau-Iraty AOP (Basque Country, known as Ardi Gasna ["sheep's milk cheese"] in Basque)*
- *Queso Manchego DOP (Spain)*

Tomme de Savoie & Co.

Characteristics

APPEARANCE Commonly known as tommes, the members of this group of cheeses come in various shapes and sizes. They are generally round but sometimes square, and can weigh anywhere from 10½ oz. (300 g) for tomettes to several pounds or kilos for larger wheels. They all have a natural rind in shades of white, gray, or brown, mottled with patches of surface molds in blue, yellow, or red. The color of the cheese ranges from white (if it is made with goat's milk) to intense yellow (if made with milk from pastured cows from breeds like Bretonne Pie Noir). Some producers add seeds and spices such as fenugreek, cumin, mustard, or pepper, as well as colorants like annatto or carotene, which both produce an orange hue.

TASTE The texture and flavor vary significantly from one tomme to another. They may be melt-in-the-mouth tender like Saint-Nectaire or dry like some Corsican sheep's milk tommes or Fiore Sardo PDO, a smoked sheep's milk tomme from Sardinia. When young, these cheeses have lovely milky notes, which may be sweet or tangy. After a few months of ripening, they tend to develop fruitier notes and more pronounced animal flavors.

Origins

It isn't easy to pinpoint the exact origins of these tomme-style cheeses, which are relatively simple to make and do not require much equipment. Over the centuries, different variations have emerged, depending on the region, terroir, and producer.

← Tomme de Savoie

Tommes can be stored for extended periods and were traditionally a means of preserving excess milk. In the past, they were primarily made in mountainous areas, but now they are produced just about everywhere. In the Mediterranean, cheeses are mainly made with ewe's milk, including tommes. With the fat-rich milk and less humid caves than elsewhere, this region also produces many hard cheeses.

> **TOME OR TOMME? THAT IS THE QUESTION**
> Both words designate a circular-shaped cheese, although "tomme" is the most commonly used spelling. Exceptions include Tome des Bauges, Tome de la Brigue, and Tome de la Vésubie. According to the *Grand Larousse Gastronomique*, both words come from the pre-Latin root "*toma*," from the verb "*tomer*," which means "to form the curd." In the Tome des Bauges AOP specifications, the word "*toma*" is said to mean "an Alpine pasture-made cheese" in the Savoie dialect. The local trade union, the Syndicat Interprofessionnel de la Tome des Bauges, has embraced this subtle spelling difference as it distinguishes Tome des Bauges AOP from other Savoyard cheeses.

How they're made

All of these tomme-type cheeses have one thing in common—they are all pressed while in their molds (see p. 37). They are meant to be kept for up to several months, so cheesemakers aim to remove as much whey from the curd as possible before the ripening stage.

Tomme-style cheeses are pressed in different ways. In simple systems, the curd is placed in perforated molds, covered with a disk called a follower (*foncet* in French), and then pressed manually or using weights. Other cheesemakers use pneumatic or mechanical cheese presses, which may be horizontal or vertical.

Before pressing, the milk is prepared differently depending on the cheese. It may be raw or pasteurized, and left whole or partially or totally skimmed. This all influences the texture and flavor of the final cheese after ripening. Tome des Bauges, for example, is made with a mixture of skimmed milk from the previous night and warm whole milk from the following morning.

After rapid coagulation, which lasts up to about a half-hour or so, the curd is cut into hazelnut-sized pieces and stirred at around 95°F–98°F (35°C–37°C)—the same temperature as when it comes out of the cow's udder. Because the curds are never heated above this temperature, these cheeses fall into the category of uncooked pressed cheeses.

Tommes are cave-ripened on wooden boards and turned regularly. *Affineurs* sometimes brush the rinds, depending on the cheese.

Saint-Nectaire is traditionally ripened in very damp caves, so it is placed on rye-straw mats to regulate the surface moisture. The rind is washed regularly to control the growth of the mold *Mucor*, known as "*poil de chat*" (cat fur in French), which gives the cheese its prized gray hue. In this environment, the cheese develops earthy notes that perfectly complement the buttery, meltingly soft texture.

Peak season

The season varies according to the type of milk, the region, and even the producer. **Goat's milk tommes** are often made in spring when the milk is plentiful, or in summer if the animals are moved to mountain pastures. **Sheep's milk tommes** are made when ewes produce milk, principally from Christmas to summer. **Cow's milk tommes** are generally produced year-round. With relatively long ripening periods, most of these cheeses can be found throughout the year. Tommes "*d'estive*," however, which are made in summer with high-mountain pasture milk, remain relatively rare and only appear in shops in fall or winter.

Food pairings

•Tommes pair effortlessly with citrus fruits and vegetables.
•To add some spice, paprika and cumin harmonize particularly well with tomme-style cheeses.
•For a delicious and surprising combination, top a slice of rye bread with ribbons of tomme, roasted or sautéed fruit (such as apricots or Mirabelle plums in summer, and pears or apples in winter), and freshly ground pepper.
•A classic partner for Ossau-Iraty is a jam or chutney made with tender and slightly sweet Itxassou cherries.

Morbier & Co.

Characteristics

APPEARANCE Mostly round but sometimes square-shaped, the members of this group can weigh anywhere between 1 and 22 lb. (500 g–10 kg). Given the semi-soft texture of the cheese, anything larger would be too fragile. For the same reason, these cheeses are never more than 4–6 in. (10–15 cm) thick—if larger, they could collapse. The rinds have a subtle orange color that differs from the mottled, grayish shades found on the tommes in the previous entry. The color of the cheese itself ranges from white to intense yellow, depending on the type of milk, breed, and season.

TASTE These semi-soft cheeses have a smooth, supple texture, and some are meltingly tender. On the palate, they offer more or less subtle hints of grass and fruit. Some artisan-produced or longer-aged versions have a more assertive character, with occasional animal overtones combined with buttery notes.

Origins

Like tommes, the members of this group are relatively simple to make and require little equipment. In the Alps and Jura Mountains, these cheeses were traditionally made when there was not enough milk available to make larger varieties. Cheesemakers used the same tools but simplified the process.

Morbier
Morbier—one of the stars in this group of pressed washed-rind cheeses—was first

← Morbier

documented in the late eighteenth century and, historically, was made on farms in the Franche-Comté region. When the weather was too harsh for farmers to take their milk to the local *fruitière* (cheesemaking cooperative), they would use it to make their own cheese. They would place curds from the evening milking in molds and cover them with a layer of ash taken "from the bottom of the cauldron" to protect them until the next day, when they would add curds from that morning's milking. This layering technique allowed them to make a thicker cheese that could be kept for longer. In the 1960s, copies of Morbier started appearing across France; since 2002, however, Morbier has been protected by an AOP and must be made with raw milk from French Simmental or Montbéliarde cows. Nowadays, Morbier producers form the cheese whole in molds, cut it in half, sprinkle it with ash, and press it back together.

Raclette de Savoie IGP

The tradition of melting cheese on a hot stone has existed for centuries in the Swiss and French Alps. During the winter tourism boom that began in the 1950s, the French appliance manufacturer Tefal expanded into the region and sought to partner with local producers to grow its business. This led to the invention of the raclette grill as we know it today, along with the flavorful Raclette de Savoie cheese, which was less "oily" than its predecessors.

Port Salut

In the Alpine valleys, producers with an abundant milk supply began to make larger cheeses than the soft varieties described in the Soft Cheeses chapter. Port Salut, for instance, was created in the late eighteenth century by Trappist monks who had fled to Westphalia, in Germany, during the French Revolution. When they returned to France in 1815, they brought their cheesemaking knowledge with them. They established the Port-du-Salut Abbey in Entrammes, Mayenne, and started crafting cheese using raw milk from the monastery's own cows. By the mid-nineteenth century, the monks had begun purchasing milk from neighboring farms to meet the growing demand for their popular cheeses. Although still made with raw milk, the artisanal cheese was now "*laitier*"—i.e., made with milk collected from more than one farm. The monks trademarked the brand "Port-du-Salut" in 1874, and in 1959 they sold the cheese and name to a company near the monastery, which produced it industrially from pasteurized milk. In 2012, the multinational Bel Group took over the company and moved production across France to Cléry, in the Meuse region. Today, Port Salut is made using partially skimmed and pasteurized milk along with microbial rennet, coloring for the rind, and natamycin—an antifungal that prevents spoilage. A far cry from the original Trappist cheese.

> **THE DIFFERENCES BETWEEN TRAPPIST, MONASTIC, AND ABBEY CHEESES**
> • Officially, **Trappist** cheeses must be made:
> - near a Trappist abbey,
> - under the monks' supervision, and
> - for the benefit of the order or charitable associations.

The most well-known variants include Mont des Cats in French Flanders; Orval and Chimay in Belgium, based on the original Port-du-Salut recipe; La Trappe in the Netherlands; and Westmalle, which is also made in Belgium. The last two are both coated Gouda-type cheeses with the lactose removed (see "How they're made" below). Also of note are Engelszell Abbey, in Austria, where cheese is beginning to be made again, and the San Pedro de Cardena abbey in Spain, where a sheep's milk tomme is produced.

• **Monastic** also refers to an association and a registered brand that groups together over two hundred orders in France and other European countries. Cheeses with the Monastic label can be made by farmers, artisans, or industrial producers. Many of the official Trappiste cheeses mentioned above fall under this umbrella. Other Monastic-labelled cheeses include Trappe d'Echourgnac and Timanoix, which are washed with walnut liqueur, and the reblochon-type cheeses made by the Abbaye de Citeaux and the Abbaye de Tamié.

• **Abbey** cheeses have no official label or appellation.

How they're made

The first stages are similar to those in the tomme-making process. Depending on the cheese, the milk is either left whole, skimmed, or partly skimmed and then thermized or pasteurized, if not used raw. It is even ultrafiltered in the case of some industrially produced varieties. The milk is then coagulated, and the curd is cut into relatively small pieces before being molded and pressed.

The production of these cheeses diverges from tommes at the ripening stage. While the latter have natural rinds, Morbier and company are regularly rubbed with brine as they age. *Affineurs* first brush the older cheeses, followed by the younger ones, which helps to spread the surface cultures that give the rinds their orange hue. These cheeses generally have a creamier texture than tommes.

To make cheeses like Morbier and Raclette de Savoie even more meltingly tender, producers wash or rinse the curd after it has been cut, replacing the whey with cold water. This reduces the lactose content and adds moisture, resulting in a softer cheese.

Peak season

Made chiefly with cow's milk in regions that enjoy mild summers, these cheeses are produced year-round.

Food and drink pairings

• Fresh fruits and vegetables—especially apricots, blackberries, grapes, or celery—are wonderful companions to these cheeses and add color to cheese plates.

• Cut into large cubes and tossed in a salad with fresh herbs and a honey vinaigrette, these cheeses live up to their delicious promise.

• For a unique twist on the traditional *café gourmand* (an espresso served with a selection of petits fours or small desserts in France), try pairing single-origin Costa Rican coffee with Morbier. Creamy, bold, and sweet.

• You could easily pair the cheeses in this family with a strong and slightly sweet Tripel ale, or opt for an authentic Trappist beer like the sublime Orval. If you prefer a white wine, a French Arbois Blanc is a good choice.

Some family members

- *Gouda (Netherlands), including Noord-Hollandse Gouda PDO and Boeren-Leidse met sleutels PDO*
- *Edam (Netherlands), including Noord-Hollandse Edammer PDO*
- *Maasdam (Netherlands)*
- *Mimolette (France)*

Gouda & Co.

Characteristics

APPEARANCE Goudas come in wheels with rounded edges and have a wax coating, while Edam and mimolette have a more spherical shape, and the latter has a natural rind. Other cheeses in this group are coated in paraffin wax (derived from petroleum) colored red, green, or even blue. Inside, the color of the cheese ranges from white in the case of goat's milk cheeses to bright orange, with different colors if flavored or sprinkled with spices such as caraway or cumin seeds. These cheeses sometimes have "eyes" (air bubbles) and can develop small tyrosine crystals when aged.

TASTE Gouda and its kin have a characteristically sweet and milky taste with notes of cream. If aged for a short period, they have a soft texture that melts in the mouth. If they are aged for a longer time, they develop sweeter notes of caramel, and their texture becomes dry and brittle with a crystalline crunch.

Origins

During the Middle Ages, dairy farming was one of the primary sources of income in the swampy regions around Gouda, a city between Rotterdam and Amsterdam in the Netherlands. From the fourteenth century, thousands of gallons of milk (as well as thousands of cattle) and many, many cheeses—including Goudas and Edams—were traded at the renowned Gouda cheese market.

In the seventeenth century, Jean-Baptiste Colbert, chief minister of French king Louis XIV, prohibited the import of all foreign cheese into France. As a result, farmers in French Flanders began producing more of their own version of Dutch Edam cheese. To distinguish it from its confrere, they used annatto to color it and left it with a natural rind instead of covering it in wax like the original. This cheese was initially called "Vieux Hollande" or "Boule de Lille," but was later christened "mimolette."

Nowadays, Gouda-type cheeses are primarily produced industrially and are made worldwide. Mimolette is produced mainly in Normandy, but also in the Loire-Atlantique since 1980. In the Netherlands, about three hundred dairies still make farmstead Gouda using raw milk known as *Boerenkaas* (literally "farmer's cheese" in Dutch) since the term "Gouda" has become generic.

How they're made

Gouda and its cousins are pressed cheeses. After the milk is coagulated, the curd is finely cut, stirred, and left to rest on the bottom of the vats. The curds are then washed in hot water at 140°F–160°F (60°C–70°C). This curd-washing step is one of the defining characteristics of this family. Beyond extracting more whey from the curds, it removes as much lactose and lactic acid as possible, resulting in a sweeter cheese. The curds are then placed in a mold and pressed.

In the low-lying Netherlands, it is not possible to dig caves in hillsides for aging cheese. Instead, climate-controlled ripening rooms are used that have no natural humidity. To preserve moisture in the cheese, it is typically covered with a layer of paraffin wax or—more often—a protective plastic coating.

Nowadays, Goudas may also be made using goat's or sheep's milk, either alone or combined with cow's milk.

As mentioned above, mimolette is not wax-coated but has a natural rind instead. During the aging process, cheese mites nibble on the rind, creating craters on the surface that promote ripening and give the cheese more complex flavors.

> **ANNATTO**
> Producers may add annatto to mimolette, Gouda, or Cheddar to give the cheese an orange color. This carotenoid-rich powder is obtained from the seeds of the achiote plant, native to South America and the Caribbean, and has been known in the Netherlands since the seventeenth century. Extracted from the red wax surrounding the seeds, annatto is stirred into milk at the start of the cheesemaking process. In large quantities, it has a slightly peppery flavor, reminiscent of nutmeg.

← Mimolette

Peak season

Gouda and similar cheeses are made year-round, particularly when industrially produced. The production period for farmstead cheeses is more closely linked to grazing periods, so ask your local cheesemonger for advice.

Food and drink pairings

• These remarkably versatile cheeses invite experimentation. Have fun combining them with contrasting flavors like red chili pepper and orange or walnuts and raisins. As a basic rule of thumb, younger cheeses work well either in cold dishes (diced and tossed in salads, for example) or melted, while the older, drier ones can be grated.
• When it comes to beverages, aged cheeses from the Gouda family pair nicely with a porter or stout, while younger ones go well with dry white wines. Or you could try Jin Xuan Oolong tea from Taiwan, which has a light, creamy flavor that complements this group's milky notes.

Some family members

- *Cantal AOP*
- *Salers AOP*
- *Laguiole AOP*
- *Fourme de Rochefort*

Cantal & Co.

Characteristics

APPEARANCE The members of this family come in large cylindrical wheels weighing 44–110 lb. (20–50 kg), with a diameter of around 16 in. (40 cm). The rind ranges from beige-brown to gray, depending on the season and ripening stage. On some cheeses, notably Salers, the surface can have a rustic, speckled look and can become very thick and cracked.

TASTE These cheeses have a supple and slightly grainy or crumbly texture while melting in the mouth. When they are young, their flavor is reminiscent of cream and butter, with light vegetal notes. As they ripen, they become more floral and eventually develop hazelnut notes. In cheeses aged for several months, peppery, spicy notes emerge.

Origins

In the mountains of the Auvergne region, the cheesemaking tradition goes back at least two thousand years. In the first century CE, Pliny the Elder mentioned cheese from the area in his work *Natural History*, although it's impossible to determine whether he was referring to a Cantal, Roquefort, or another type of cheese. As in other mountainous areas, the winters are long and harsh, but in summer farmers move their livestock to higher altitudes for fresh grass so that they can cut and dry the grass in the valleys for winter reserves.

Back then, living conditions in the high mountains were spartan. Dairy farmers would stay in *burons*—stone huts with slate or stone roof tiles—during the summer grazing season. There, they would make large, long-keeping cheeses that they could eat throughout the winter. In the fifteenth century, monks took Auvergne cheesemaking techniques with them to Aubrac—where Laguiole is produced—to make the most of the summer pastures on the surrounding plateaus. It wasn't until the early twentieth century that dairies first appeared in the region.

Cantal was awarded AOC status in 1956, coinciding with the sector's increasing industrialization. As if in reaction, Salers obtained its AOC in 1961. The latter must be made the traditional way following the exact techniques used before industrialization. Farmstead by definition, Salers can only be made with milk from a single herd between April 15 and November 15, when the cows graze on summer pastures. Producers must use traditional tools like *gerles* (wooden vats). Salers cheese that is made exclusively with milk from Salers cows also carries the word "Tradition" on its label.

Laguiole received an AOC in 1960, despite a significant decrease in its production due to the two World Wars and the modernization of the farming sector. Thanks to the creation of a cooperative in Laguiole, a small group of dairy farmers were able to keep producing the cheese.

A small handful of cheesemakers, also in Auvergne, produce Fourme de Rochefort around the town of Rochefort-Montagne in the Puy de Dôme department. The production process is simplified, but not standardized, and each of the eight producers makes the cheese in their own way.

How they're made

Laguiole and Salers are made from whole, non-standardized raw cow's milk, while pasteurized milk is sometimes used for Cantal. The production process begins very similarly to that used to make tommes and other uncooked pressed cheeses.

The next steps are unique to the Cantal family. After the curd is cut and drained, it is pressed into a mass, known as a "*tome*," in the vat and left to rest. The *tome* is then wrapped in linen, pressed and turned several times, and is left to ripen, forming a compact slab.

After this resting period, the slabs of curd are milled and then pressed into molds to give the cheese its final shape. This process explains why Cantal and its kin have a slightly grainy texture, as the curds do not always knit together seamlessly. The cheese is then ripened in a damp cave with 90 percent relative humidity. These are the general steps used to make the three AOP cheeses in this category, although each cheese has its own specificities. Salers, for instance, is made using wooden *gerles*—open wooden vats in which the fresh milk is transformed into curd—and Laguiole and Salers Tradition can only be made with milk from certain cattle breeds.

← Cantal

The flavor of Salers varies depending on the type of pasture the cows grazed on and the native microbes present in the *gerle*. If made with rich milk from cows that grazed on summer pastures, the cheese will have notes of gentian and a slight bitterness. As the cheese ages, it develops strong animal overtones.

POUTINE AND ALIGOT HAVE "TOMES" IN COMMON
The unripened, unsalted, uncooked pressed cheese used as the base for milled curd cheeses like Laguiole and Cheddar is known as "tome fraîche" in French. This is one of the main ingredients in the Aubrac specialty *aligot*: cheesy mashed potatoes mixed with cream, butter, and garlic (see recipe p. 203). It is also used to make *truffade auvergnate*, another hearty potato and cheese dish. Tome Fraîche de l'Aubrac was granted IGP status in October 2023. The cheese curds used to make poutine (a dish of French fries and cheese curds topped with brown gravy), which is popular in Quebec and sometimes called *"couic-couic"* or "squeaky cheese," are also made of tome fraîche.

Peak season

These cheeses are produced throughout the year, although those made with milk from pastured cows are more complex in aroma. Notable exceptions are Salers (made exclusively between April 15 and November 15, when the cows graze on fresh grass) and Laguiole "Buron" (see dates below). Ripening times range from a minimum of one month for Cantal, three months for Salers, and four months to over a year for Laguiole. The quality varies from one producer to another, so it is worth asking your cheesemonger for advice.

BURON-MADE
Certain Laguiole labels may feature the term "Buron." This refers to the dwellings where dairy farmers lived during the summer. A Laguiole may be labeled "Buron" if it is produced:
- between May 25 and October 13,
- from the milk of a single herd grazed at over 3,000 feet (1,000 m), and
- in a permanent dairy of solid construction (as opposed to a shelter made of wooden boards, for example), located near the grazing area.

Food and drink pairings

• Black cherry jam provides a sweet, bold contrast to mature cheeses in this group.
• Try these cheeses grated over beef carpaccio. They are also excellent in gratins and soufflés, or melted over toasted bread tartines or pizzas.
• Sip apricot or mango nectar with Cantal and its kin.
• Vermouth, with its notes of citrus and spice, is a great match. A cold wheat beer is just the thing for a young cheese, while an older one calls for an IPA or a gueuze.
• Salers pairs well with a dry white wine like Collioure or Saint-Chinian.

Some family members

- *Cheddar*
- *Cheshire*
- *Caerphilly*
- *Red Leicester*
- *Lancashire*

Cheddar & Co.

Characteristics

APPEARANCE Depending on the producer and season, the color of the cheese can range from shades of yellow (light to straw-colored) to orange, if dyed with annatto. Whole Cheddars (and other similar British cheeses) are traditionally sold as "truckles": large round wheels that are often clothbound and have gray rinds with the occasional hint of red. They come in many different sizes, from small 7-oz. (200-g) cheeses to large wheels weighing around 55 lb. (25 kg). The majority of Cheddars for mass-market sale come in blocks that are vacuum-packed or coated with wax.

TASTE The cheeses in this family are crumbly with a buttery, melt-in-the-mouth texture. They boast subtle notes of milk and cream, with the occasional hint of nuts and herbs. Some of the more unique artisanal or farmstead versions, such as Scotland's Isle of Mull Cheddar, may show notes of leather and an attractive bitterness.

Origins

Previously, we mentioned the milled and pressed cheeses of France's Auvergne mountains. Well, the techniques used for this type of cheese were also developed in the British Isles. Did one region inspire the other? It's hard to say, but it is safe to assume that the many exchanges between England and southeastern France over the centuries also included cheesemaking techniques.

Each English county had its own cheese, made in more or less the same way, including Cheshire, Cheddar, Double Gloucester, Lancashire, and Red Leicester. Made on farms, these cheeses were primarily sold in large urban centers.

Everything changed with the Industrial Revolution in the nineteenth century. The first Cheddar factory was built in the US in 1851, and from then on inexpensive American and then New Zealand Cheddar gained the upper hand over English farmstead versions. In the early twentieth century, pasteurization became more widespread, which not only proved to be a boon for public health (aiding in the fight against tuberculosis, for instance), but also boosted the dairy industry by making milk less perishable. This led to the decline of traditional cheesemaking, as Cheddar production was industrialized to compete with the cheaper versions being made overseas. Furthermore, the introduction of rationing in the UK during World War II forced all factories to produce only standardized cheese that was easy to distribute and preserve, leading to the disappearance of many varieties. In 1939, around a thousand farms were turning their milk into cheese. Twenty years later, only 140 farmstead producers remained, and by 1974 there were only 62 left in the entire country.

However, by the early 1980s, a handful of dairy farmers, cheesemakers, and creameries launched an English cheese renaissance, and today a few hundred farmstead producers are making traditional cheeses that had all but disappeared. They have also created new varieties by simply adapting recipes for traditional tangy chèvres and bloomy-rind or cooked pressed cheeses. Long live Cheddar!

CHEDDAR IS WORLD FAMOUS
Cheddar cheese is named after the village of Cheddar in Somerset, in southwestern England, where it was originally made. Fans of prehistory will also be familiar with the name, as it is the site where Britain's oldest complete human skeleton, dating back 10,000 years, was discovered—and it is known, quite simply, as the Cheddar Man!

How they're made

All of these cheeses are "cheddared"—yes, cheddar can be both a noun and a verb. Blocks of curd that have matted together on the bottom of the cheese vats are left to rest on a draining table, where they are regularly piled and turned until they reach the desired consistency and level of acidity. The curd is then milled or cut into pieces and placed in molds. Different counties and individual producers create unique cheeses by varying factors like texture and ripening time.

Unlike Cantals and other French milled-curd varieties, Cheddar and its cousins are wrapped the moment they are removed from their molds. This locks in moisture and prevents a rind from forming. Traditionally, producers used cloth and lard, making what are known as clothbound cheeses. Today, cloth has largely been replaced by wax or food-grade shrink-wrap, particularly for mass-market sale.

← Cheddar

Peak season

These cheeses are produced year-round, as grass thrives in the mild, wet climate of the British Isles. To make Traditional Welsh Caerphilly PGI, the cows must graze for at least three hundred days a year, which is no problem in a country renowned for its lush pastures.

Food and drink pairings

• For a simple cheese plate, serve members of the Cheddar family with apples, grapes, celery, and honey.
• You can't go wrong with the classic British combination of melted Cheddar and Worcestershire sauce on toast; Welsh rarebit takes it up a notch with a flavorful roux-thickened cheese sauce made with Guinness or another stout (see recipe p. 244).
• These milled-curd cheeses go well with fresh thyme, mint, and nutmeg, and make a delicious addition to tart fillings, with zucchini, shallots, and pepper.
• As for drinks, Madeira, port, lager, or green tea are all good options.

Unjustly overlooked members of this family

→ West Country Farmhouse Cheddar PDO
Protected by a PDO since 1996, this Cheddar from southwestern England is exclusively farmstead. Square or cylindrical in shape, it is made from curds heated to 102°F–106°F (39°C–41°C) and then left to cool to form blocks. These are turned and stacked by hand (i.e., cheddared), before being cut and salted, and placed in molds and pressed. The cheese is then wrapped (cloth, wax, and shrink-wrap are all permitted) and aged for at least nine months. It has a delightfully crumbly texture and nutty notes.

→ Lancashire PDO
Also PDO-certified since 1996, Lancashire is produced in the eponymous county around the city of Manchester in northwestern England. Curds made with whole cow's milk are lightly pressed, then drained and dried overnight. These curds are milled together with fresh curds, mixed with salt, and placed in molds. After the cheese is shaped, it is bound in cloth, waxed, or buttered, and left to mature for at least a month, but usually around six months. Lancashire cheese is less dense and firm compared to traditional Cheddar, and it has a buttery, tangy, slightly sharp flavor.

→ Traditional Welsh Caerphilly/Caerffili
This cheese, which is native to Wales, obtained PGI status in 2017. Made with raw or pasteurized cow's milk, it comes in round, flat wheels and has a slightly lemony taste when eaten young, as it typically is. Traditional Welsh Caerphilly/Caerffili is not to be confused with cheeses labeled simply "Caerphilly," which are produced industrially, sold in shrink-wrapped blocks, and have a milder flavor and a lumpy rather than crumbly texture. Despite sharing the same name, these two cheeses are very different.

Some family members

- *Stilton PDO (United Kingdom)*
- *Fourme de Montbrison AOP*
- *Bleu de Termignon*
- *Cabrales DOP (Spain)*
- *Castelmagno DOP (Italy)*

Stilton & Co.

Characteristics

APPEARANCE These cheeses come in cylindrical wheels of different sizes. Fourme de Montbrison AOP, for instance, typically weighs between 4½ lb. and nearly 7 lb. (2–3 kg). It has a diameter of 5–5¼ in. (12–14 cm) and is 7–8¼ in. (17–21 cm) tall. In contrast, Bleu de Termignon weighs 18–22 lb. (8–10 kg), has a diameter of 6–8 in. (15–20 cm), and is 12–14 in. (30–35 cm) tall. The rinds range in color from orange to gray, with occasional white or red spots. The cheese has a white, crumbly texture with blue veins throughout. In French, these cheeses are known as "*persillés*" due to their marble-like veining, as opposed to the blue-lined cavities found in Roquefort.

TASTE The texture can range from melt-in-the-mouth to dry, depending on the cheese and ripening stage. The characteristic blue notes can be mild or powerful. Although most of these cheeses are made from cow's milk, some may mix the cow's with goat's or sheep's milk, including Cabrales, Castelmagno, and some "*persillé*" cheeses in Savoie, which may or may not have blue veins. Cheeses made with goat's or sheep's milk have a more powerful and sometimes sharp flavor.

Origins

Most of these cheeses are crafted in remote mountainous regions during the summer season, when the animals are grazing in alpine pastures. Fourme de Montbrison (AOC since 1972 and AOP since 2009), for instance, is made at altitudes of over 2,000 feet (700 m). In the seventeenth century, it was produced on *jasseries*—the term for both the summer pasture farms high up in the Monts du Forez in Auvergne and the rye- or broom-thatched stone dwellings where the cheese was made.

Cabrales (DOP since 1981) is produced in the Picos de Europa mountains in Asturias, northern Spain. Herdsmen grazing their animals in the alpine pastures in summer began ripening their cheeses in the natural caves in the area from a very early date.

Castelmagno DOP is also a mountain cheese, hailing from the Piedmont region in northwestern Italy. Although versions are produced year-round in the Valle Grana, formerly part of Occitania, the words "Prodotto della Montagna" (mountain product) or "di Alpeggio" (from summer Alpine pastures) on the label confirm their mountain origins. The former guarantees the cheese has been made at altitudes above 2,000 feet (600 m), while the latter indicates it was produced above 3,000 feet (1,000 m).

Stilton is unique in this group as it is not made in the mountains, but rather in the rolling hills of the English counties of Derbyshire, Leicestershire, and Nottinghamshire. During the nineteenth century, sales of Stilton took off and its fame spread worldwide.

BUT STILTON IS NOT FROM STILTON
Stilton takes its name from the village of that name in Cambridgeshire, eastern England, some 80 miles (130 km) north of London. But it has never actually been made there! In the eighteenth century, the village was a staging post on the main road between London and Edinburgh, where travelers could stay en route. Cooper Thornhill, the astute proprietor of the Bell Inn in Stilton, served guests cheese that he purchased from a farm in the Earldom of Leicester, over 50 miles (80 km) to the northwest. This played a key role in spreading the cheese's fame.

How they're made

To make the cheeses in this family, the milk is usually coagulated quickly. The curd is then broken down into pieces the size of corn kernels or even grains of rice. After stirring, it is left to settle into blocks at the bottom of the vats.

The blocks of curd are then drained and, in some cases, left to ferment in the open air and/or in whey from previous batches. Stilton is left out for around ten hours, while Castelmagno curd is left to rest for twenty-four hours and then immersed in whey for between two and four days. In the case of Bleu de Termignon, half of the curd used in each batch is left to ferment in whey for two days (see p. 131).

After this more or less lengthy fermenting phase, the curd is ground, salted, and transferred to molds, or hoops as Stilton molds are called. Depending on the cheese, it may or may not be pierced with stainless steel needles during the ripening period to allow blue veins to develop through it.

Stilton →

Fourme d'Ambert and Stilton are made using techniques similar to those used for their neighbors Cantal and Cheddar (see pp. 119 and 123 respectively).

Peak season

These cheeses were traditionally made with cow's milk in mountain pastures from May to October. Some, like Cabrales or Castelmagno, included sheep's or goat's milk during spring and summer. Today, most of these cheeses are produced year-round, although Bleu de Termignon and Castelmagno di Alpeggio are still seasonal.

> **PORT AND STILTON: AN INSEPARABLE PAIR**
> In the early eighteenth century, England was at war with France (yet again!), so no longer had access to the French wine market. Merchants turned to Portuguese wine producers to supply them with this precious beverage. Some merchants came up with the idea of adding brandy to the wine, which stopped the fermentation process and resulted in a sweet, concentrated blend. Port wine was born and put an end to the contents of barrels turning to vinegar! At the same time, Stilton began to make a name for itself, and the two proved an irresistible combination. The luxury food store Fortnum & Mason popularized the pairing with its potted Stilton and port packaged in stylish ceramic jars.

Food and drink pairings

• All of these milled-curd blues are dynamite when infused with sherry, Madeira, or port.
• Mushrooms, pears, cauliflower, and broccoli all make good partners for these cheeses in salads, tarts, and on cheese platters.
• Artisanal pear juice mixed with a little sparkling water makes a refreshing, alcohol-free accompaniment to this family of blues.
• Many alcoholic beverages pair well with these cheeses, including stout or porter, farmhouse cider, a demi-sec or sweet (moelleux) white wine, or a medium to full-bodied robust red wine. Port is traditionally drunk with Stilton, particularly at Christmas time (see above).

Bleu de Termignon

Savoyard, unique, rare, little-known—all are good adjectives for describing Bleu de Termignon (as opposed to *"très mignon"* ["adorable" in French], as it's occasionally misnamed). A handful of *crémiers* have brought this cheese back into the spotlight, but production remains limited and vulnerable to change, as there are fewer than ten producers.

Characteristics

APPEARANCE Bleu de Termignon comes in attractive 13–15-lb. (6–7-kg) wheels with a cream-colored rind that browns with age. The cheese itself may be ivory-hued when young, and sometimes has blue marbling.

TASTE This Savoyard blue has a crumbly, grainy texture and a honeyed flavor that is balanced by blue notes as the cheese ages. Toward the end of the ripening process, it develops notes of barnyard and leather.

Interesting facts

Only a few producers in the Parc de la Vanoise region make this distinctive cheese, which takes several days to prepare. For each batch, they mix fresh curd with two-day-old curd that has been left for forty-eight hours in a wooden bucket filled with fermented whey.

After mixing the two types of curd, cheesemakers manually grind the mixture using a hand-operated grinder. They then roll the small curd pieces between their hands while adding salt, using a technique similar to that for hand-rolling couscous. The mixture is transferred to molds and pressed by hand. No cultures are added to the cheese, as the cheesemakers rely instead on microbes that are naturally present in the cheesemaking environment, including blue molds of the *Penicillium* genus.

Various factors influence this completely natural process, including time, place, terroir, and the individual producer, so the results are not predictable. Each wheel of Bleu de Termignon cheese boasts an astonishing array of flavors, and no two wheels are the same. Only a few artisans continue this tradition, and they do not depend solely on it for their livelihood. They also transport milk from the valley to the local cooperative, and may work a second job during winter.

Hard Cheeses

Gruyère & Co. 135

Abondance & Co. 141

Emmental & Co. 143

Grana & Co. 147

Pecorino & Co. 153

Provola & Co. 159

Some family members

- *Gruyère AOP (Switzerland)*
- *L'Etivaz AOP (Switzerland)*
- *Beaufort AOP (France)*
- *Gruyère de France IGP*
- *Storico Ribelle (Italy)*

Gruyère & Co.

Characteristics

APPEARANCE These long-keeping cheeses come in large wheels that weigh between 40 lb. (18 kg) in the case of L'Etivaz and nearly 160 lb. (70 kg) in the case of Beaufort. The rinds are dry and range in hue from light- to orange-brown. The color of the cheeses' smooth, uniform texture may vary from light yellow to straw-yellow, with a few holes or "eyes" smaller than a hazelnut.

TASTE When young, these cheeses have a smooth, creamy texture and grassy notes. As they age, they become more intense, acquiring notes of leather, nuts, and even spice.

Origins

Named after the Gruyère district in Switzerland's Fribourg canton, Gruyère cheese is the oldest member of this family. The production techniques were perfected and spread during the fourteenth and fifteenth centuries, first across the Jura Mountains, and then throughout the Swiss and French Alps. Gruyère-type cheeses are typical of mountainous regions with long, harsh winters. In these areas, rural populations sought ways to make optimal use of abundant summer grass, turning it into nourishment for their animals and making use of it for themselves. During the warmer months, cows were sent up to graze in the alpine pastures (*alpage*), while the grass down in the valleys was harvested for hay. In the *alpage* areas, producers made large cheeses that would keep until the following year. It takes a lot of milk to make these cheeses, as about fifty cows are needed for just one wheel.

← Beaufort

THE FIRST CHEESEMAKERS

During the fourteenth and fifteenth centuries, farmers took turns processing their own milk and that of their neighbors, and would then age the cheese themselves. Over time, they built specific facilities for cheesemaking and ripening. As some individuals were more skilled than others, they began to specialize, and the profession of cheesemaker was born.

The pooling of milk and cheesemaking work led to the creation of small cooperatives known as "*fruitières*." Written evidence attests to their presence in the fourteenth century, but they became more prevalent in the seventeenth century, particularly in the valleys. In the early nineteenth century, the same recipe was used in the Alps, Jura, and Vosges mountain ranges to make a cooked pressed cheese called Gruyère in Switzerland and vachelin or "Gruyère-style cheese" in France. From 1850 onward, the name Gruyère predominated.

Up until the nineteenth century, these Gruyère family cheeses were made exclusively in the mountains, either at high elevations (*en alpage*) or lower down, in *fruitières*. But as demand increased, milk production and cheesemaking gradually moved into the valleys, where it was more cost-effective. The reputation of these alpine cheeses suffered as their quality was inconsistent due to sometimes dubious ripening conditions, and many imitations emerged. When the Stresa Convention established agreements on the use of cheese denominations and appellations of origin in 1951, the name "Gruyère" was recognized for both Switzerland and France, unlike "Emmental" (see p. 143). In the second half of the twentieth century, each of these Gruyère-style cheeses sought to differentiate itself from the rest, and there came a gripping twist in the family saga:
- "Gruyère de Comté" became "Comté AOC" in 1958.
- "Gruyère de Beaufort" was similarly shortened, becoming "Beaufort AOC" in 1968.
- French producers in towns bordering the Beaufort and Comté appellations obtained a PGI for—can you guess?—Gruyère (yes, really!) in 2013.

In 1932, Alpine cheesemakers (*alpagistes*) in the Pays d'Enhaut in Switzerland had joined forces in a cooperative and built a communal aging facility. From this point on, the cheese they made, L'Etivaz, took a different path from Swiss Gruyère, with a distinct approach to cheesemaking. Today, L'Etivaz is produced in the traditional way on a small scale—seventy *alpagistes* produce around 400 metric tons a year. Gruyère, meanwhile, is made in both valleys and high-mountain pastures, with 160 dairies and around 60 *alpagistes* producing about 30,000 metric tons per year. These cheeses vary significantly depending on how they're produced. In France, Beaufort is mainly made in valley dairies, but there are some rare, renowned high-mountain ones bearing the label Beaufort Chalet d'Alpage AOP (see p. 139). Comté is produced exclusively in *fruitières*.

How they're made

These large, slow-ripening cheeses have much in common in terms of the way they are made. They are meant to be kept for a long time, so the techniques used eliminate as much water as possible from the curds, resulting in characteristically dense textures.

To make Gruyère and company, cheesemakers mix fresh warm morning milk with milk from the previous evening, which has been left overnight in a cool place. This encourages the microflora in the milk to develop and the cream to rise to the surface. The cream is partially skimmed off using a "*poche*" (a small shovel).

Rennet is added, so coagulation is quick, and the resulting curd is supple and solid. The curd is then cut into pieces the size of wheat kernels to release as much water as possible.

After a short resting period, the mixture is stirred to prevent the curds from clumping together. The temperature is slowly raised to 122°F–131°F (50°C–55°C); this is done gradually to prevent a skin from forming on the curd (*coiffage*). The temperature and stirring are maintained for about an hour.

Knowing when the curd is ready and it's time to stop stirring is a critical moment that demands considerable experience. This heating process serves a double purpose: it encourages the curds to expel as much whey as possible and eliminates unwanted microbes, allowing only the desired heat-resistant (thermophilic) strains to survive. These strains play a key role in fermentation and aroma formation.

After the hot curds are placed in molds, they are pressed gradually over a period of about twenty hours to extract more liquid. After pressing, the wheels are transferred to a cold ripening cellar with a temperature ranging from 50°F to 59°F (10°C–15°C). The cheese is ripened on spruce boards, and is surface-salted and turned regularly. During the first two to three weeks, a rind gradually forms on the cheese. After that, the wheels are regularly turned and washed with *morge*—a mixture of brine and ripening cultures such as *Brevibacterium linens*.

These cheeses can be kept for several months and develop an array of aromas and flavors during the ripening period.

BEAUFORT: CREAMIER THAN THE REST OF THE FAMILY
Beaufort's milk is not skimmed, resulting in a slightly higher water content than other Gruyère family members. This gives Beaufort the buttery and melt-in-the-mouth texture it's famous for in the Beaufort, Haute Tarentaise, and Maurienne valleys, but it also results in a shorter shelf life compared to its cousins.

Peak season

These cheeses are now produced and consumed year-round, but winter remains the preferred season. The most popular varieties are those made with milk from pastured cows, especially *en alpage*.

Food and drink pairings

• These well-rounded cheeses pair beautifully with walnuts, almonds, or any other nut, alongside a fruit paste like quince or apricot.

• For an easy meal, take a cue from the brilliant Irish food writer Trish Deseine: top toasted bread with thin slices of banana, cover with Comté, season with pepper, and place under the broiler for 2–3 minutes. To spice things up, add a touch of sweet chili powder or mango chutney. Or, if you feel like cooking, add any of these cheeses to a quiche, fondue, or *gougères* (French cheese choux pastry puffs).

• For an original pairing, try Chinese oolong tea accompanied by a young Comté with sweet, creamy notes—a tried-and-tested combination from the Comité Interprofessionnel de Gestion du Comté. The result is almost dessert-like, evoking panna cotta with berries.

• White wines like Chasselas and Chardonnay from the Annecy region perfectly complement Gruyère family cheeses, proving the old adage that what grows together goes together. If you're melting the cheese, try a blonde ale like Saison Dupont.

Beaufort Chalet d'Alpage AOP

This rare, remarkable gem is the product of age-old mountain traditions and considerable hard work.

Characteristics

APPEARANCE From the outside, it can be difficult to distinguish between Beaufort wheels produced in the high mountains and those made in the valleys. The only valid indication is a subtle marking on the side of the cheese, which unfortunately is not always immediately obvious to the buyer.

TASTE Beaufort Chalet d'Alpage AOP is typically more aromatic and flavorful than its valley-made counterpart, reflecting the diversity of flora in the Alpine pastures where the cows graze. It is firm when you bite into it, but then melts in the mouth.

Interesting facts

Each producer of Beaufort Chalet d'Alpage AOP makes the cheese from June to October in chalets located at altitudes of over 5,000 feet (1,500 m), using milk from a single herd. This cheese represents less than 8 percent of all the wheels made within the Beaufort appellation, with an annual production of around 400 metric tons. It's a labor-intensive cheese that requires a great deal of passion, as milking starts at dawn to bring in warm milk for the day's first batch, which is made throughout the morning. After lunch, the farmers return to milking their cows and continue with the second batch of the day.

Producers of Beaufort Chalet d'Alpage AOP spare no effort in making cheeses that most fully express the diverse flora of the Alpine pastures and their cows' fragrant milk. Enjoying the fruits of their labor is one delicious way to help preserve these unique landscapes and ancestral practices.

L'Etivaz and Gruyère d'Alpage are made in a similar way.

Some family members

- *Abondance AOP (France)*
- *Raclette du Valais AOP (Switzerland)*
- *Appenzeller® (Switzerland)*
- *Tête de Moine AOP (Switzerland)*
- *Fontina DOP (Italy)*
- *Asiago (Italy)*

Abondance & Co.

Characteristics

APPEARANCE Made in wheels, these cheeses resemble Gruyère, Comté, and Beaufort in shape, but they are smaller in size and usually weigh around 22 lb. (10 kg) each. Just like their larger cousins, they have a brownish-orange rind, range from ivory to pale yellow in color, and are sometimes dotted with holes or "eyes."

TASTE These cheeses have a firm and dense texture, yet melt in the mouth. Creamy notes dominate in young cheeses, while nutty flavors become more pronounced with age.

Origins

This group of semi-cooked pressed cheeses shares characteristics and history with the Gruyère family. Most are made in the Alps, straddling the three countries around Mont Blanc: Switzerland, Italy, and France. Abondance, Raclette du Valais, and Fontina are made using the same techniques as Gruyère, but adapted to obtain a smaller cheese.

Livestock rearing practices are similar, with an early June ascent to the mountain pastures and a late September descent. Beyond that, each valley and region has developed its own characteristics:
- As with Beaufort, Abondance has concave sides, making it easier to transport down the mountain on muleback.
- Famous for its superior melting qualities, Raclette du Valais is made with curd that is rinsed slightly to remove just the right amount of lactose, so it melts perfectly.

← Abondance

How they're made

The production process is similar to that of Gruyère-type cheeses, except that the curd is heated and stirred at a lower temperature and for a shorter period of time. Abondance AOP and Fontina DOP curds are heated to 113°F–122°F (45°C–50°C), Raclette du Valais AOP curds are heated to 97°F–113°F (36°C–45°C) and rinsed slightly, and Tête de Moine AOP curds are heated to 115°F–127°F (46°C–53°C). After heating, the curds are generally gathered into a linen cloth, placed in a mold, and then pressed.

This results in smaller cheeses with a slightly softer texture, which also require shorter ripening times: a minimum of 80 days for Fontina and 100 days for Abondance. Appenzeller® is not an AOP but a brand. Its special feature is that it is regularly rubbed with an herbal brine whose recipe is a closely guarded secret.

Peak season

These cheeses are produced year-round, but consumption peaks in late autumn to early spring, when the highest-quality *alpage* cheeses are available.

Food and drink pairings

• These semi-cooked pressed cheeses all pair beautifully with charcuterie, and not just as part of a classic raclette meal (see recipe p. 249). Try lardons, *viande des Grisons* (Swiss air-dried beef), or Rosette de Lyon sausage.
• Pickles provide a crisp, refreshing contrast to a rich fondue or raclette made with any of these cheeses (see recipes pp. 247 and 249).
• Abondance and company are excellent in gratins and cheese-rich baked or grilled dishes, including quiches, tarts, stuffed vegetables, tartines, and baked pasta dishes.
• When choosing a wine, try a dry white like Apremont. As to beer, an amber ale or peaty porter are good choices. These cheeses also work well with pineapple juice or apricot nectar.

Some family members

- *Emmentaler AOP (Switzerland)*
- *Emmental de Savoie IGP (France)*
- *Allgäuer Emmentaler IGP (Bavaria, Germany)*
- *Emmental Français Est-Central IGP (France)*
- *Leerdamer (Netherlands)*
- *Masdaam (Netherlands)*

Emmental & Co.

Characteristics

APPEARANCE The members of this group, often referred to generically as "Swiss cheese," are easily recognizable by their holes. No, mice have not been nibbling on them! These large "eyes" or openings in the cheese can sometimes be as large as a walnut. Emmental and company come in large straw-colored to brownish-yellow wheels that are gently rounded on top. They can weigh up to 265 lb. (120 kg), making them the heavyweight champions among all the known cheeses.

TASTE The flavors are straightforward and fruity, and the texture of the cheeses is firm yet supple. The longer-aged 18-month Emmentaler AOP, produced on a small scale, has more character and a meltingly soft texture, with the occasional tyrosine-crystal crunch.

Origins

The first written records of an "Emmental cheese" ("*Emmentaler käss*") can be traced back to the sixteenth century; they are found in books documenting donations or gifts made in the Bern canton of Switzerland. Yet, once again, it's best to exercise caution, as there is no guarantee that these cheeses were the same as the Swiss Emmentals we know today. What is certain is that the cheeses in this family take their name from the Emme River, which runs alongside the canton of Lucerne.

During the eighteenth century, cheese dairies flourished in the lush, pine-rich Emme Valley. Cowherds there had a more abundant grass supply than their Alpine-based colleagues, so they could have more animals, which also produced more milk.

In the nineteenth century, as exports grew, customs duties were determined by the number of wheels rather than weight, which is why Swiss Emmental eventually averaged 220 lb. (100 kg) per wheel.

The recipe for Swiss Emmental, propelled by the sweet smell of success, was exported to neighboring regions—particularly Savoie and Franche-Comté. The first Savoie *fruitière* (cooperative) dedicated to Emmental production was established in 1822.

In the late nineteenth century, competition grew fierce between the Swiss Gruyères and Emmentals and their French counterparts. Initially a favorite of the French, Emmental began to lose its popularity in the twentieth century. Before long, it was renamed "Gruyère d'Emmental," which caused lasting confusion among consumers. This was followed by repeated disputes between Switzerland and France regarding the use of the names and the need to differentiate between the origins of each cheese. A copy of Emmental was even made in Germany. At the 1951 Stresa Convention, which forged historic international agreements concerning cheese denominations and appellations of origin, the Swiss roots of Emmental were officially recognized.

This meant that countries other than Switzerland could not use the Swiss Emmentaler AOP label. In France, protected versions go by other names, including Emmental de Savoie IGP and Emmental Français Est-Central IGP, from the Vosges and Jura mountain ranges and the northern Alps. But 90 percent of French Emmental-style cheese comes from Brittany, the country's leading dairy region. The dairy giant Entremont, based in Savoie, opened its first plant in Brittany in the late 1960s.

IT'S ALL IN THE HOLES

Prior to the second half of the twentieth century, Emmental had bigger holes and more of them than its competitor, Gruyère. But in the 1960s, Gruyère producers in Switzerland and later in France decided to put an end to the confusion by eliminating the famous "eyes" or holes in the cheese. They achieved this by lowering the ripening temperature, resulting in fewer eyes, or even none at all.

How they're made

Emmental family members are made in exactly the same way as Gruyère. The difference comes at the ripening stage. After pressing, both types of cheese are placed on spruce boards in a cold cellar with a temperature range of 50°F–59°F (10°C–15°C). The wheels are regularly turned and surface-salted, allowing the rind to form.

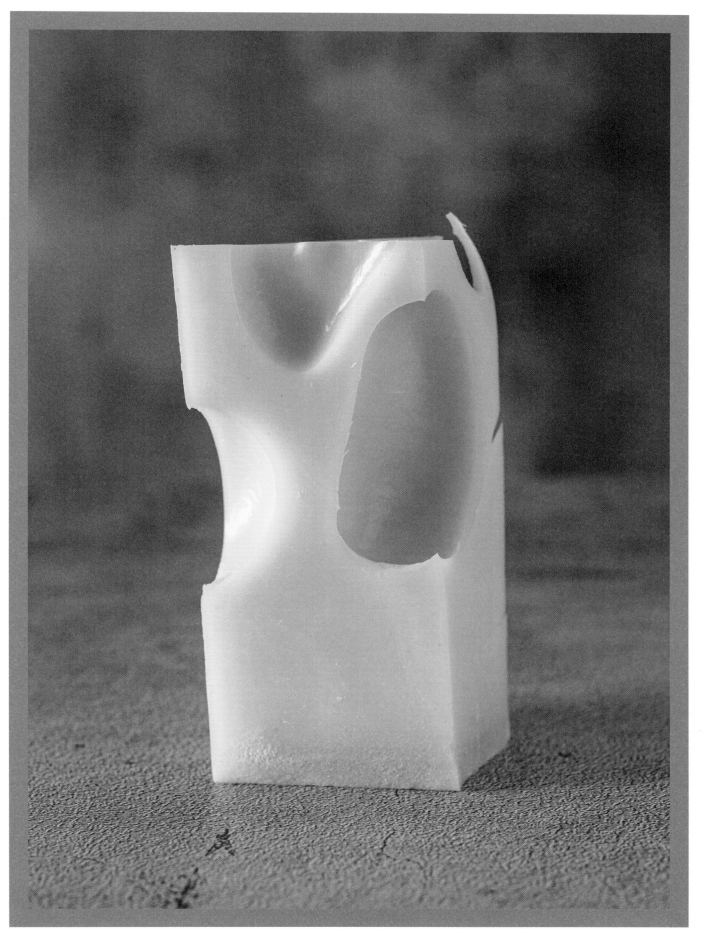

Emmental-style cheeses are then moved to a warm cellar (68°F–77°F/20°C–25°C). This encourages the growth of propionibacteria—either naturally present in the milk or added at the beginning of the cheesemaking process. These bacteria produce carbon dioxide, which causes the characteristic "eyes" to appear and the cheese to swell.

After a few weeks in this warm environment, Emmental family cheeses are transferred to a cool cellar to stop the propionic activity and encourage the proteins to break down and release new flavors.

Industrial versions of these Emmental-type cheeses are made with skimmed, pasteurized milk as opposed to whole raw milk like their artisanal and farmstead counterparts. Microbial rather than animal rennet is also used. The cheese is then ripened in shrink-wrapped blocks to retain moisture and prevent a rind from forming. This makes the cheese particularly smooth and meltable—and more profitable, too, as after forty days of ripening the cheese is ready to be sold.

> **A LAUGHING MATTER**
> Before the mid-twentieth century, wheels occasionally imploded in the warm cellars due to excessive microbial activity. These defective cheeses were then melted to make processed cheeses such as La Vache Qui Rit (The Laughing Cow; see pp. 101–103).

Peak season

These cheeses are produced and consumed year-round.

Food and drink pairings

•All of these cheeses are delicious on a sandwich, along with good ham, a little Dijon mustard, and cornichons—simple yet classic—or melted on a hamburger or croque-monsieur.
•For a mouthwatering twist on yakitori skewers, wrap slices of beef carpaccio around sticks of Emmental, drizzle with soy sauce, and grill for a few minutes.
•Top any of these cheeses with a hint of bitter orange marmalade. Believe it or not, this surprising and contrasting combination works beautifully.
•Why not accompany these cheeses with a wonderfully bitter herbal cocktail? We suggest a Santenberg Spritz: 1 part gin, ⅔ part Génépi liqueur, and 1 part freshly squeezed grapefruit juice. Cheers!

Some family members

- *Parmigiano Reggiano DOP (Italy)*
- *Grana Padano DOP (Italy)*
- *Trentingrana DOP (Italy)*
- *Sbrinz AOP (Switzerland)*

Grana & Co.

Characteristics

APPEARANCE These large cheeses are made in wheels that weigh up to 88 lb. (40 kg). They are typically eaten as pieces that have been broken off rather than cut into slices, or grated. The straw-colored hue varies in intensity depending on the season and ripening stage.

TASTE These cheeses are characterized by their hard texture, which is crumbly and grainy on the palate ("*grana*" means "grain" in Italian). Depending on the age of the cheese, it may have tiny "eyes" measuring less than $1/16$ in. (2 mm) in diameter. Most long-aged versions have small white specks of tyrosine crystals throughout. These cheeses are famous for their rich umami notes.

Origins

The origins of this cheese family can be traced back to at least the Middle Ages. Cistercian and Benedictine monks living in the region around Parma and Reggio Emilia during the twelfth and thirteenth centuries produced large wheels of cheese suitable for long preservation. The cheese got its name from these two provinces located in the Po Valley in northern Italy. Abundant fertile land in the area provided the means to produce large amounts of milk, which in turn made it possible to make large cheeses. The first written record of the sale of this type of cheese appears in a notarial deed drawn up in 1254 in Genoa, in northwestern Italy, proving that *caseus parmensis* ("cheese from Parma" in Latin) was known and traded beyond its home region by this date.

Demand for Grana-style cheeses continued to grow over the following centuries. Production became more organized on dairy farms, which used milk from their own herds and from neighboring tenant farmers to make the cheese. As milk became more plentiful, the size of the cheese wheels grew, too, reaching up to 40 lb. (18 kg). These could be kept for longer and sold further afield, such as in France and Spain.

Sbrinz: The Swiss version of Grana

Grana-style cheese was highly popular for its flavor and keeping qualities, and the recipe made its way to other countries, including Switzerland. The first written accounts of Swiss Sbrinz date back to 1530. The name is thought to derive from "*lo sbrinzo*," meaning "from Brienz" in Italian, referring to the town located in the canton of Bern. Mules transported the cheese from Lucerne and the surrounding area to northern Italy. Even today, the production process is still very similar to that of the rest of the Grana family.

Protection from imitators

Back in Italy, the Duke of Parma sought to protect the cheese whose success had bred imitation. On August 7, 1612, he formally recognized the name Parmigiano in a deed, establishing that it could only be used for cheeses made in the Parma and Modena provinces. In 1934, dairies in Parma, Reggio Emilia, Modena, and Mantua joined forces and formed the Consorzio Volontario Interprovinciale Grana Tipico, now known as the Consorzio del Formaggio Parmigiano-Reggiano. This consortium adopted the oval-shaped hot-iron mark for compliant wheels that is still used today. On June 1, 1951, the Stresa Convention forged an international agreement on cheese names and styles, and made a distinction between Parmigiano Reggiano and Grana di Lodi, which later became Grana Padano.

How they're made

The production process is the same for all of these cooked pressed cheeses. The evening's milk is placed in large vats, and the cream that rises to the surface overnight is carefully skimmed off the following day. Fresh morning milk is then added, along with cultures and rennet.

To extract the maximum amount of water, the curd is cut into tiny, pinhead-sized granules and stirred in the whey. The temperature is gradually increased to around 133°F (56°C).

Left to rest for one hour, the curds settle to the bottom of the vat. They are then wrapped in a linen cloth and hung from a wooden rod to drain. The next step is to extract as much moisture as possible from the curds, then let the cheese mature for as long as possible (up to ten years in rare cases).

These are the cheeses that require the most milk to make. To obtain 2¼ lb. (1 kg) of cheese, at least 4 gallons (15 liters) of milk are needed, which equates to

Parmesan →

130–160 gallons (500–600 liters) per wheel! Four breeds of cow are used to produce these cheeses: Friesian (Holstein) and Bruna Alpina (Brown Swiss)—the most productive—and Rossa Reggiana and Bianca Modenese (see below)—local breeds that are actively being preserved.

What's the difference between Parmigiano Reggiano DOP and Grana Padano DOP?
Although these two cheeses have a very similar production process, the specific rules that the makers must follow differ significantly. As with all PDO cheeses, quality can vary greatly from one producer to another.

	Parmigiano Reggiano	Grana Padano
Appellation	Designation of origin and strict guidelines since 1954	Designation of origin and strict guidelines since 1955
Production zone	5 provinces	33 provinces
Milk source	4 cattle breeds: Bruna Alpina (Brown Swiss), Holstein, Rossa Reggiana, and Bianca Modenese, exclusively fed on grass and hay	All breeds and diets permitted
Cultures	Native cultures from the previous day's batch	Lab-grown cultures allowed a maximum of once per month
Additives	None	Lysozyme permitted
Milk treatment	Partially skimmed raw milk (from the previous evening's milking)	Skimmed raw milk (from the previous evening's and the morning's milking)
Affinage	At least 12 months 24 months on average	At least 9 months 15 months on average

Note that in certain countries, including the US, it is against the law to use the term "Parmigiano Reggiano" for any cheese that is not produced in the designated Italian area. The word "Parmesan" is not restricted, however, and it is used indiscriminately in the American cheese industry.

Products bearing the label "Parmesan" run the gamut: they may be semi-hard rather than hard, and made with skimmed or even powdered milk, which may be whitened or artificially colored and fortified with added vitamin A. Finely grated versions of the product may have cellulose mixed in to prevent clumping.

Parmigiano Reggiano made with Bianca Modenese cow's milk

In the 1960s, there were around 140,000 Bianca Modenese cows, but by 2002 the number had fallen to only 200. The breed is a cross between the Reggiana Rossa and the Podolica, native to Puglia in southern Italy. This docile breed, used in the past as a draft animal, is especially prized today for its high-quality meat and milk. It also features among the Presidia of the Slow Food movement, which is dedicated to preserving the world's culinary heritage (see p. 12).

Currently, only two dairies in the Apennines produce Parmigiano cheese solely from Bianca Modenese milk. Due to its lower fat content compared to other cow's milks, the cheese is aged for 30–36 months to fully reveal its flavor and aromatic potential.

Trentingrana

The production of Grana-style cheese developed in the mountainous Trentino region in the 1920s. A local cheesemaker, originally from the area, returned home and began using the techniques he had learned in the Modena region. Today, seventeen dairies process milk from farms located at altitudes of over 5,900 feet (1,800 m) to make Trentingrana cheese.

Although included in the Grana Padano PDO, Trentingrana stands out from the rest. The cows' feed comes exclusively from this mountainous area, and silage and other fermented fodder are forbidden, as is the additive lysozyme.

Furthermore, two dairies produce a high-mountain version supported by the Slow Food movement. Known as Mountain Trentingrana (*"di alpeggio"* in Italian), this cheese is made in the summer months using only milk from cows that have grazed on selected Alpine pastures.

Peak season

These Grana-style cheeses have long ripening times, although they can be eaten relatively young, after just nine months of aging. They keep very well, and it is not unusual to find a 48-month Parmesan. This ripening process means that these cheeses are available year-round at different ages.

Food and drink pairings

•These cheeses are perfect in *pesto alla Genovese*. Freshly grated, they boost the flavor of meat, fish, and pasta. If added at the end of cooking, they also lend creaminess to a number of dishes.
•Clean Parmesan rinds add flavor and depth to minestrone and other soups.
•Grana-style cheeses are especially delicious with balsamic vinegar from Modena. Broken up into bite-size pieces and drizzled with balsamic vinegar, they are perfect with cocktails. This classic pairing offers a harmonious balance of buttery notes and acidity.
•When young (aged 12–24 months), Grana-style cheeses pair beautifully with white wines, especially sparkling ones like the Italian Franciacorta, which is made from three varietals: Chardonnay, Pinot Noir, and Pinot Blanc. Longer-ripened Granas (aged 36–48 months) can easily be paired with more structured red wines.

Some family members

- *Pecorino Balze Volterrane DOP (Italy)*
- *Pecorino Romano DOP (Italy)*
- *Pecorino Sardo DOP (Italy)*
- *Pecorino Siciliano DOP (Italy)*
- *Pecorino Toscano DOP (Italy)*

Pecorino & Co.

Characteristics

APPEARANCE These hard sheep's milk cheeses ("*pecora*" means "sheep" in Italian) come in a range of sizes, depending on the appellation. On the smaller end of the spectrum, wheels of Pecorino Toscano DOP weigh 2¼–6⅔ lb. (1–3 kg), while Pecorino Romano DOP wheels can weigh up to 55 lb. (35 kg). When fresh, the cheeses do not have rinds, and they tend to be white. As they age, they gradually turn off-white and then pale yellow, while the rind turns dark yellow to dark brown.

TASTE These pecorino family cheeses range from semi-hard to hard in texture, depending on how long they have been aged. As they mature, they become crumblier, and the flavor intensifies, turning sharp or even pungent. When young, they have a mild, milky flavor with plenty of fresh notes.

Origins

The Mediterranean region is ideal for sheep farming. Almost half of the world's sheep's milk is collected here, and it is used to make hard cheeses that can be kept for several months. Pecorino-style cheeses are found all over the Italian peninsula, as well as in Spain, Portugal, the Balkans, and Greece.

In Italy, the pecorino-making process has as many subtle differences as there are regions. Already appreciated in ancient Rome, pecorino was traditionally crafted on an artisanal scale on small farms. It was mentioned by the Greek author Homer in

the late eighth century BCE and by the first-century CE agronomist Columella in his work *On Agriculture* (*De Re Rustica* in Latin). But, as with many historical references, there is no way of being 100 percent certain that the cheeses mentioned were actually pecorinos.

American superstar
Let's fast-forward in time to talk about hard facts. In the twentieth century, Pecorino Romano, produced in the Lazio region around Rome, experienced a significant boom. Large-scale Italian emigration to the United States made Pecorino Romano well known Stateside, and it became the most exported Italian cheese, surpassing even Parmesan—a position it would hold until the 1990s. Production in Lazio alone was no longer enough to keep up with the demand. Dairies were built in Sardinia, famous for its sheep farming, and the island eventually became the primary production area for Pecorino Romano. Unfortunately, this came at the expense of the local artisanal production of Pecorino Sardo and Fiore Sardo, which are discussed later in this entry (see p. 157).

Pecorino Romano has been protected at national level in Italy since 1951. The same goes for Pecorino Siciliano (since 1955), Pecorino Sardo (since 1993), and Pecorino Toscano (since 1996). Additionally, smaller-scale products more deeply rooted in local traditions and terroir have also been granted their own DOPs: Pecorino di Filiano, Pecorino di Picinisco, Pecorino Crotonese, Pecorino delle Balze Volterrane, and Pecorino del Monte Poro. All of these are well worth seeking out.

How they're made

Pecorino is a hard cheese made exclusively from sheep's milk. That's about the only thing all Italian pecorinos have in common. Beyond that, each one follows its own path.

The differences begin at the curd-cutting stage. For cheeses intended to be eaten young, the curd is cut into hazelnut-sized pieces. If the cheese is going to be ripened, the curd is cut into smaller pieces—the size of corn kernels, or even grains of rice—to obtain a drier wheel.

In some cases, the curds are heated—to 108°F (42°C) for Pecorino Toscano, 109°F (43°C) for Pecorino Sardo, and up to 118°F (48°C) for Pecorino Romano. To make Pecorino Siciliano DOP, cheesemakers stir the curds and then add hot water at 160°F (70°C) to encourage the curds to expel whey—a phenomenon known as syneresis.

There are also many different approaches to ripening. Some pecorinos are rubbed with oil, and others, like Fiore Sardo, are smoked. Some are even covered with clay, as in the case of Axridda di Escalaplano, a Sardinian pecorino registered as a Slow Food Presidium.

← Pecorino

155

Peak season

Production is mainly concentrated between October and May, or sometimes until early summer, depending on the region and the weather. As pecorinos are left to ripen from a few weeks to several months, depending on the cheese, different varieties can be found throughout the year.

Food and drink pairings

• The ways in which pecorinos can be used are as diverse as the cheeses themselves. They can boost the flavor of a creamy sauce like carbonara, made with egg yolk and guanciale, and seasoned with pepper. They also round out vegetable stuffings and tart fillings.

• When young, pecorinos are perfect for grating into a variety of Mediterranean-style dishes. As they age, the flavors become more concentrated, and they're best used as a condiment. They are excellent over tuna or pasta, for instance.

• Pecorino pairs well with the earthy flavors of cauliflower, broccoli, walnuts, fava beans, and other types of beans.

• For a simple dessert, serve thin slices of pecorino with quartered pears and a drizzle of honey, preferably acacia.

• Pecorino is a delicious match for smoked black tea such as lapsang souchong from the Fujian province in China, or a white wine like Chardonnay or Riesling. As for cocktails, try using pecorino as a salt substitute for a margarita. Simply coat the rim of a glass with lemon juice, then dip it in finely grated pecorino.

Shepherds' Fiore Sardo

Traditionally, Fiore Sardo was the preeminent shepherd's cheese on Sardinia, the second largest Mediterranean island after Sicily. The name is thought to come from the flowers carved into the bottom of the wooden molds that were once used to shape the cheese (*fiore* means "flowers" in Italian). These flowers were often asphodels, which thrive in the island's limestone soil. Another possible explanation for the name is that thistle flowers were once used to coagulate the milk—a common practice in the Mediterranean. Fiore power!

Characteristics

APPEARANCE Weighing around 9 lb. (4 kg), wheels of shepherd-made Fiore Sardo have shiny, oil-rubbed rinds with a brownish-gray hue. Inside, the cheese is pale yellow, and has a hard, grainy, crumbly texture that is reminiscent of Parmesan.

TASTE Fiore Sardo has a characteristic smoky flavor. When young, it has a milky taste that acquires notes of sheep's leather as it ages. A hint of smoke lingers on the finish, which may be slightly piquant.

Interesting facts

In the twentieth century, Pecorino Romano became the most widely produced cheese in Sardinia (see p. 155), due to growing demand for this variety, as well as the expansion of the dairy industry. As a result, Fiore Sardo production plummeted. Yet the latter has survived and remains a highly unique, artisanal cheese. It has been protected by a PDO since 1996, but poorly written specifications have favored industrial production. Factory-made versions are largely sold in Puglia, and weak support for traditional production methods has jeopardized the original shepherd-made cheese.

In the early 2000s, Slow Food decided to make traditional Shepherds' Fiore Sardo a Presidium. The aim was to safeguard age-old production methods in the mountainous Barbagia region in the center of the island, where Fiore Sardo originated.

Today, around twenty shepherds in the region still practice transhumance and make their Fiore Sardo in the traditional way, using raw sheep's milk and natural rennet that they have prepared themselves. They press the curds manually and smoke the cheese at the start of the ripening phase. As the cheese ripens, they regularly rub the rinds with a mixture of olive oil, wine vinegar, and salt, producing extraordinary wheels said to capture the very essence of Sardinia.

Some family members

- *Provola (Italy)*
- *Caciocavallo AOP (Italy)*
- *Ragusano AOP (Italy)*
- *Pallone di Gravina (Italy)*

Provola & Co.

Characteristics

APPEARANCE Most provola-style cheeses are pear-shaped and can weigh anything from a couple of pounds to several kilos. Larger versions are known as provolone, which means "large provola" in Italian. The necks are often tied with raffia, or even rope in the case of the largest cheeses, while others, like Ragusano, come in blocks. Other family members are made in similar ways and come in even more unique shapes, such as the rolled-up Slovenská Parenica or the braided korbačik, both made in Slovakia. Provola-style cheeses have smooth rinds that range from light to dark yellow. After prolonged ripening, the rinds can be gray and rough. The cheese has a paler hue than the rind, and it is sometimes dotted with small holes called "partridge eyes." Small horizontal cracks are considered a defect.

TASTE When young, these cheeses have a remarkably mild flavor. Delicate, very lightly salted, and tender, they seem to melt in the mouth. As they mature, the texture becomes drier and the flavor more piquant. Some have notes reminiscent of beef broth with hints of nuts.

Origins

Provola-type cheeses are not only found in southern Italy, but also in the Balkans and throughout southeastern Europe, as well as in Turkey, Syria, and Lebanon. This is because the production technique used to make these cheeses is well suited to the Mediterranean climate. The curd sets quickly in the region's warm temperatures,

← Provola

resulting in rather dry cheeses. Although relatively little milk is available, it is particularly rich in fat, which partly explains why these cheeses become sharp as they age.

Although the exact origins are disputed, the name of the southern Italian cheese caciocavallo may provide some evidence of the recipe's journey. Some say the name comes from "*kash*," the Farsi word for cheese, and Kaval, in reference to the Greek town of Kavala, believed to be the first production center for this cheese. Others claim that this type of cheese was a specialty of Romanian communities throughout the southern Balkans. However, others still claim caciocavallo refers to the way in which it is matured; it is hung in pairs over wooden beams, like saddle bags, hence the name, which literally means "horse cheese" in Italian.

No matter the exact origins, we can say with certainty that this cheese has benefited from the many exchanges between Mediterranean peoples. It has developed in different ways all across the region. Today, kashkaval, a cousin of provola, is eaten young and tender with nuts or honey in the Balkans and Turkey, while in Albania restaurants serve it fried.

By the late nineteenth century, provolas and caciocavallos faced the same problem as pecorinos (see p. 155). The supply was no longer sufficient to meet the demands of either the local population or that of the Italian diaspora, particularly in the United States. To cater to the growing demand, the Po Valley dairies (the same ones making Parmesan), with their abundant and, therefore, inexpensive milk, produced a new ripened *pasta filata* cheese. This later became known as Provolone Valpadena DOP.

How they're made

These cheeses are made following the same *pasta filata* (stretched-curd) technique used for the mozzarella family (see pp. 51–55).

The curd is cut into small pieces and left to settle on the bottom of the vats, where it forms a compact mass. It is then covered with very hot water and mixed to stretch the curd. Once it is sufficiently stretched, it is hand-pressed to expel as much whey as possible and obtain a smooth surface.

After the cheese is formed, it is plunged into cold water to help it solidify. The cheese is then soaked in brine for salting. Finally, it is tied with either raffia or rope, depending on its size, and hung to age for several weeks to several months.

Aged provolas with a particularly intense, sharp flavor (known as "*piccante*" in Italian) are typically made with kid rennet rather than calf rennet.

Provola-style cheeses are sometimes smoked. Calabrian cheesemakers smoke their cheese for a few days in a windowless room to make provola affumicata. In Sardinia, the cheese is left for a few hours in a smokehouse with aromatic herbs.

Ragusano DOP

A type of caciocavallo, Ragusano DOP is made from raw cow's milk from November to May only, when the animals graze in pastures in southern Sicily. The cheese is molded into rectangular blocks weighing 26–35 lb. (12–16 kg). It is then hung from beams by rope and ripened for at least three months.

Caciocavallo Silano DOP

This semi-hard cheese is made using raw or thermized cow's milk in the southern regions of Italy, including Abruzzo, Puglia, and Campania. In the Naples area, a version of this cheese is ripened in natural caves for at least six months. Its elongated melon shape, fire-stamped logo, and rope trim make it a particularly elegant-looking cheese.

Slovenská Parenica IGP

This Slovakian cheese, made with raw sheep's milk or a mixture of sheep's and cow's milk (at least 50 percent sheep's milk), has an unusual "S" shape. To produce it, cheese-makers stretch the curd mass in hot water into long strips that are rolled up into the characteristic spiral shape. The cheese is then dried and smoked.

ZERO-WASTE PROVOLA EQUALS RICOTTA!
Producers make two types of ricotta with the leftover sweet whey from caciocavallo and other provolas: a fresh one and a ripened one. To make the latter, they combine the remaining sweet whey with acid whey, resulting in a coarser ricotta, which is then dried and used grated as a condiment throughout the year. These ripened ricottas were generally preserved in salt (hence their name of ricotta salata) for slow, controlled aging. Traditionally, the surface was cleaned, and the cheese was sometimes boiled to soften it before eating. Sicily's ricotta infornata is drained for two days and then dried in the oven at 350°F–400°F (180°C–200°C) for 30 minutes. This produces a delicate brown rind that protects the cheese and gives it caramelized notes.

Peak season

Milk is available year-round, although the grazing period depends on the production zone. Due to variations in size, ripeness, and producing areas, these highly popular Italian cheeses are available in one form or another throughout the year.

Food and drink pairings

• For a surefire hit, slice one of these cheeses ½ in. (1 cm) thick, top with a little garlic, tomato sauce, vinegar, and a sprinkling of sugar, and place on a hot grill until the slices turn crisp and brown and are just melted in the center. Alternatively, make a tartine: place slices of the cheese on bread, add fresh tomatoes and a pinch of oregano, and melt under the broiler.
• Serve these cheeses in a salad with thinly sliced fennel (use a mandolin, if possible). Add green olives and a lemon vinaigrette.
• Grate or shave any of these cheeses over pasta for a no-fail classic pairing.
• A sweet sparkling wine is a perfect accompaniment for these cheeses.
• Artisanal grape juice pairs well with young provola-style cheeses, while a Corsican red wine is a good match for the group's longer-aged members.

Tips

How to Buy Cheese with Confidence

It is not always easy to differentiate between a truly good and an average cheese. This may be especially true in France, where cheese is so highly revered and the selection is so vast. But there is no single standard for excellence, a fair price, or the perfect amount—we each have to figure out our own criteria. It's also important to trust the experts and let them guide us. Ultimately, selecting the right cheese comes down to how much we want to spend and what is available in our area.

If you're on a budget and have a grocery store nearby:

• Avoid precut or flavored cheeses and any cheese with a slick marketing campaign—that's never a good sign. Always look at the price per pound or kilo to determine what is really good value and don't forget to check the label as some cheeses contain large amounts of preservatives and artificial ingredients.

• Whenever possible, purchase PDO (Protected Designation of Origin) cheeses or, even better, organic PDOs. Whether at the cheese counter or the grab-and-go section, the choice is up to you. And be sure to pick up accompaniments, like crackers, bread, fruit (fresh or dried), and jam, to compose your own cheese board at home.

If you have a more generous budget and are after higher quality, head to your local cheese shop or farmers' market:

Are you someone who rarely goes to specialty cheese shops or has never dared to enter one at all? Every day, the coauthor of this book—a cheesemonger—sees people wavering at the door of his store, hesitant to go in. Many customers are shy or fearful of sounding like they don't know what they're talking about. They don't realize they can enter the shop just to browse, find out more, or simply have a conversation with the cheesemonger about his cheeses. Good cheesemongers love to talk about cheese, so don't be afraid to ask questions. Who makes this cheese? Where and how do they work? Why do you think this cheese is so good? Remember, it's not your job to know everything—it's the job of the team in the shop. They should be able to answer your questions and not just read the label. So, feel free to ask for a sample—politely, of course. By tasting the cheese before you buy it, you can avoid disappointment back home.

In all cases, it's important to know how to read the labels and to recognize the following European certifications:

• AOC/AOP: Appellation d'Origine Contrôlée/Protégée

This is the premier official label in France, protecting cheeses and other agricultural products from imitations and fraud. The label also guarantees a strong link with a specific terroir and ensures that all producers use the same time-honored methods. Obtaining an AOC certification is a collective endeavor, and lawful use of the label is enforced by independent bodies. Specifications have become stricter over time, and older ones have even been revised to be more stringent. This name-protecting system was harmonized at the European level in 1996, when all French AOCs became AOPs and were recognized EU-wide. Other countries use different acronyms for the same certification, such as PDO in English for Protected Denomination of Origin, or DOP in Italian and Spanish for Denominazione di Origine Protetta and Denominación de Origen Protegida, respectively. As of July 2023, there were two hundred PDO cheeses in eighteen European countries, including fifty-three in Italy, forty-six in France, twenty-seven in Spain, and twenty-two in Greece.

• **IGP: Indication Géographique Protégée**
Known in English as PGI (Protected Geographic Indication), this label also protects products at the European level but is less stringent than PDO and has more flexible criteria regarding geographical boundaries, production methods, history, and other factors. PGIs are not generally eligible for PDO status. As of July 2023, there were around fifty-six PGI cheeses in seventeen European countries, including seven in the UK, eight in Slovakia, and nine in France (including Raclette de Savoie, Saint-Marcellin, and Soumaintrain).

• **Label Rouge**
This French certification, which is rare among cheeses, recognizes products that are superior to other identical ones in terms of taste. There are no specific restrictions on the geographical origin of the milk or the production method. Label Rouge has been awarded to Brie made with thermized milk, raclette without natamycin, aged mimolette, and Emmental made with raw milk, to give a few examples. This label is largely geared toward the dairy industry and supermarkets. A product cannot carry both the Label Rouge and AOC-AOP labels at the same time.

• **AB: Agriculture Biologique (Organic Agriculture)**
Recognized at the EU level, this label certifies that a product is made in an environmentally friendly way that respects animal welfare:
- The animals must be pastured whenever possible, and at least 60 percent of their feed must come from the farm.
- The use of antibiotics is restricted.
- Synthetic fertilizers, pesticides, and GMOs are prohibited.
The AB label guarantees the quality of the raw materials used and encompasses respect for biodiversity and natural resource conservation. AOC- and AOP-certified products can also carry the AB label simultaneously. Other labels, such as Nature & Progress or Demeter (for biodynamic products), are even more demanding.

Cutting with Confidence

Many of us have experienced a look of horror from fellow diners when we've cut the tip off a wedge of Brie, or when our slices of Comté were too thick or too thin. It's time to put our doubts to rest as after committing such cheese-cutting faux pas, many of us have developed a fear of doing it wrong. Well, we've got good news for you. Here, we won't be giving you any strict rules about *the* way to cut this or that type of cheese because we think it's impossible to memorize those geometrical patterns, which are more mysterious than the Sphinx's riddles. More importantly, we believe that the spontaneous pleasure of enjoying cheeses with others should come first. And no amount of stress or heated discussion about the thickness of that particular slice of Sainte Maure de Touraine—should it have been precisely 1.12 or 1.94 cm?—should spoil it.

Here are our recommendations:

• **Equip yourself with a cutting board and good knives that are sharp but not serrated and have a pointed tip.** These are essential and are as important as good ingredients in cooking. Immersing the blades of the knives in hot water just before cutting can make the job easier. We like to use large or small santoku-type knives (Japanese chefs' knives with a flat edge and long curving blade). To serve cheeses that are soft, oozing, or very ripe and risky to pick up without getting sticky fingers, we recommend using a simple pie server.

• Serving several different cheeses? **Provide one knife for each type of cheese, to avoid mixing flavors.**

• When it comes to the cutting itself, there is only one essential rule in our opinion: **think of the person who will eat the last piece.** If that person ends up with just the rind, or the heel (edge of the wheel), you've played your cards wrong. In short, cut the cheese so that each slice has all the layers of flavor, from the interior to the rind.

As a general rule of thumb, it's best to start cutting wheels or square-shaped cheeses from the center using the tip of the knife. This will give you triangular wedge-shaped slices. Cut cylindrical cheeses like logs crosswise into rounds. As for pyramid-shaped cheeses, it's best to cut them into quarters. If you have a slab cut from a large wheel of cheese like Abondance, Swiss Gruyère, or Comté, slice it into rectangular sticks. This is the only exception to our rule about the final slice being all rind.

When serving runny cheeses such as Mont d'Or or Serra da Estrela, use a thin-bladed, pointed knife to carefully cut the top of the rind off without damaging the sides (too) much. This will serve as a lid if there's any cheese left over at the end of the meal. Use a spoon to help yourself, which is always better than a knife for these extremely soft cheeses.

> **FOR YOUR NEXT CHEESE PLATE, CUT EVERYTHING**
> It's easier to eat what's already been cut. Due to the same fear of cutting mentioned earlier, if you cut all the cheese on your board in advance, your guests will thank you. Otherwise, leave the pieces as you purchased them if you want any leftovers.

Composing a Harmonious Cheese Board

Just like the proper way to cut cheese, the right way to put together a cheese board or plate is a source of ongoing, passionate debate. Fortunately, there are no definitive answers. First and foremost, when assembling your selection of cheeses, you should focus on what you like and what you think your guests will enjoy, too, especially if that means introducing them to ones they are unfamiliar with.

The basics: How much cheese do you need?

• **For the end of a meal** (in France, cheese is served *before* dessert): Plan on between 2–2¾ oz. (60–80 g) per person, depending on the preceding dishes and number of guests. So, if there are four people, a nice piece weighing 7–10½ oz. (200–300 g) is enough to wrap things up.

• **For a pre-meal aperitif:** Count on 2¾–3½ oz. (80–100 g) per person, depending on what you'll be serving later.

• **For a cocktail party:** Serve 3½–5¼ oz. (100–150 g) per person, depending on the other nibbles.

• **For a cheese and charcuterie buffet:** Set out about 7 oz. (200 g) cheese, 5¼ oz. (150 g) charcuterie, and 8¾ oz. (250 g) bread per person.
• **For a cheese-tasting soirée:** Plan on about 8¾ oz. (250 g) per person.
• **For raclettes and fondues:** You'll need about 8¾ oz. (250 g) cheese per person, or 10½ oz. (300 g) if your guests are real enthusiasts.

The great cheese-plate debate: Which styles and formats to include?

To settle this question once and for all, our coauthor-cheesemonger likes to serve a single cheese, preferably an unfamiliar one. You could even make your choice based on the number of guests, for example:
- one round of Mont d'Or for about fifteen people,
- one wheel of sheep's milk tomme for about thirty people, or
- one wheel of Brie de Meaux for about fifty people (lucky guests!).

If you want to offer a choice—either because your guests will prefer it or you are hoping there will be plenty left over for the week—three different cheeses may suffice. For larger gatherings, you can offer a greater variety. If you have ten guests, you'll need 1–1¾ lb. (500–800 g) of cheese, so five different cheeses will be more than enough. Serving more than that might lead to frustration as crowd-pleasers run out while other, often lesser-known varieties go untouched.

> **WHAT ABOUT SEASONAL CHEESES?**
> In specialty cheese shops, the selection is generally seasonal. Keep in mind that different cheeses reach their fullest flavor potential at different times of the year. The best season can also be a matter of personal taste: in France, cheeses with a creamy yellow texture, which reflect the nuances of pasture-based milk, are appreciated, while Italians tend to prefer cheeses that have a creamy, whiter texture. The "right season" for a given cheese depends largely on where it's from and the weather in that particular year. Add to this the cheesemaker's personality, mood, and tastes, and you've got a huge number of parameters to consider before making your choice. Ask your cheesemonger to guide you.

A few useful tips to keep in mind when selecting cheeses for a cheese plate or board:
- Include cheeses made from **one of three different types of milk:** cow's, goat's, or sheep's.
- Offer **a variety of textures,** with one relatively creamy cheese, another with a melt-in-the-mouth texture, and a third, firmer cheese.
- Alternatively, you can make a themed plate with **only goat cheeses or hard cheeses,** for instance. Just be sure to consider your guests' preferences, to ensure that everyone will enjoy the selection.

A cheese plate for each season

You can also compose your cheese plate around seasonal cheeses and flavors. Here are some potential combinations:
• **Spring**
- Goat cheese, as this is the peak season, when chèvres galore return to market stalls
- Brocciu and other fresh cheeses for which it is easy to vary the accompaniments
- Soft cheeses made with the first pasture-based milk of the season
- Cooked pressed cheeses aged between twelve and twenty-four months

- **Summer**
  - Goat cheeses
  - Tommes made in the spring
  - Soft *alpage* cheeses like reblochon or Munster
  - Younger cooked pressed cheeses, aged for around eight, ten, or fifteen months
- **Fall**
  - Goat cheeses
  - Vacherins
  - Tommes made in the spring
  - Morbier or other mountain tommes
  - Cooked pressed cheeses aged between twelve and twenty-four months
- **Winter**
  - Vacherins, which are at their peak in winter
  - Summer mountain cheeses (*fromages d'estive*), such as sheep's milk tommes from the Pyrenees or semi-cooked pressed cheeses like Abondance
  - Pressed cheeses aged for eighteen months, such as Comté, Beaufort, or Gruyère
  - Mozzarella di bufala (yes, really!)
  - Soft cheeses
  - Note that lactic goat's milk cheeses are less readily available in winter.

Tasting with All the Senses

Take a moment to taste a cheese. Do you have the words to describe the flavors and sensations, or to list the particular qualities or drawbacks? If not, don't worry! With a bit of practice, you can learn to taste cheese like a pro. This gustatory journey begins with the senses, and it's always better to embark on it with other enthusiasts, so you can share your impressions and reflections. There is just one mantra to keep in mind: trust yourself. No one is an absolute expert when it comes to taste. Everyone has their own personal perceptions based on their own experience and references.

WHY AND HOW TO SERVE CHEESE AT THE RIGHT TEMPERATURE
Cheeses are alive and constantly evolving, so we recommend storing them in the refrigerator, or a wine cellar for those lucky enough to have one. At around 39°F (4°C), bacteria are much less effective at their job, so the cheeses do not change too quickly. Yet these low temperatures also dull the cheese's aromas and flavors, and solidify its texture. That is why it's a good idea to remove it from the refrigerator and bring it to room temperature before serving. Although the exact timing depends on several factors, including the ambient temperature, the type of cheese, and how long it will be left out, a minimum of twenty to thirty minutes is the general consensus. Keep the cheese wrapped in its original paper or box and unwrap it just before serving.
- **Special cases:** When the weather is very hot, certain firm cheeses like Comté or sheep's milk tommes tend to "sweat" quickly. This particularly affects the texture and can make the cheese less enjoyable to eat. As for mozzarella, even if you want it to be a little on the cool side, you still need to take the bag out of the refrigerator at least one hour before serving it, as the brine needs to warm up before the cheese does.

In fact, Neapolitans never refrigerate fresh mozzarella—but they don't keep it for days, either, as it is best eaten as soon as possible after it is made.
•If you slice the cheese in advance, cover the plate with plastic wrap or a clean dish towel so the pieces don't dry out. Keep the plate in the refrigerator until shortly before serving. About fifteen minutes should be enough, since thin slices warm up quickly.

Look at the cheese

Before you even touch a piece of cheese, take some time to examine it attentively. What is the texture? What color is the rind? Are there any cracks, colored veins, or other particularities? What color is the cheese itself? An intense yellow color, for example, may indicate that the cows grazed on fresh grass, rich in carotene. Can you see the label? What do you like and dislike about the cheese's appearance?

Touch the cheese

The way the cheese feels beneath your fingertips gives you additional clues about it. Touch the rind and press down gently. Try to guess the temperature. Is the cheese soft, supple, firm, or hard? Take a little piece and try to break it in half, if possible. Is it crumbly, and is the break clean, or is it difficult to split in two? Different cheeses have an incredible array of textures—now is the time to appreciate this quality.

Smell the cheese

This is a particularly delicious kind of yoga! Inhale deeply through your nose and then exhale, clearing your mind of stray thoughts. Then inhale deeply again while bringing a piece of cheese toward your nose—but not too close. Lightly wave the cheese toward your face to create a gentle waft of scents. Smell the rind. Smell the inside of the cheese. Although taste is closely linked to smell, concentrating on the cheese's scent before eating it can reveal different aromas than tasting it directly. Does it smell herbaceous, milky, floral, fruity, or earthy? Does it recall hazelnuts or caramel? The nose can detect an incredible variety of nuances, including sharp, oily, or musty scents, as well as notes of leather or animal.

Finally, taste the cheese

Place a small piece of cheese on your tongue and let it sit there for five seconds. What do you notice? Close your eyes if you wish. Start chewing slowly. As you chew, inhale deeply a few times through your nose. Switch to inhaling a little air through your mouth and then exhaling it through the nose. This releases a flood of impressions and—dare we say it—emotions. Does the cheese taste differently from what the aroma suggested? Does it melt in your mouth, or is it dry, crumbly, or gooey? Is it brittle and hard with bits of crunch? Think about where it falls on the spectrum between sweet, tangy, sour, savory, and bitter. Some flavors may appear at the beginning and disappear immediately, while others may emerge later and persist on the finish. Have the sensations ended? Take another bite to find out.

EQUIP YOURSELF WITH WORDS

Are you having trouble describing the flavors and aromas you perceive? It's all about practice and trusting your senses. Just say what comes to mind, rather than trying to use fancy, complicated, or pretentious terminology. Express your memories and impressions in your own words, using the names of foods like spices or fruits. If you'd like some inspiration, look for a "flavor wheel" online for a list of different terms to describe tastes.

Choosing the Right Bread

Bread, like wine, is a product of fermentation and is an all-time classic partner for cheese, but which breads pair best with which cheeses? Here are some suggestions. Be sure to try the breads toasted, too.

- **Traditional baguettes:** With a crisp crust and tender crumb, baguettes are an excellent match for all kinds of cheese. They are especially good with soft, spreadable cheeses like Brie de Meaux and creamy goat cheeses.
- **Sourdough bread:** With their open yet chewy crumb and rustic, tangy flavor, sourdough-based breads pair beautifully with a fruity Comté or soft and ever-so-slightly tangy cheeses like reblochon or Morbier. This is our top choice.
- **Whole-grain bread:** The distinct grain flavors and occasional dried fruit and hazelnut notes in whole-grain bread pair beautifully with Mont d'Or or Cheddar.
- **Rye bread:** The nutty, toasted grain flavors in rye bread are perfect with Saint-Nectaire, Munster, Salers, or Brillat-Savarin.
- **Heritage-grain bread (Einkorn, buckwheat, etc.):** Try these with bold cheeses like the blues for a refreshing change from the classic Roquefort and fig-walnut bread pairing, which is a little too sweet, rich, and overpowering for our taste. In fact, we prefer fig-walnut or even apricot bread with goat cheeses for a more harmonious balance of flavors, rather than a noisy clash of heavyweights.

> **JAM OR NO JAM, THAT IS THE QUESTION**
> Let's just say that if you do pair jam with cheese, you should use it sparingly. You can always add another small spoonful, if you are really hooked on the combination. We recommend trying artisanal fruit pastes, such as quince, instead. For cocktail parties, it can be fun to create small bites of cheese and fruit paste with contrasting colors and shapes.

- **Hazelnut bread:** This bread's mild, lightly sweet flavor pairs well with cooked pressed cheeses and goat cheeses like Sainte Maure de Touraine.
- **Sesame bread:** this bread provides a nice contrast to full-flavored Manchegos, thanks to its slight crunch and a flavor reminiscent of hazelnuts, but with a little more tang. And why not toast it and top it with a little paneer?
- **Corn-flour bread:** Made from fine cornstarch (cornflour), as opposed to traditional American-style cornbread which uses cornmeal, this bread has a mild sweetness that contrasts well with the salty, assertive notes of blue cheeses, Ossau-Iraty, or long-aged mimolettes.
- **Olive fougasse:** This savory fougasse nicely complements salty cheeses. Try it with pecorino for a sharp edge or pélardon for a more harmonious duo.
- **Crackers:** Like baguettes, crackers are eminently versatile. Crisp and mildly wheat-flavored (unless seasoned with aromatic herbs or seeds), they are perfect with melt-in-the-mouth cheeses like chèvre, Stilton, Mont d'Or, or Brie.

Pairing Cheese with Drinks

There is a perfect drink for every type of cheese, whether you're looking for something with or without alcohol. You can go with similar flavors or opt for a compelling contrast. Here are some of our recommendations. But most importantly, feel free to experiment and discover your own favorite combinations.

Wine

Wine is the ultimate partner for cheese, particularly in France, where it is considered its natural counterpart in terms of culinary heritage. With more than 360 wine AOCs (Appellations d'Origine Contrôlée), France is the world's second-largest consumer of wine, and these pairings are guaranteed to please—drinking the wine in moderation, of course.

Our advice: choose red wines carefully
- When combined with the fat in cheese, the astringent tannins in red wine can leave a dry, chalky feeling in the mouth. The salt in the cheese can reinforce this sensation.
- Older red wines have softer tannins, but cheeses can easily overpower the wine's subtle flavors.
- Ultimately, it comes down to choosing the right bottle.

Here are a few pairings that work every time:
- Brie, Neufchâtel, and Camembert pair well with fruity, low-tannin, non-woody red wines, such as Côte de Beaune, Côtes-du-Rhône, or an older Saint-Émilion.
- Cantal, Saint-Nectaire, and aged mimolette enjoy the company of mature Bordeaux reds such as Médoc or Pomerol.
- Slightly ripened goat cheeses (like Valençay and Crottin de Chavignol) pair well with fruity Beaujolais Gamays or even a Saint-Nicolas-de-Bourgueil from the Loire Valley.

In our opinion, white wine offers a broader range of options:
- With their refreshing, fruity notes, white wines perfectly complement the richness of cheese.
- Ranging from dry to sweet, white wines can be paired with cheeses on all points of the ripening spectrum.

Cheeses	Wines
Fresh cheeses (brocciu or fresh goat)	*Vin doux naturel* (Muscat), *moelleux* (Gewurztraminer or Jurançon)
Lactic goat cheeses (Selles-sur-Cher or Mâconnais)	A fruity, dry white wine (Chablis, Pouilly-Fuissé, Vouvray Sec, Sancerre, or Pouilly-Fumé) or a demi-sec (Montlouis)
Bloomy-rind cheeses (Camembert, Chaource or Brillat-Savarin)	A sparkling Vouvray or a Blancs de Blancs from Champagne
Assertive washed-rind cheeses (Livarot or Pont-l'Évêque), reblochon, Époisses, or one of the vacherins	A highly aromatic dry white wine (Riesling or Meursault) or a sweeter one (like a late-harvest Pinot Gris)
Blue cheeses (Stilton, Bleu d'Auvergne, or Fourme d'Ambert)	Sweet wines like *vins doux naturels* (Banyuls, Rivesaltes) or *liquoreux* (Quarts-de-Chaume or Sauternes)
Cow's milk tommes from the Alps or sheep's milk tommes from the Pyrenees	Crisp, dry white wines (such as Roussette de Savoie, Saint-Joseph, Irouleguy, or dry Jurançon)

Beer

Carbonated drinks generally work very well with cheese, and beer is no exception. Beer holds a special place in our hearts as cheese lovers. Given the incredible diversity of beers available, it's possible to find unique cheese pairings that few have tried before. France alone has around 2,300 breweries—the highest number in any European country.

Cheeses	Beers
Long-aged pressed, uncooked blue cheeses (Roquefort or Laguiole)	A powerfully hoppy IPA
Camembert, Brie, or another bloomy-rind cheese	Fruit beers flavored with raspberries, strawberries, or cherries that contrast with the cheese's creamy texture and flavor
Triple-cream or fresh cheeses	Sour beers like lambics or gueuzes, or a Belgian-style saison, which contributes a wonderful freshness and complexity with its spicy notes
Aged Gouda or aged mimolette, or a washed-rind or blue cheese	Stout, or, if you prefer something stronger, a robust, complex barley wine with flavors of malt, candied fruit, and caramel
Mozzarella, burrata, lightly aged goat cheeses, young tommes	Light wheat beers with delicate fruity notes and effervescence that complement the sweetness in these cheeses without overpowering it
Cooked pressed cheeses (like Comté or Appenzeller)	A smoked amber lager, which emphasizes the hazelnut, dried fruit, and caramel notes of these cheeses
Mild blue cheese (Gorgonzola Dolce)	A Belgian Dubbel, with malt, dried fruit, and spice flavors that complement the creamy richness and tang of the cheese and linger on the finish
Washed-rind cheeses (like Maroilles or Bleu de Termignon)	Porters with toasted malt, chocolate, and coffee flavors that highlight the sharp notes in these cheeses

Hard apple or pear cider

If you ever enter a Camembert-ripening cellar, you'll notice a scent of green apples. It's not surprising, then, that a good brut apple cider or a pear cider (perry) would pair well with the cheese. A demi-sec or sweet cider is best for older, more powerful Camemberts. Avoid overly tannic ciders, as they can overpower the cheese. Tried-and-true combinations include a Loire Valley goat cheese with pear cider or a mild blue cheese with ice cider.

Spirits

For maximum flavor, use one large ice cube rather than many smaller ones to refresh your spirits. Larger cubes melt more slowly, keeping your drink colder for longer without watering it down as much.

Our favorite pairings of the moment:

Cheeses	Spirits
Long-aged smoked Fiore Sardo or another long-aged hard cheese (such as Comté or Parmesan)	A peaty whisky with smoky, earthy notes for an extraordinary tasting experience
Stilton, Roquefort, aged Gouda, aged Manchego (*viejo*)	A white port, with its sweet taste reminiscent of dried fruit and honey, or a dry vermouth
Lightly aged goat cheeses	Pineau des Charentes, with yellow fruit and honey notes and a mellow sweetness that complement the salty, tart, and herbaceous flavors in goat cheese
Blue cheeses	Pear brandy, with fruity, sweet notes that offset the peppery intensity of blue-veined cheeses
Gouda	Bourbon, whose vanilla and oak notes accentuate Gouda's caramel and dried fruit flavors
Aged Basque sheep's milk tomme	Cognac, which has a rich, woody side that perfectly contrasts with the sweet, robust cheese
Langres	Gin, with citrus and herb overtones that pair effortlessly with the cheese's salty notes

Fruit juice

Fruit juices pair well with cheese as their natural sweetness plays a complementary role, as do fruit nectars, which offer a subtle contrast. Choose high-quality juices (preferably cold-pressed or fresh-squeezed) rather than those made from concentrate. Here are a few suggestions:

Cheeses	Fruit juice or nectar
Fresh cheeses	Red berry nectar
Soft, bloomy-rind cheeses	Apple, pear, or quince juice, or similar
Soft, washed-rind cheeses	White grape or litchi juice
Gruyères	Pineapple juice
Goat cheeses	Apricot juice
Mountain tommes	Dark fruit juice (blueberry, black currant, etc.)
Blue cheeses	Pear juice

Storing Cheese Correctly

When you purchase cheese, be sure to ask your cheesemonger if it is ready to eat now, how many days it will last, and how best to store it, as this can vary from one cheese to another.

When in doubt, follow these simple rules:

- **Store cheese in the lower part of your refrigerator,** and even in the crisper drawer if there is room. The ideal temperature for cheese is 43°F–46°F (6°C–8°C).
- **Protect it,** individually wrapped, in cheese paper. The inside of this special paper is lightly waxed, which makes it airtight. If you have the original paper around the cheese, respect the creases when re-wrapping it to minimize contact with the air. Otherwise, be neat and tidy when folding, as if you were wrapping a gift. No rough crumples, please. Some other alternatives, which are less effective in terms of preservation, include natural reusable beeswax wraps or plastic wrap. Another option is vacuum-packing, which is convenient for long trips, as long as the cheese is kept in an insulated bag with enough cold packs. Once you've reached your destination, store the cheese in the refrigerator, wrapped in one of the packaging materials mentioned earlier. Otherwise, it may become too damp and spoil more quickly.
- **Don't use cheese storage containers.** These designated containers help limit refrigerator odors, but condensation collects in them, and different cheeses stored together can transfer flavors to one another.
- **Don't buy too much cheese at once.** When purchasing cheeses with a short shelf life, limit yourself to amounts suited to your needs, to best enjoy them and avoid food waste.
- **If there's mold on the cheese, look carefully before throwing it away.** Whether you need to toss it or not depends on the type of cheese. If you have a hard cheese like Comté, Parmesan, Cheddar, or Gruyère, you can often scrape off just the surface mold and/or cut off the surrounding parts. If a cheese starts to become too strong for your liking, try cooking it with other cheeses in a tart or gratin. Cooking will help mellow out the flavor.

Cheese and Health: The Facts

The media frequently touts the health benefits of cheese—it's nutritious (beyond supplying calcium), digestible, and a pleasure to eat! But the arguments are often simplistic, especially given the limited number of studies on the link between milk and health. Here are some key points that are worth considering.

Milk production methods have changed significantly over time. In the past, farmers used to keep only a few cows, goats, or sheep, but today it is common to find herds numbering in the tens of thousands. Once exclusively grazed on pastures or rangeland (zones with diverse wild flora, especially shrubs), the animals are now often given concentrated feed such as silage and oil cakes. The use of genetic tools in livestock breeding has also affected milk composition. Dairy production today is mainly intensive and caters to large-scale milk processing plants. However, some farmers still use traditional, grass-based methods that respect the animals' natural cycles.

Sugars

Milk contains 4–5 percent sugars, mainly in the form of lactose. When we are infants, our bodies produce an enzyme called lactase that breaks down lactose, a complex sugar, into simple sugars. However, this enzyme tends to disappear from our bodies as we grow. Our tolerance to lactose can depend on our ethnic background and, above all, our individual genetic makeup. Those who are intolerant to lactose can experience bloating and other types of abdominal discomfort after consuming it. Cow's, goat's, and sheep's milk all contain lactose.

Lactose intolerance affects a large majority of the population in regions of the world where milk consumption has long been virtually non-existent, such as East Asia and Equatorial Africa. In his book *Atlas de l'alimentation*, food geographer Gilles Fumey suggests that the transformation of milk into yogurt or cheese in temperate northern countries may have led to genetic evolution favoring lactose tolerance. Cheesemaking involves fermenting lactose into lactic acid, so cheese contains much less lactose than milk in its original form. The final lactose content of the cheese depends on various factors, including the cheesemaking techniques used and the duration of the ripening process.

Cheesemaking technique	Final lactose content per 3½ oz. (100 g)
Milk	4–5%
Fresh cheese	2.5–4.1%
Goat cheese	Around 1%
Mozzarella	Around 1%
Blue cheese	Less than 0.8%
Soft cheese	Less than 0.2%
Uncooked pressed cheese	Less than 0.1%
Cooked pressed cheese	Traces of lactose
Long-ripened pressed cheese	Lactose-free

Fats

According to regulations in many countries, including France, the US, and the UK, whole milk must contain a minimum of 3.5 percent fat, but cow's milk from some heritage breeds can contain up to 5.5 percent. Goat's milk contains more like 3.5–4 percent fat, while sheep's milk has 7 percent. When cheesemakers separate the curd from the whey, they obtain a concentrated mixture of milk solids and, consequently, a higher concentration of fat. Using partially or fully skimmed milk in some cheeses can result in a lower fat content, but remember, fat is the source of many flavors and aromas in cheese. Fat adds taste! Besides the fat content, which not all experts agree is unhealthy, consider the type of animal feed used, as this plays a major role in the quality of the fatty acids in the cheese.

Type of cheese	Fat content per 3½ oz. (100 g)
Lightly ripened goat cheese	15–20%
Dry goat cheese	24–28%
Camembert	20–24%
Cantal	28–31%
Roquefort	30–32%
12-month Comté	32–35%
24-month Parmesan	30–32%
Brillat-Savarin	35–40%

Proteins

Cheese is an excellent source of protein, comparable to meat, fish, and legumes. This, apart from the pleasure of eating it, is perhaps its most important benefit. However, individuals with Type I or Type III hypersensitivities to milk proteins, which is extremely rare in adults, should avoid consuming milk and its derivatives entirely. If someone is intolerant to cow's milk protein, they may still be able to consume products made with goat's or sheep's milk.

Type of cheese	Protein content per 3½ oz. (100 g)
Brillat-Savarin	8–10%
Lightly ripened goat cheese	22–26%
Dry goat cheese	20–24%
Camembert	20–24%
Cantal	24–28%
Roquefort	18–20%
12-month Comté	25–30%
24-month Parmesan	32–36%

A FEW TIPS

If we were to pick just a few of the many recommendations from doctors and nutritionists, in addition to maintaining a balanced lifestyle and diet, we would say:
• Take a leaf out of the Germans' book, and eat cheese in the morning rather than in the evening. When we wake up, our bodies produce more of the enzymes that help to digest the cheese's lipids and proteins.
• Opt for cheeses made with milk from animals fed exclusively on grass and/or hay.
• Remember that the drier and more concentrated the cheese, the higher the fat content will be.

Vitamins and minerals

Cheese is especially rich in calcium and a great source of phosphorus, potassium, and vitamin B12. In fact, with the exception of lactic cheeses (including goat cheeses like Selles-sur-Cher, picodon, and Rocamadour), cheese contains far more calcium than other foods, including eggs, shellfish, and crustaceans.

Salt

As we learned earlier, salt is a crucial ingredient in cheesemaking. Yet health experts warn that we consume too much salt in this day and age. This is particularly problematic for people with high blood pressure, diabetes, or anyone who is overweight. Although industrially made cheeses often contain more sodium than other types (they need more to enhance the flavor), all cheeses are usually considered high-sodium foods that are best avoided or limited. The saltiest cheeses, such as blue cheese, can contain between 3 and 4 percent sodium, but the least salty ones, including Gruyère and Parmesan, contain less than 1 percent, which may surprise some people. Cheese is an excellent source of calcium and protein, and is low in lactose and fat. Depending on our preferences and dietary considerations, we can all find cheeses that are right for us.

Microbes

The microorganisms found in cheese may be the most interesting components in terms of human health. Although harmful bacteria can develop in cheese—like *Salmonella*, enterohaemorrhagic *E. coli*, and *Listeria monocytogenes*, which is why producers are obliged to regularly check their products to ensure they are safe to eat—other microbes found in cheese can help keep the body healthy. Some, such as *Lactobacillus bulgaricus* (a yogurt starter culture) and *Propionibacterium freudenreichii* (responsible for the holes in Emmental), have anti-inflammatory properties. Like all fermented foods, cheese helps enrich and strengthen the microbiota in our gut, which can aid in the digestive process. The (good) bacteria present in large quantities in cheese and other dairy products can withstand digestion and reach our stomachs intact.

> **BILLIONAIRE CHEESE**
> When we eat a 1-oz. (30-g) slice of Emmental made with raw milk, we're consuming around 30 billion bacteria, according to Gwenael Jan, research director at the French National Institute for Agricultural Research (INRA). "Emmental is undoubtedly the most effective and least expensive *Propionibacterium freudenreichii*-based probiotic," says Jan. Do you have zero tolerance for bacteria? When raw milk cheeses are adequately cooked, such as in dishes baked in the oven, they no longer pose a threat. However, they won't do much for your microbiota either.

Microbes from cheese do not directly enter the consumer's microbiota, as Marc-André Selosse, microbiologist and professor at the French National Museum of Natural History and author of *Jamais seul, ces microbes qui construisent les plantes, les animaux et les civilisations* (Never alone: The microbes that build plants, animals, and civilizations) points out. Yet, as they pass through the digestive system, their presence favors the growth of beneficial bacteria and overall gut health. In contrast, the freeze-dried microorganisms sold in capsule form over the counter in health food shops and parapharmacies (the famous "probiotics") do not survive the long digestive process.

The increase of certain diseases, including metabolic conditions such as diabetes and obesity; immune system disorders such as asthma, multiple sclerosis, and Crohn's disease; and nervous system disorders like autism, Alzheimer's, and Parkinson's, has been partially attributed to the depletion of our microbiota—all the more reason (as if one were needed!) to eat cheese.

> **RAW MILK CHEESE COULD PREVENT ALLERGIES**
> Since 2002, the European birth cohort study *PASTURE* (Protection Against Allergy: Study in Rural Environments) has tracked a thousand families living in rural areas of Germany, Austria, Finland, France, and Switzerland. The results suggest that exposure to animals, a varied diet, and consumption of raw milk cheese during pregnancy and infancy can significantly reduce the likelihood of children developing allergies, eczema, and asthma.

Our final recommendations

• Whenever possible, **purchase cheeses with an appellation (a PDO at the European level).** Many industrially produced French cheeses are made with milk from intensive farming operations, whether in France or abroad. Appellations ensure that the milk comes from animals raised in a particular area and fed a reasonably healthy diet, and that the cheese has been made without industrial methods that can degrade the raw materials.

• **Choose products with the Agriculture Biologique (AB) label.** The AB label prohibits the use of pesticides (like the lipophiles that can be found in cow's milk), chemical fertilizers, and synthetic hormones, and strictly controls the use of antibiotics. This label does not relate to how the cheese tastes, however.

• **Remain open-minded and curious!** To complicate matters, some cheeses without an appellation can be just as good or better than those with PDO and/or AB labels.

• **Ask your cheesemonger (or your local cheesemaker) questions.** Talk to them regularly so you can learn the types of cheeses you prefer and they can guide you to choose the best ones.

>> Review the European labels and appellations on pages 164–65.
>> Not sure which questions to ask your cheesemonger? See page 164.

Recipes

Basic Recipes
with Cheese

Lyon-Style Herbed Cheese Spread

Cervelle de canut

Place the fromage blanc in a fine-mesh sieve lined with cheesecloth set over a bowl. Let drain for at least 30 minutes.

Meanwhile, peel the garlic and shallot.

Place the drained fromage blanc in a food processor with the remaining ingredients. Blend until the garlic and shallot are finely chopped and the texture is thick.

Alternatively, finely chop the garlic and shallot using a knife, then stir them into the fromage blanc along with the herbs, oil, and vinegar.

Season with salt and pepper to taste.

Serve chilled, drizzled with olive oil and topped with fresh herbs or microgreens. It is delicious on its own or spread thickly over toasted bread.

SERVES 4

Active time **10 minutes**
Draining time **At least 30 minutes**

INGREDIENTS

· 1 cup (9 oz./250 g) fromage blanc (or ricotta, or faisselle, which contains more water so will produce creamier results)
· ½ clove garlic
· 1 shallot
· 2 tbsp finely chopped fresh herbs of your choice (dill, tarragon, chives, chervil, parsley, etc.), plus more for garnish (optional)
· ½ tsp extra-virgin olive oil, plus more for drizzling
· 1 tsp red wine vinegar
· Microgreens (optional)
· Salt and freshly ground pepper

Fresh Sheep's Milk Cheese Balls

Place the fresh cheese in a bowl. Using a fork, mash and stir to loosen.

Divide the cheese into 5 equal quantities (about 3 oz./80 g each). Place one quantity in a bowl and stir in the charcoal powder until well combined; the cheese should be evenly colored. Shape into small balls, about the size of large marbles.

Shape the remaining cheese into balls of the same size. Roll one quantity in the poppy seeds to coat, another in the pistachios, and another in the sesame seeds. Roll the remaining balls in the paprika.

Chill the balls for 30 minutes to firm up the cheese. Serve with small wooden food sticks to skewer.

SERVES 6

Active time **20 minutes**
Chilling time **30 minutes**

INGREDIENTS

- 14 oz. (400 g) fresh sheep's milk cheese (*fromage frais de brebis*)
- 1 tbsp bamboo charcoal powder
- 1 tbsp poppy seeds
- 1 tbsp finely chopped pistachios
- 1 tbsp toasted sesame seeds
- 1 tbsp paprika

Baked Camembert

Wash the potatoes and cook them in a saucepan of boiling salted water for 20 minutes, or until tender. Drain, peel, and keep warm.

Preheat the oven to 340°F (170°C/Gas Mark 3).

Take each Camembert wheel out of its wooden box and remove the wrapper, then return the cheese to the box. Set the box lids aside for baking. Using the tip of a paring knife, cut a circle around the top of each Camembert and peel off the top layer of rind.

Peel and thinly slice the garlic cloves. Stick garlic slices and a few pieces of rosemary sprig into each cheese, then put the lids on the boxes and bake for 10 minutes.

As the cheese bakes, roughly chop the nuts and place them in a bowl. Place the endive leaves in a separate bowl and drizzle with the olive oil and vinegar. Remove the Camemberts from the oven, carefully remove the lids, and season with a few grinds of fresh pepper.

Serve immediately, accompanied by the warm potatoes in a shallow dish and the endive leaves on the side. Dip the potatoes first in the melted cheese and then in the chopped nuts to coat.

SERVES 4

Active time **15 minutes**
Cooking time **30 minutes**
Chilling time **30 minutes**

INGREDIENTS

· 2¼ lb. (1 kg) small, waxy potatoes (such as new or fingerling potatoes, Yukon gold, or Charlotte)
· 2 × 9-oz. (250-g) raw-milk Camembert wheels in their wooden boxes (or 1 Camembert per person for larger appetites)
· 2 cloves garlic

· 1 large sprig rosemary, cut into pieces
· 4 small handfuls shelled walnuts, hazelnuts, or other nuts of your choice
· 1 red endive (or radicchio or another slightly bitter salad green)
· 4 tbsp extra-virgin olive oil
· 2 tbsp vinegar of your choice
· Salt and freshly ground pepper

Cheddar Crackers

One day ahead
Sift the flour into the bowl of a stand mixer fitted with the paddle beater, or a large bowl if mixing by hand. Season with salt and pepper. Add the butter and beat until the mixture is well blended and crumbly. Mix in the cheese until evenly distributed.

With the mixer running on low speed, mix in 3–4 tablespoons water, one at a time, until the dough comes together into a ball after a few minutes. Cover the dough with plastic wrap and chill it overnight.

The following day
Preheat the oven to 350°F (180°C/Gas Mark 4). Roll out the dough on a sheet of parchment paper to a thickness of about ⅛ in. (3 mm). Using a rolling pizza cutter, cut the dough into 30–40 squares. Alternatively, use a cookie cutter to make other shapes of your choice, removing the excess dough between the shapes. Carefully transfer the parchment paper and dough to a baking sheet. If using toppings, scatter them over the top and press them down lightly.

Bake the crackers for 15–20 minutes, or until lightly golden.

MAKES 30–40 CRACKERS

Active time **20 minutes**
Chilling time **Overnight**
Cooking time **20 minutes**

INGREDIENTS

· 2 cups (9 oz./250 g) all-purpose flour
· 4 tbsp (2 oz./60 g) unsalted butter, well chilled and diced
· Scant 2 cups (7 oz./200 g) shredded Cheddar
· 3–4 tbsp water
· Salt and freshly ground pepper

· Toppings of your choice (optional): pink peppercorns, poppy seeds, herbes de Provence, sesame seeds, etc.

Smoked Mackerel and Fresh Cheese Dip

Remove the skin from the mackerel fillets. Break the flesh into small pieces in a large serving bowl.

Cut open the chili pepper and remove the seeds. Chop the pepper finely and add it to the fish in the bowl.

Finely grate the zest of the lime and then juice it.

Add lime zest and juice and remaining ingredients to the mackerel mixture. Stir until well combined. Season with salt and pepper to taste.

Serve with assorted raw vegetables, such as bite-size cauliflower florets, and carrot and celery sticks, for dipping, or spread on lightly toasted slices of sourdough bread.

SERVES 4

Active time **10 minutes**

INGREDIENTS

· 2 smoked mackerel fillets, with or without pepper (about 9½ oz./270 g)
· 1 fresh bird's eye chili pepper
· 1 lime
· 1 small pinch ground nutmeg
· 1 small pinch ground cumin
· 3½ oz. (100 g) fresh cheese of your choice (such as cream cheese, fromage blanc, or crème fraîche)
· 1 level tbsp strong Dijon mustard
· Salt and freshly ground pepper

To serve
· Assorted raw vegetables, cut into bite-size pieces (cauliflower florets, carrot and celery sticks, etc.)
· Sourdough bread, sliced and lightly toasted

Marinated Goat Cheese
Fromage de chèvre mariné

Preheat the oven to 240°F (115°C/Gas Mark ½). Thoroughly wash and dry a glass jar slightly taller than the length of the cheese and wider in diameter.

Sprinkle the cumin over a plate, roll the cheese log in it, and chill for 30 minutes.

Spread the nuts in a single layer on a baking sheet lined with parchment paper. Toast them in the oven for 20 minutes, stirring every 5 minutes to prevent them from burning. Transfer to a plate and let cool, then chop roughly.

Using the channel knife of a citrus zester or a vegetable peeler, work around the orange or lemon to remove 3 strips of zest about 4 in. (10 cm) long, taking care not to remove the white pith as well. If using a peeler, cut the zest into thin julienne.

Cut the cheese crosswise into thin slices and stack them in the jar. Add the nuts, zest, and fennel seeds, if using.

Cut the chili pepper in half lengthwise and remove the seeds. Slice the pepper thinly and add to the jar.

Pour in enough walnut or olive oil to cover the cheese, close the jar, and let marinate in the refrigerator for 2–3 days, to allow the flavors to meld.

Remove the jar from the refrigerator 2 hours before serving to allow the cheese to come to room temperature.

SERVES 4

Active time **15 minutes**
Chilling time **30 minutes**
Cooking time **20 minutes**
Marinating time **2–3 days**

INGREDIENTS

· 1 large pinch cumin
· 1 × 5¼-oz. (150-g) bûche de chèvre (goat cheese log with a rind; not too creamy)
· 1 handful shelled nuts of your choice
· 1 small orange or 1 lemon, preferably organic
· 1 heaping tbsp fennel seeds (optional)
· ½ fresh red chili pepper
· Walnut or extra-virgin olive oil

Fresh Cheese with Chili-Tahini Sauce

Gebnah

Cut the cheese into approximately ¾-in. (2-cm) dice and place in a serving bowl.

Wash and thinly slice the mint leaves.

In a bowl, whisk together the tahini and olive oil, then whisk in the lime juice, chili pepper, and black pepper. Stir in the mint, reserving some for garnish. Transfer the sauce to a small glass pitcher.

Place the cheese in a serving dish and drizzle with the sauce. Sprinkle over the remaining mint, black pepper, and ground red chili pepper.

If you wish, add fresh mango slices and/or pitted and chopped medjool dates to the bowl with the cheese.

You can also serve *gebnah* on toast, as a side dish for pasta or meat, or alongside assorted salads as part of a meze platter.

SERVES 4

Active time **10 minutes**

INGREDIENTS

· 7 oz. (200 g) feta or Gebnah bēda ("white cheese" from Sudan, known as Domiati in Egypt)
· 1 handful fresh mint leaves
· 2 tbsp tahini
· 2 tbsp extra-virgin olive oil
· 1 tsp lime juice
· 1 tsp ground red chili pepper (such as cayenne), plus more for garnish
· Freshly ground black pepper
· Fresh mango slices and/or pitted and chopped medjool dates (optional)

Baked Mont d'Or

Preheat the oven to 375°F (190°C/Gas Mark 5).

Peel and thinly slice the garlic clove. Remove any wrappers or labels from the cheese box, leaving the cheese inside. Place on a baking sheet.

Cut 8–10 slits in the top of the cheese using the tip of a paring knife. Tuck the garlic slices into the slits and pour the white wine over the cheese. If you are using rosemary, place tiny pieces in the slits. Bake for 20–30 minutes.

While the cheese is baking, prepare the chosen accompaniments.

• Smoked sausage or charcuterie
To prepare the Morteau sausage, place it in a saucepan of cold water, bring to a simmer, and cook over medium heat for 25–30 minutes, until cooked through. Alternatively, prepare a charcuterie platter with your choice of deli meats (cured ham and sausage, mortadella, etc.) and cornichons.

• Potatoes
Cook the potatoes in a large saucepan of boiling salted water for 15–20 minutes, or until tender. Drain well and keep warm.

• Broccoli and cauliflower
Place the florets in a saucepan of boiling salted water and cook for about 5–10 minutes, until crisp-tender. Serve warm drizzled with vinaigrette.

• Bread
Toast the bread slices just before the cheese is taken out of the oven.

When the Mont d'Or is ready, remove it from the oven and serve immediately with the accompaniments of your choice.

SERVES 4

Active time **10 minutes + time to prepare accompaniments**
Cooking time **About 30 minutes**

INGREDIENTS

• 1 large clove garlic
• 1 Mont d'Or cheese (1 lb./500 g) in its original spruce packaging (see Notes)

• 3½ tbsp (50 ml) dry white wine, such as Savagnin from the Jura region or Chardonnay
• 1 sprig fresh rosemary (optional)

SUGGESTED ACCOMPANIMENTS

• 1 smoked sausage (preferably Morteau) or assorted charcuterie (cured ham and sausage, mortadella, etc.)

• Cornichons
• 12 firm-fleshed new potatoes
• Broccoli and cauliflower florets
• Vinaigrette of your choice
• Thinly sliced bread
• Sesame grissini

NOTES Make sure the box is stapled and not glued, as the glue may come unstuck during baking.

Savory Recipes
with Cheese

Cheesy Mashed Potatoes

Aligot

Peel the potatoes, cut them into large pieces, and rinse under running water to remove some of the starch.

Place the potatoes in a large saucepan of cold salted water and bring to a boil. Cook over medium to high heat for 20–25 minutes, until tender.

Meanwhile, cut the tome fraîche into small pieces or shred it coarsely using a grater. Warm the milk in a small saucepan over low heat, then remove from the heat and cover.

Drain the potatoes thoroughly. While the potatoes are still hot, pass them through a food mill or potato ricer back into the saucepan, then gradually stir in the butter and crème fraîche until well blended. Do not use a food processor, as this will develop the gluten too much and make the mixture elastic.

Gradually stir in the warm milk, until the texture is smooth and creamy and is neither too stiff nor too runny.

Place the saucepan over low heat and add the cheese. It is now time for some elbow grease: using a wooden spoon, stir in the same direction every 2 minutes, for a total of 10–15 minutes. Take care not to incorporate too much air, which will cool the aligot excessively.

Continue stirring until the aligot is smooth, pulls away from the sides of the pan, and can be stretched with the spoon (see photo).

Season with pepper, add the garlic, and give one final stir to combine.

Serve immediately with a green salad, thick slices of bread, and sausage and/or bacon.

SERVES 4

Active time **20 minutes**
Cooking time **40 minutes**

INGREDIENTS

- 2¼ lb. (1 kg) floury (starchy) potatoes
- 14 oz. (400 g) tome fraîche (see Notes)
- ¾ cup (200 ml) whole milk
- 4 tbsp (2 oz./60 g) butter, diced and at room temperature
- ¼ cup (2 oz./60 g) crème fraîche
- 2 cloves garlic, finely chopped
- Freshly ground pepper

To serve (optional)
- Green salad, thickly sliced bread, and sausage and/or bacon

NOTES This dish from the Auvergne region is traditionally made with tome (or tomme) fraîche: lightly fermented hard-pressed curd similar in texture to mozzarella. If tome fraîche is unavailable, use firm, cooking mozzarella instead.

Cheese-Filled Ravioli in Broth

Bouillon de ravioles

Wash the vegetables for the broth, peeling them if necessary, and cut them into pieces. Sauté in a saucepan over medium heat with a little olive oil and a generous pinch of salt until softened and browned in places.

Cover with the water and bring to a boil. Reduce the heat and let simmer for 30 minutes. Taste for salt and add more if necessary.

Remove the vegetables and strain the broth through a fine-mesh sieve.

Wash and thinly slice the zucchini, scallions, and mushrooms. Bring the broth to a simmer and add the vegetables.

Let the vegetables cook for 3 minutes, until just tender, then carefully add the ravioli to the broth. When they float to the surface, they are ready.

Divide between four bowls and serve immediately.

SERVES 4

Active time **20 minutes**
Cooking time **35 minutes**

INGREDIENTS

Vegetable broth
- 1 leek
- 1 onion
- 2 carrots
- 2 shallots
- 3½ oz. (100 g) button mushrooms
- 1 head fennel
- 1 stalk celery
- Olive oil
- 1 generous pinch salt, plus more as needed
- About 4 cups (1 liter) water

To serve
- 1 zucchini
- 4 scallions
- 8 button mushrooms
- 1 package fresh cheese-filled ravioli

Spaghetti Carbonara

Whisk together the egg yolks, 1 pinch of salt, 2 pinches of black pepper, and most of the grated Parmesan (1½ oz./40 g) in a bowl large enough to hold the cooked spaghetti.

Fill a large saucepan with water, add 2 pinches of salt, and bring to a boil.

Meanwhile, cut the pancetta into thin slices and brown it over medium heat in a skillet large enough to hold the cooked pasta. Remove the pancetta and set the skillet aside, without draining off the fat from the pancetta.

When the water comes to a boil, add the pasta and cook until al dente, following the recommended time on the package.

Just before the pasta is ready, scoop out 2 tablespoonfuls of the pasta cooking water and gradually pour it into the egg yolk mixture, whisking continuously. Warm the skillet containing the pancetta fat, if necessary.

Drain the spaghetti, leaving some water clinging to the strands. Working quickly, pour the spaghetti into the skillet with the pancetta fat, add the olive oil, and toss until evenly coated.

Transfer the still-hot pasta to the large bowl containing the egg yolk mixture. Toss to combine, then add the pancetta and remaining black pepper.

Sprinkle with the remaining Parmesan and serve immediately.

SERVES 4

Active time **15 minutes**
Cooking time **10 minutes**

INGREDIENTS

- 6 egg yolks
- 3 pinches salt
- 4 pinches black pepper
- ½ cup (2 oz./50 g) freshly grated Parmesan
- 2 oz. (50 g) pancetta
- 10½ oz. (300 g) dried spaghetti
- 1 tbsp extra-virgin olive oil

Veal Cordon Bleu

Escalopes cordon bleu

Place the veal cutlets between two sheets of parchment paper. Using a rolling pin or meat mallet, pound the cutlets to a thickness of about ⅛ in. (3 mm).

Place the flour in a shallow dish. Whisk the egg in another shallow dish and season with salt and pepper. Combine the breadcrumbs and Parmesan in a third shallow dish.

Lightly dust one side of each cutlet with flour, shaking off the excess. Dip in the egg until coated, then dredge in the breadcrumb mixture to coat one side. Lay flat on a baking sheet, breadcrumb-side down.

Top each cutlet with a slice of ham and scatter one-quarter of the shredded Emmental over the ham. Chill for 30 minutes.

Coat a skillet with a little olive oil and warm over low heat. Carefully place the cutlets, breadcrumb-side down, in the skillet. Cook for about 10 minutes, keeping a close eye on them, until browned and the meat is cooked through and the cheese has started to melt.

Carefully transfer to plates and fold each cutlet over to enclose the ham and cheese.

Serve immediately, with lemon wedges to squeeze over and some microgreens, if you wish.

SERVES 4

Active time **20 minutes**
Chilling time **30 minutes**
Cooking time **10 minutes**

INGREDIENTS

- 4 veal cutlets (also known as scaloppini or escalopes)
- Flour, for dusting
- 1 egg
- 1½ cups (5¼ oz./150 g) Panko breadcrumbs
- 1 cup (3½ oz./100 g) finely grated Parmesan
- 4 slices baked ham
- 1⅓ cups (7 oz./200 g) shredded Emmental
- Extra-virgin olive oil
- Salt and freshly ground pepper

To serve (optional)
- Lemon wedges
- Microgreens

Maroilles Tart

Flamiche au maroilles

Heat the water until it is just lukewarm (no hotter than 115°F/46°C; about 15 seconds in a microwave). Pour it into a mixing bowl. Crumble in the fresh yeast, add the sugar and salt, and stir until dissolved.

Let sit for 5 minutes, then whisk in the olive oil. Add one egg and whisk quickly, by hand, to blend, then add the second egg and whisk even more vigorously.

Add the flour and whisk it in until just smooth. Avoid over-whisking, which could make the dough dry. Cover and let rise for 30 minutes at room temperature.

Line two 9½-in. (24-cm) tart pans with parchment paper. Divide the dough into two equal pieces and place in the tart pans. Using a flexible spatula or your hands, press the dough evenly over the bases of the pans and up the sides. The dough layer will be thin, but it will rise when baked.

Remove the rinds from the sides of each Maroilles square, but leave the top and bottom rinds on. Cut the cheese into slices and arrange in a crisscross pattern over the dough, leaving a 1¼-in. (3-cm) border. Sprinkle the tops lightly with grated nutmeg. Let rise for about 40 minutes at room temperature.

Preheat the oven to 400°F (200°C/Gas Mark 6) on fan setting. Bake one tart at a time for about 30 minutes, or until deeply golden.

MAKES 2 × 9½-IN. (24-CM) TARTS

Active time **40 minutes**
Rising time **About**
1 hour 10 minutes
Cooking time **1 hour**

INGREDIENTS

- ⅓ cup (80 ml) water
- ⅔ oz. (20 g) fresh (cake) yeast
- 1 tsp superfine sugar
- ½ tsp salt
- ¼ cup (50 ml) extra-virgin olive oil
- 2 eggs
- 1⅔ cups (7 oz./190 g) all-purpose flour
- 2 × 7-oz. (200-g) squares Maroilles cheese
- A little freshly grated nutmeg

Smoked Scamorza Frittata

Wash the unpeeled potatoes and cook them in a large saucepan of boiling salted water for about 20 minutes, or until tender.

Meanwhile, wash and deseed the bell pepper and cut it lengthwise into thin strips. Trim and thinly slice the spring onions. Sauté both in a nonstick skillet with the olive oil over medium heat until softened and browned in places.

Stir in the spinach and cook for 2 minutes, until wilted.

Drain and peel the potatoes. Cut the potatoes and the scamorza into small dice and scatter them over the vegetables in the skillet.

Whisk the eggs together and pour them into the skillet. Reduce the heat to very low, cover, and cook for 7–8 minutes.

When the frittata is almost cooked, place a large plate upside down over the skillet, upturn the skillet and plate, then slide the frittata off the plate back into the skillet to cook the other side. Continue to cook for a few minutes, until the egg is fully set.

Cut into small squares or wedges to serve at cocktail hour. Alternatively, for a light meal, serve accompanied by a salad.

SERVES 4

Active time **20 minutes**
Cooking time **About 35–40 minutes**

INGREDIENTS

• 2 medium waxy potatoes (such as Yukon gold or Charlotte)
• 1 red bell pepper
• 2 spring onions
• 3 tbsp extra-virgin olive oil
• 1 bag baby spinach (3½ oz./100 g)
• 1–2 approximately 9-oz. (250-g) balls smoked scamorza cheese
• 8 eggs

To serve (optional)
• Salad of your choice

213

Grilled Cheese Sandwich

Spread one side of each slice of bread with butter, then spread mustard over two of the slices, if you wish.

Cut the slice of ham in half, and place a half-slice on two of the slices of bread. Divide the cheese in half and place on top of each ham slice.

Place the other two slices of bread on top to close the sandwiches. Toast them in a sandwich press until the cheese has melted and the bread is lightly golden.

Alternatively, lightly butter the outsides of the bread slices, too, and toast the sandwiches in a skillet over medium-low heat, turning them over halfway through the cooking time.

Variation
You could also add sautéed button mushrooms to the sandwiches before toasting them.

SERVES 2

Active time **5 minutes**
Cooking time **5 minutes**

INGREDIENTS

· 4 slices sandwich bread
(with or without the crust)
· 2 tbsp (1 oz./30 g) butter, softened
· Wholegrain mustard (optional)
· 1 large slice baked ham
· 1 generous cup (4¼ oz./120 g)
shredded Emmental or Cheddar

Georgian Cheese-Filled Bread
Khachapuri

Preparing the dough
Whisk together the yogurt, crème fraîche, and baking powder in a large bowl. Add the egg and salt and whisk to blend. Add the flour and begin stirring it in using a spoon. Switch to your hands and knead until the dough is uniform, smooth, and still a little sticky. This should take no more than 5 minutes.

Add the olive oil and knead for a few more minutes, until fully incorporated. At first, the dough will no longer be sticky, but as soon as it starts sticking to your hands again, stop kneading. Cover the dough with plastic wrap and let rest for 10 minutes.

Preparing the cheese filling
Crumble the feta into a large bowl and add the Emmental. Using a fork, stir the cheeses together, mashing the feta slightly. Add the egg, then mix and mash until the mixture is well blended and compact. Divide the mixture into 5 balls weighing 3 oz. (85 g) each and set aside. Place the dough on a lightly floured surface and shape it into a ball, using the flour to prevent sticking.

Shaping and baking the *khachapuri*
Preheat the oven to 350°F (180°C/Gas Mark 4). Divide the dough into 5 pieces weighing about 5 oz. (140 g) each. Shape them into balls, dusting with flour as needed to prevent sticking. Cover with plastic wrap to prevent them from drying out.

Working with one at a time, flatten each ball slightly to make an approximately 5-in. (12-cm) disk. Place a cheese ball in the center, then fold the sides up over the cheese to form a pouch. Pinch all the seams together well to prevent any leaks during baking.

Dust the pouch with flour and place it on the work surface. Using your hands (not a rolling pin), flatten the pouch into an approximately 6½-in. (16-cm) disk. Be sure to dust the work surface regularly with flour to avoid tearing the dough. Repeat with the remaining dough balls.

Place the shaped *khachapuri* on a baking sheet lined with parchment paper, without crowding them. Bake them in batches for about 30 minutes, until they are golden. As soon as you remove them from the oven, brush the crust with melted butter.

SERVES 5

Active time **45 minutes**
Resting time **10 minutes**
Cooking time **30 minutes per batch**

INGREDIENTS

Dough
- 1 cup (9 oz./250 g) firm plain yogurt
- 1 tbsp crème fraîche
- 1 level tsp baking powder
- 1 egg
- 1 heaping tsp salt
- 3¼ cups (14 oz./400 g) all-purpose or pastry flour, plus more for dusting
- 1 tbsp extra-virgin olive oil

Cheese filling
- 5¼ oz. (150 g) feta (or cottage or cream cheese)
- Scant 1½ cups (9 oz./250 g) shredded Emmental
- 1 egg, beaten

To finish
- 2 tbsp (1 oz./30 g) lightly salted butter, melted

Georgian Cheese and Herb-Stuffed Dumplings

Khinkali qvelit

Preparing the dough

Place the flour, egg, and salt in a food processor and pulse to blend. Gradually add the water, pulsing until the dough pulls away from the sides of the bowl. Cover with plastic wrap to prevent the top from drying out and crusting. Let rest for 30 minutes.

Preparing the cheese filling

Meanwhile, wash, dry, and finely chop the cilantro and mint. Place in a large bowl with the ricotta, crème fraîche, and eggs. Season with salt and pepper and stir until well combined.

Shaping and cooking the dumplings

Divide the dough into several balls, about the size of ping-pong balls. On a lightly floured work surface, roll each ball into a 4–5-in. (10–12-cm) disk. Hold a disk in the palm of your hand and place 2 teaspoons of filling in the center. Fold the edges of the dough over the filling, pressing gently to release air, and form pleats all the way around. Pinch the tip to seal. Place on a floured surface and repeat with the remaining dough balls.

Bring a large saucepan of water to a boil and season with salt. Using a slotted spoon, gently lower several dumplings into the water, one at a time. Cook until they float to the surface (7–8 minutes for each batch). Lift out using the spoon and transfer to a serving dish. Repeat until all the dumplings are cooked.

Serve warm with a few grinds of pepper over the top.

SERVES 4

Active time **45 minutes**
Resting time **30 minutes**
Cooking time **7–8 minutes per batch**

INGREDIENTS

Dough
- 4 cups (1 lb. 2 oz./500 g) all-purpose flour
- 1 egg
- 1 large pinch salt
- 1 cup (250 ml) lukewarm water

Cheese filling
- ½ bunch fresh cilantro
- ½ bunch fresh mint
- 2 cups (1 lb./500 g) ricotta
- Scant ½ cup (3½ oz./100 g) crème fraîche
- 3 eggs
- Salt and freshly ground pepper

219

Mac and Cheese

Preheat the oven to 350°F (180°C/Gas Mark 4).

Fill a large saucepan with water, add 2 pinches of salt, and bring to a boil. Add the pasta and cook until al dente, following the recommended time on the package. Drain and place the cooked pasta in a large bowl.

Heat the milk in a microwave.

Melt the butter in a saucepan over low heat. Whisk in the flour and cook, whisking continuously, until the mixture is smooth (about 3 minutes).

Using a spatula, gradually pour in the hot milk, stirring constantly. Still stirring, cook until the mixture thickens, then stir in 1 generous cup (5¼ oz./150 g) of the shredded Cheddar and a few pinches of ground nutmeg. Season with pepper.

Immediately pour the cheese sauce over the cooked pasta in the bowl and stir until well combined. Transfer to an 8 × 10-in. (20 × 26-cm) baking dish; the pasta layer should be about 1½ in. (4 cm) thick.

Combine the remaining Cheddar with the breadcrumbs and scatter over the pasta. Bake for 30 minutes, or until golden.

Serve hot or warm with a seasonal salad, if you wish.

SERVES 4

Active time **10 minutes**
Cooking time **45 minutes**

INGREDIENTS

- 2 pinches salt
- 9 oz. (250 g) macaroni (straight tubes or elbows)
- 2½ cups (600 ml) whole milk
- 2 tbsp (1 oz./30 g) butter
- 1½ tbsp (15 g) all-purpose flour
- Scant 2 cups (7 oz./200 g) shredded Cheddar
- Ground nutmeg
- ½ cup (25 g) breadcrumbs (preferably Panko)
- Freshly ground pepper

To serve (optional)
- Seasonal salad of your choice

Breaded Fresh Goat Cheese with Spiced Quince Paste

Place the quince paste, vinegar, Espelette or Aleppo pepper, and lemon juice in a food processor. Blend until smooth. Transfer to a small serving bowl.

Combine the thyme and breadcrumbs in a large bowl. Cut the cheese log into 12 equal rounds and coat them lightly with flour.

Beat the egg in a bowl using a fork. Brush the cheese rounds with the egg, then gently roll them in the breadcrumb mixture to coat.

Drizzle a little olive oil into a large nonstick skillet and warm over high heat. Cook the breaded cheese slices for about 2 minutes on each side, until golden and crisp. Season with a little salt.

Transfer to a plate lined with paper towel to drain.

Serve immediately with the quince paste.

SERVES 4

Active time **15 minutes**
Cooking time **4 minutes**

INGREDIENTS

- 7 oz. (200 g) quince paste
- 2 tbsp sherry vinegar
- 8 g ground Espelette or Aleppo pepper
- 1 tbsp lemon juice (from about ½ lemon)
- 1 tbsp dried thyme
- 1 cup (3½ oz./100 g) dried breadcrumbs
- 1 × 8-oz. (230-g) bûche de chèvre frais (fresh goat cheese log)
- Scant ½ cup (2 oz./50 g) all-purpose flour
- 1 egg
- Extra-virgin olive oil
- Salt

Brazilian Cheese Bread

Pão de queijo

Preheat the oven to 350°F (180°C/Gas Mark 4).

Combine the milk, water, and oil in a saucepan, then bring to a boil.
Remove from the heat.

Combine the tapioca flour and salt in a large bowl. Pour over the hot liquid and, using a spatula, stir until well blended.

Stir in the eggs one at a time until fully incorporated.

Gradually stir in the grated cheeses, until well combined. The dough should be stretchy and dense.

Grease your hands with a little oil and shape the dough into walnut-size balls. Place on a baking sheet lined with parchment paper (see Notes).

Bake for about 30 minutes, until puffed up and deeply golden.

SERVES 4

Active time **15 minutes**
Cooking time **30 minutes**

INGREDIENTS

- ⅔ cup (150 ml) whole milk
- ⅔ cup (150 ml) water
- ⅔ cup (150 ml) neutral oil (such as canola or grape-seed), plus more for greasing
- 4½ cups (1 lb. 2 oz./500 g) tapioca flour
- 1 tsp salt
- 3 eggs
- 1¾ cups (7 oz./200 g) grated Emmental
- ½ cup (1¾ oz./50 g) grated Parmesan

NOTES You can freeze some of the balls after shaping them, although they won't puff up as much as fresh ones when baked. Bake as indicated without thawing, adding about 10 minutes to the cooking time.

Spinach and Bell Pepper Pastilla

Preheat the oven to 350°F (180°C/Gas Mark 4).

Wash, deseed, and finely chop the bell peppers. Sauté them in the olive oil in a skillet over medium heat until just softened.

In a separate skillet, melt 2 tablespoons (1 oz./30 g) of the butter over medium heat. Add the spinach and cook until wilted, stirring regularly. Remove from the heat.

Melt the remaining butter. Take one sheet of brik pastry and brush it with the butter, then place it in the base of an 8½-in. (22-cm) round springform pan. Repeat with 3 more sheets of pastry, layering them over the first.

Add the spinach, bell peppers, cream, and cheese in layers, repeating until they are all used up. Sprinkle with ground red chili pepper.

Brush the remaining brik pastry sheets with melted butter, one at a time as above, and layer them over the filling. Tuck the edges down inside the pan.

Brush the top with the remaining melted butter. Bake for about 15 minutes, until the pastry is golden. Toward the end of the baking time, scatter sliced almonds over the top, so that they toast slightly without burning.

SERVES 4

Active time **40 minutes**
Cooking time **15 minutes**

INGREDIENTS

- 1–2 red bell peppers
- 2 tbsp extra-virgin olive oil
- 7 tbsp (3½ oz./100 g) butter, divided
- 1 lb. 5 oz. (600 g) baby spinach
- 10 sheets brik pastry (or phyllo dough)
- ¾ cup (200 ml) heavy cream (min. 35% fat)
- 1¾ cups (7 oz./200 g) grated Emmental
- Ground red chili pepper
- Sliced almonds

Pesto

There are two methods for making pesto: the traditional method, by hand, and the quicker, more practical method, using a food processor or blender.

Wash the basil leaves and leave them to dry on a clean dish towel.

Preparing the pesto the traditional way
In a mortar and pestle, pound the garlic and pine nuts into a paste.

Add a pinch of coarse salt and the basil leaves, then continue to pound.

Add the Parmigiano Reggiano and pecorino, then pound again.

Continue pounding as you gradually drizzle in the olive oil.

Preparing the pesto the not-so-traditional but practical way
Place the garlic, pine nuts, basil, and cheeses in a food processor or blender with a pinch of coarse salt. Pulse until finely chopped.

With the machine running on low speed, slowly drizzle in the olive oil and process until the pesto is smooth.

Taste for salt and adjust if necessary.

This pesto is best served as soon as possible, tossed with your pasta of choice.

**MAKES ENOUGH
FOR 4 PASTA SERVINGS**

Active time **About 10 minutes**
(longer if you're making it by hand, and shorter if using a food processor!)

INGREDIENTS

· 2 oz. (60 g) fresh basil leaves
· 1 clove garlic, peeled
· Generous ¼ cup (1½ oz./40 g) pine nuts
· Generous ½ cup (2 oz./60 g) freshly grated Parmigiano Reggiano
· Generous ¼ cup (1 oz./30 g) freshly grated pecorino
· Generous ¼ cup (60 ml) extra-virgin olive oil
· A few pinches coarse salt

To serve
· Pasta of your choice, cooked until al dente

NOTES Pine nuts can be quite expensive. Sunflower seeds are a more economical substitute—our apologies to Italian gourmets!

Four-Cheese Pizza

Preheat the oven to 400°F (200°C/Gas Mark 6).

Stretch the pizza dough over a large rectangular baking sheet covered with parchment paper.

Spread the crème fraîche over the dough in an even layer, then scatter over the shredded Gruyère.

Cut the raclette cheese, mozzarella, and goat cheese into slices and distribute evenly over the top, finishing with the goat cheese. Sprinkle with pine nuts.

Bake for 15 minutes, until the crust and cheese are golden.

Remove the pizza from the oven, scatter over the basil leaves, and serve immediately.

SERVES 4

Active time **15 minutes**
Cooking time **15 minutes**

INGREDIENTS

· Dough for 1 pizza to serve 4 (store-bought or homemade)
· 2 tbsp crème fraîche
· Scant 1 cup (3½ oz./100 g) shredded Gruyère
· 3½ oz. (100 g) raclette cheese
· 1 ball mozzarella
· 1 × 5¼-oz. (150-g) bûche de chèvre (goat cheese log with a rind)
· Pine nuts
· A few leaves fresh basil

Quesadillas

Cook the bacon in a skillet over medium-high heat until crisp. Drain on paper towel.

Wash the tomatoes and thinly slice them crosswise. Thinly slice the scallions and jalapeño (if using). Wash and roughly chop the cilantro. Crumble the fresh goat cheese into a bowl.

Melt a little butter in a skillet over low heat.

Place one tortilla in the skillet and scatter one-quarter of each ingredient over one half, then sprinkle with smoked paprika. Fold the other half over the top.

Cook for a few minutes, until the tortilla is lightly browned on the bottom, then turn it over and cook until the cheese is melted and the other side is lightly browned. Remove from the skillet and keep warm. Repeat with the remaining tortillas.

Sprinkle with dukkah immediately before serving. Serve with salsa and sliced avocado on the side, if you wish.

SERVES 4

Active time **20 minutes**
Cooking time **20 minutes**

INGREDIENTS

· 8 slices bacon
· 1–2 firm tomatoes, such as Roma
· 2 scallions
· 1 small pickled jalapeño (or ground Espelette pepper or chili flakes)
· A few fresh cilantro leaves + a few sprigs for garnish
· 7 oz. (200 g) fresh chèvre (goat cheese)
· Butter

· 4 × 9–10-in. (23–25-cm) corn or wheat tortillas
· Scant 2 cups (7 oz./200 g) shredded Cheddar or Gouda
· 1 tsp smoked paprika

To serve
· 1 tbsp dukkah
· Mexican-style salsa
· 1 avocado, thinly sliced (optional)

Brocciu-Stuffed Sardines

Sardines farcies au brocciu

Preheat the oven to 400°F (200°C/Gas Mark 6).

Scale and gut the sardines, then remove the heads and central spine.

To prepare the filling, wash and finely chop the parsley and mint leaves, reserving some for garnish. Place in a bowl with the brocciu, egg, and garlic, then stir until well blended. Season with salt and pepper.

Open the sardines, skin side down, and place a spoonful of filling on one side of each. Close the sardines.

Place the stuffed sardines in a baking dish greased with olive oil.

Bake for 10–12 minutes, until the fish is cooked through.

Season with pepper, garnish with a few parsley and mint leaves, and serve immediately.

SERVES 4

Active time **15 minutes**
Cooking time **10–12 minutes**

INGREDIENTS

- 16 fresh sardines
- A few leaves fresh parsley
- A few leaves fresh mint
- 9 oz. (250 g) brocciu (see Notes)
- 1 egg, beaten
- 1 clove garlic, finely chopped
- Extra-virgin olive oil
- Salt and freshly ground pepper

NOTES If brocciu—a soft, creamy cheese from Corsica (see p. 60)—is unavailable, you can use ricotta instead.

Cheese Sauce

Melt the butter in a large saucepan over low heat, then stir in the cream. When the cream is hot, stir in the shredded Emmental.

Continue to cook over low heat for 7 minutes, until the sauce is smooth, stirring often.

Remove from the heat and whisk in the egg yolk to thicken the sauce.

Add the nutmeg and season with ground five-peppercorn blend, salt, and freshly ground black pepper. Stir until well blended.

Serve the sauce hot, while it is still melted and pourable. Drizzle over pasta or another dish of your choice, and sprinkle with fennel seeds for texture and flavor if you wish.

SERVES 4

Active time **10 minutes**
Cooking time **10 minutes**

INGREDIENTS

· 1 tbsp butter
· ¾ cup (200 ml) heavy cream (min. 35% fat)
· 3½ oz. (100 g) freshly shredded Emmental
· 1 egg yolk, at room temperature
· 2 pinches ground nutmeg
· A few pinches ground five-peppercorn blend
· Salt and freshly ground black pepper

To serve
· Pasta of your choice, cooked until al dente (or anything else you'd like to drizzle the sauce over)
· Fennel seeds (optional)

NOTES If you like bold flavors, add a few drops of Tabasco sauce for a spicy kick.

Parmesan Soufflé

Place a baking sheet on the oven floor and preheat the oven to 400°F (200°C/Gas Mark 6).

Melt 3 tablespoons (1½ oz./40 g) of the butter. Brush the insides of eight individual soufflé dishes, with a 7-oz. (200-ml) capacity, with the melted butter to grease them well. Chill until using.

Bring the milk to a boil in a saucepan.

Melt the remaining butter in a separate saucepan over low heat. Sprinkle the flour over the butter and whisk constantly until the mixture is frothy and white.

Still whisking constantly over low heat, gradually pour in the hot milk and cook for about 3 minutes, until the sauce mixture becomes mousse-like.

Remove from the heat and season with salt, white pepper, and a little ground nutmeg. Let cool slightly.

Place the egg whites in a bowl and beat them until they begin to hold their shape. Add the powdered milk and continue beating until the whites form firm peaks.

Gradually incorporate the egg yolks into the cooled sauce, followed by the grated Parmesan. Gently fold in the beaten egg whites.

Divide the mixture between the dishes. Carefully transfer to the preheated baking sheet. Bake for about 20 minutes, until well risen and golden brown on top.

Serve immediately, with a spinach and tomato salad or a green salad of your choice.

SERVES 8

Active time **20 minutes**
Cooking time **20 minutes**

INGREDIENTS

· 7 tbsp (3½ oz./100 g) butter, divided
· 2 cups (500 ml) whole milk
· ½ cup (2 oz./60 g) all-purpose flour
· Ground nutmeg
· 8 eggs, separated
· 4 tsp (20 g) powdered milk
· 1½ cups (5 oz./150 g) freshly grated Parmesan
· Salt and white pepper

To serve
· Spinach and tomato salad or a green salad of your choice

Tartiflette

Wash the potatoes. Place them unpeeled in a large saucepan of boiling salted water and cook for 20 minutes, or until just tender.

Preheat the oven to 200°F (100°C/Gas Mark ¼).

Cut the bacon into approximately ¼-in. (5-mm) lardons. Place them in a small saucepan with enough water just to cover. Bring to a simmer over medium heat. As soon as the water starts to bubble, remove and drain the lardons.

Peel the onions and cut them crosswise into rounds.

When the potatoes are cooked and cool enough to handle, peel them and cut them crosswise into rounds.

Melt the butter in a large sauté pan over medium-high heat. Add the lardons and onions and cook for about 3 minutes, until they start to brown. Add the wine and a little grated nutmeg if you wish. Add the potatoes and cook for 2–3 minutes, stirring often using a wooden spoon.

Remove from the heat, stir in the crème fraîche, and season with pepper. Stir until well combined, then transfer to a 9 × 13-in. (24 × 34-cm) baking dish.

Cut the reblochon in half crosswise to obtain two equal rounds and place over the potatoes with the rinds facing up. For an extra-decadent version, cut a second reblochon into slices and arrange around the first.

Bake for 20–30 minutes, or until golden, stirring once or twice during the baking time.

Serve immediately, with a green salad on the side dressed with walnut oil vinaigrette, if you wish.

SERVES 4

Active time **30 minutes**
Cooking time **About 1 hour**

INGREDIENTS

· 2¼ lb. (1 kg) firm, waxy potatoes (such as Yukon gold or Charlotte)
· 7 oz. (200 g) smoked bacon
· 2 large onions (7 oz./200 g)
· 1 tbsp butter
· Scant ½ cup (100 ml) dry white wine
· Freshly grated nutmeg (optional)
· ⅔ cup (5½ oz./160 g) crème fraîche
· Freshly ground pepper
· 1 × 9-oz. (250-g) round reblochon cheese, preferably farmstead (or 2 for large appetites)

To serve (optional)
· Green salad with walnut oil vinaigrette

Parmesan Tuiles

Finely grate the Parmigiano Reggiano.

Melt the butter in a nonstick skillet over medium heat. Using a paper towel, wipe out the excess melted butter, leaving just a thin coating.

Cook the tuiles in batches. Using a large spoon, place several small mounds of the grated cheese in the pan, making sure they have space to spread in a thin layer. If you'd like perfectly round tuiles, you can place stainless steel baking rings on the skillet and melt the cheese inside the rings.

Cook for a few seconds, until the cheese melts and the edges start to brown.

Using a palette knife, lift out the tuiles once cooked. While they are still warm, drape them over a rolling pin or a glass on its side, so that they harden into a curved shape as they cool.

Let the tuiles cool briefly, just until crisp. Serve immediately, either with an aperitif or alongside a soup or an appetizer.

SERVES 4

Active time **15 minutes**
Cooking time **A few seconds per tuile**

INGREDIENTS

· 5¼ oz. (150 g) Parmigiano Reggiano
· 1 generous tbsp (20 g) butter

NOTES Feel free to season the grated Parmigiano Reggiano with herbs or spices before cooking the tuiles. Ground pepper, nutmeg, and rosemary are all good options.

Welsh Rarebit

Preheat the broiler.

Melt the butter in a medium saucepan over low heat.

Using a wooden spoon, stir in the flour and cook for 2–3 minutes, stirring continuously, to obtain a roux.

Gradually pour in the beer, still stirring constantly.

Remove the saucepan from the heat and stir in the mustard and Cheddar. Keep stirring until the cheese has melted.

Toast the bread lightly in a toaster, then place on a baking sheet.

Spread the cheese sauce over the toast. Place under the broiler for about 1 minute, until the cheese is bubbly and browned in places. Let cool slightly.

Just before serving, top with a few drops of Worcestershire sauce.

SERVES 4

Active time **15 minutes**
Cooking time **20 minutes**

INGREDIENTS

- 3 tbsp (1¾ oz./50 g) unsalted butter
- 3 tbsp all-purpose flour
- 1 cup (250 ml) stout beer (such as Guinness) or brown ale
- 1 tsp English mustard
- Scant 2 cups (7 oz./200 g) shredded Cheddar
- 4 relatively thick slices bread, preferably sourdough
- Worcestershire sauce

Fondue

One day ahead
Cut the bread into 1½–2-in. (4–5-cm) cubes and let dry, uncovered, overnight.

The following day
Remove the rinds from the cheese(s). Cut the cheese into large dice or grate it through the large holes of a box grater if you want it to melt more quickly.

Peel the garlic, cut it in half lengthwise, and use it to rub over the inside of a fondue pot (*caquelon*), preferably made of enameled cast iron, which retains heat well.

Warm the white wine in a small saucepan over very low heat.

To make a roux, cut the butter into small pieces and melt it in the fondue pot over low heat. Do not let the butter brown. Sprinkle the flour over the melted butter and whisk vigorously to combine. Continue to cook, whisking continuously, until the mixture thickens, without letting it brown. When the roux is bubbly and frothy, it is ready.

Pour the warm wine into the fondue pot with the roux over low heat. Stir in a figure-eight pattern using a wooden spoon.

Add the cheese to the pot. Stir occasionally with the wooden spoon until the cheese has melted completely and the mixture is smooth and creamy. Take care not to overheat it, as this can cause the cheese to seize up into clumps.

Season with pepper and stir in kirsch, eau-de-vie, or brandy if using. You can also stir in a little ground nutmeg or other spices of your choice. Immediately transfer the fondue pot to its holder (*réchaud*) to keep it warm, without heating it excessively.

Serve with the dried bread cubes and fondue forks for dipping.

SERVES 4

Active time **10 minutes**
Cooking time **30 minutes**

EQUIPMENT

Fondue set, preferably with an enameled cast-iron pot

INGREDIENTS

· 10½–14 oz. (300–400 g) bread, preferably sourdough
· 1¾–2¾ lb. (800 g–1.2 kg) hard or semi-hard cheese (Gruyère, Emmental, etc.: see Variations)
· 1 clove garlic
· ¾ cup (200 ml) dry white wine, such as Chardonnay, Pinot blanc, Riesling, Viognier, or Gewurztraminer
· 1 generous tbsp (20 g) butter
· 1 tbsp all-purpose flour
· Freshly ground pepper
· 3½ tbsp (50 ml) kirsch, eau-de-vie, or brandy (optional)
· Ground nutmeg or other spices of your choice (optional)

VARIATIONS

● Fondue Fribourgeoise: Vacherin Fribourgeois cheese only
● Fondue "*moitié-moitié*": Half-Swiss Gruyère and half-Vacherin Fribourgeois
● Fondue Savoyarde: Your choice of three of the following cheeses: Comté, Beaufort, Gruyère de Savoie, Emmental de Savoie, or Abondance
● Fondue au Vacherin Mont-d'Or: Mont d'Or cheese and nothing else (see Baked Mont d'Or, p. 198)

Raclette

Wash the potatoes and cut them in half if they are large. Place peeled or unpeeled in a large saucepan of boiling salted water and cook for about 20 minutes, or until a paring knife inserted into the center meets no resistance. Drain and set aside on a serving dish.

Cut the raclette cheese into slices approximately ¼ in. (5 mm) thick and arrange on a large plate.

Arrange all the charcuterie on a serving plate with the pickles.

Turn on the raclette grill, following the manufacturer's instructions, and let the fun begin! Let guests help themselves to potatoes and their choice of accompaniments, place the cheese slices on the small trays and melt them under the heating element, then pour over the potatoes, meats, etc., and repeat.

SERVES 4

Active time **20 minutes**
Cooking time **20 minutes**

EQUIPMENT

Raclette grill

INGREDIENTS

· 2¾ lb. (1.2 kg) firm, waxy potatoes (such as Yukon gold or Charlotte)
· 2¼ lb. (1 kg) raclette cheese
· 1¼ lb. (600 g) charcuterie of your choice (baked ham, cured ham, coppa, air-dried Grisons beef, etc.)
· Pickles (cornichons, assorted vegetables, pearl onions, caper berries, etc.)

Red Kuri Squash Stuffed with Spelt and Cantal

Preheat the oven to 350°F (180°C/Gas Mark 4).

Wash and dry the squash. Cut off the top to create a lid. Scoop out the seeds using a spoon.

Place the squash in a baking dish, replace its top, drizzle with olive oil, and bake for 45 minutes, or until tender.

Meanwhile, rinse the spelt. Bring a large saucepan of salted water to a boil, add the spelt, and simmer until al dente (about 40 minutes, or follow the recommended time on the package). Drain.

Peel and finely dice the carrots. Clean and thinly slice the mushrooms. Peel and finely chop the shallots.

Warm a little olive oil in a sauté pan over medium heat. Add the shallots and sage leaves, and cook for 5 minutes, or until the shallots have softened. Add the carrots and mushrooms, and cook for 15 minutes, stirring often.

Cut the bacon into pieces. Add it to the skillet and let cook for 7 minutes. Add the spelt and broth, and stir until well combined. Taste and adjust the seasonings as needed.

Crumble the Cantal, add it to the skillet, and stir to combine.

Using a large spoon, stuff the squash with the filling and replace the lid. Bake for 20 minutes. Serve immediately.

SERVES 4

Active time **30 minutes**
Cooking time **1 hour 15 minutes**

INGREDIENTS

- 1¾–2¼ lb. (800 g–1 kg) red kuri squash (or 2–3 smaller ones, if preferred)
- Extra-virgin olive oil
- 7 oz. (200 g) whole spelt
- 3 carrots
- 7 oz. (200 g) button mushrooms
- 2 shallots
- Leaves of 1 sprig sage
- 6 slices bacon
- 1 cup (250 ml) vegetable broth
- 3½ oz. (100 g) Cantal (or Comté or Beaufort)
- Salt and freshly ground pepper

Puff Pastry Cheese Straws

Feuilletés au fromage

Preheat the oven to 350°F (180°C/Gas Mark 4).

Unroll the puff pastry sheet and brush it with egg. Sprinkle over the grated cheese(s) of your choice and season with pepper.

Cut the pastry into strips about ¼ in. (5 mm) wide and place on a baking sheet lined with parchment paper (see Notes).

Bake for 20 minutes, until puffed and golden.

SERVES 4

Active time **15 minutes**
Cooking time **20 minutes**

INGREDIENTS

• 9-oz. (250-g) sheet ready-rolled puff pastry
• 1 egg, beaten
• ¾ cup (2½ oz./70 g) grated cheese (such as Emmental, Cheddar, or Parmesan)
• Freshly ground pepper

NOTES Alternatively, you could make different shapes from the dough strips (palmiers, spirals, etc.).

Sweet Recipes
with Cheese

Cheesecake

Preheat the oven to 400°F (200°C/Gas Mark 6).

Place the speculoos and Petit Beurre cookies in a food processor and pulse them into fine crumbs. Alternatively, place them in a large freezer bag, seal the bag, and pound them into fine crumbs using a rolling pin.

Place the cookie crumbs in a large bowl with the softened butter. Stir together until the mixture has the consistency of wet sand. Press the mixture evenly into the bottom and up the sides of a 9½-in. (24-cm) springform pan; the crust should be about ¼ in. (5 mm) thick. Bake for 8–10 minutes, then let cool. Keep the oven switched on.

Whisk together the cream cheese, crème fraîche, sugar, and vanilla extract in a large bowl for about 1 minute, or until smooth.

Add the eggs and fromage blanc, and sprinkle the potato starch over the top. Whisk until just combined.

Pour the filling into the crust and bake for 5 minutes at 400°F (200°C/Gas Mark 6), then lower the oven temperature to 325°F (160°C/Gas Mark 3) and continue to bake for 35–40 minutes. At this point, turn the oven off and leave the cheesecake resting inside for 1 hour, without opening the oven door, to prevent the top from cracking.

Remove the cheesecake from the oven and let it cool for 1 hour at room temperature. Chill for at least 6 hours before serving.

Serve drizzled with fruit coulis or dusted with confectioners' sugar.

SERVES 6

Active time **25 minutes**
Cooking time **50–55 minutes**
Resting time **1 hour**
Cooling time **1 hour**
Chilling time **6 hours**

INGREDIENTS

- 4½ oz. (125 g) speculoos (Lotus Biscoff) cookies
- 4½ oz. (125 g) Petit Beurres or another similar all-butter cookie
- 1 stick + 1 tsp (4 oz./120 g) salted butter, softened
- 2½ cups (19 oz./550 g) cream cheese
- ½ cup + 2 tbsp (5¼ oz./150 g) crème fraîche
- ¾ cup + 1 tbsp (5½ oz./160 g) sugar
- 1 tbsp vanilla extract
- 3 large eggs, beaten
- ½ cup + 2 tbsp (5¼ oz./150 g) fromage blanc (or ricotta or quark)
- 1 tbsp potato starch

To serve (optional)
- Fruit coulis of your choice
- Confectioners' sugar

Corsican Cheesecake

Fiadone

Preheat the oven to 350°F (180°C/Gas Mark 4).

Grease an 8–9-in. (20–23-cm) tart pan with the softened butter and sprinkle with 1 heaping tablespoon (20 g) of the sugar. Shake the pan a little while tapping the bottom to distribute the sugar evenly.

Whisk together the eggs (see Notes), remaining sugar, and eau-de-vie or brandy in a large bowl. Finely grate the lemon zest, taking care to avoid the bitter white pith. Whisk the zest into the egg mixture.

Gently transfer the brocciu to the bowl. Using a fork, mash the cheese and stir it into the other ingredients until well combined.

Pour the batter into the prepared pan and bake for 20–30 minutes, keeping a close eye on the cheesecake. The surface should have a few cracks and be golden brown.

Let cool slightly and serve warm or at room temperature.

SERVES 6

Active time **20 minutes**
Cooking time **20–30 minutes**

INGREDIENTS

· 1 tbsp butter, softened
· 1 scant cup (6 oz./180 g) superfine sugar, divided
· 6 eggs
· 1 tbsp eau-de-vie or brandy
· 1 lemon, preferably organic
· 1 lb. 2 oz. (500 g) brocciu (or ricotta)

NOTES For a lighter, airier version, separate the eggs. Whisk together the egg yolks, sugar, and eau-de-vie or brandy as indicated. Whisk the egg whites and fold them into the batter after adding the cheese.

Bengali Cheese Sweets
Sandesh

Combine the vinegar and the scant ½ cup (100 ml) water in a bowl. If you are using saffron, place it in a small bowl with a little water. If using threads, leave them to infuse; if using powder, stir to dissolve. Set aside.

Warm the milk in a large saucepan over medium heat. As soon as it starts to bubble, remove from the heat. Using a wooden spoon, stir in the vinegar-mixture until the milk curdles. Let the milk continue to curdle and cool for 10 minutes.

Drape cheesecloth or a thin, clean dish towel over a bowl, ensuring that the edges extend well beyond the bowl. Pour in the curdled milk, then pour some cold water over it to stop the cooking and remove the vinegary taste. To strain the curds, twist the top of the cheesecloth to close it and gently squeeze out as much liquid as possible.

Transfer the curds (*chenna*) to a large dish with high sides. Add the sugar, cardamom, and cornstarch, then press down gently using the palms of your hands to mix the ingredients together. Continue until the mixture is well combined and smooth, and does not stick to your fingers. Shape into a ball, then flatten into a disk.

Warm an ungreased skillet over low heat and add the *chenna* dough disk. Cook for about 5 minutes on each side, or until it softens a little; flatten it slightly using a wooden spoon or flexible spatula to ensure even cooking. Transfer the dough to a plate and cover with plastic wrap to prevent it from drying out. Let cool for 5 minutes.

Shape the dough into small balls about the size of a walnut and arrange them on a serving dish. Dip a finger in the saffron-tinged water and press down on the top of each ball to make a yellow-hued divot. If desired, add a few saffron threads to each.

Serve immediately.

SERVES 4

Active time **20 minutes**
Cooling time **15 minutes**
Cooking time **10 minutes**

INGREDIENTS

- 3½ tbsp (50 ml) white vinegar
- Scant ½ cup (100 ml) water
- 1 small pinch saffron threads or saffron powder (optional)
- 8 cups (2 liters) whole cow's milk, preferably fresh and organic (and even raw)
- Scant ⅓ cup (2 oz./60 g) superfine sugar
- ½ tsp ground cardamom
- 1½ tbsp (15 g) cornstarch

Cheese Blintzes

Preparing the blintz batter
Sift the flour into a large bowl. Make a well in the center and add the eggs and salt. Split the vanilla bean lengthwise and scrape in the seeds.

Gradually pour in the milk, water, and melted butter, whisking until well combined and smooth. Let the batter rest for 2 hours at room temperature.

Preparing the cheese filling
Whisk together all the filling ingredients in a large bowl until well blended.

Cooking the blintzes
Melt a little butter in a large skillet over medium heat, then pour in a ladleful of batter. When the edges begin to curl up, turn the blintz over. Spread a little of the cheese filling over the blintz and fold it like a burrito or roll it up, folding in the sides, to enclose the filling. Cook until golden on both sides. Repeat until the batter has been used up.

To serve
Serve the blintzes plain or dusted with confectioners' sugar, accompanied by fresh fruit or a coulis of your choice.

SERVES 4

Active time **20 minutes**
Resting time **2 hours**
Cooking time **20 minutes**

INGREDIENTS

Blintz batter
· 2 cups (9 oz./250 g) all-purpose flour
· 4 eggs, beaten
· 1 tsp salt
· 1 vanilla bean
· 1¼ cups (300 ml) whole milk
· 1 cup (250 ml) water
· 3 tbsp (1½ oz./40 g) butter, melted, plus more for cooking

Cheese filling
· 1½ cups (12 oz./350 g) ricotta
· 2¼ cups (3½ oz./100 g) cream cheese
· ½ cup (3½ oz./100 g) sugar
· A few drops lemon juice

To serve (optional)
· Confectioners' sugar
· Fresh fruit or coulis of your choice

Tiramisu

Whisk together the egg yolks and sugar in a large bowl until thickened and pale. Whisk in the mascarpone until the mixture is thick and smooth.

In a separate bowl, whisk the egg whites until stiff peaks form. Gently fold them into the mascarpone mixture using a flexible spatula. The mixture should be light and airy.

Pour the coffee into a shallow dish and dip half the ladyfingers horizontally into it one by one, so they are half-coated (fully immersing them would make them too soggy).

Arrange the ladyfingers to cover the base of an 8-in. (20-cm) square dish.

Pour half of the mascarpone cream over the ladyfingers and spread it into an even layer using a spatula. Cover with a second layer of ladyfingers, dipped into the espresso as above.

Cover with the remaining mascarpone cream and smooth it over, then press plastic wrap over the surface. Chill for at least 6 hours.

Just before serving, dust the top of the tiramisu with cocoa powder.

SERVES 4

Active time **20 minutes**
Chilling time **6 hours**

INGREDIENTS

- 3 eggs, separated
- ⅓ cup (2¾ oz./75 g) sugar
- 1 cup (9 oz./250 g) mascarpone
- 2 cups (500 ml) cold espresso or very strong black coffee
- 24 ladyfingers
- ¼ cup (1 oz./30 g) unsweetened cocoa powder

Gouda Nougat

Line a 4 × 10-in. (10 × 25-cm) loaf pan with plastic wrap.

Remove the rind from the Gouda. Fit a food processor with the shredding disk and, with the motor running, push the cheese down the feeder tube until it is finely shredded.

Warm the milk in a large saucepan over low heat. When it is warm to the touch, add the Gouda and stir to melt completely.

Add the baking soda, nuts, and cranberries, and stir until well blended.

Pour the mixture into the prepared loaf pan. Let it cool completely, then cover tightly with plastic wrap. Chill overnight.

The following day, turn the nougat out of the pan, peel off the plastic wrap, and cut into slices to serve.

SERVES 4

Active time **20 minutes**
Chilling time **Overnight**

INGREDIENTS

- 14 oz. (400 g) aged Gouda
- Scant ½ cup (100 ml) whole milk
- 1 pinch baking soda
- Scant 3 tbsp (20 g) whole almonds
- Scant 3 tbsp (20 g) whole hazelnuts
- 3 tbsp (20 g) shelled pistachios
- 3 tbsp (20 g) dried cranberries

Turkish Sweet Cheese Pastry
Kunefe

Preparing the syrup

Heat the water and sugar in a saucepan until the sugar dissolves, then bring to a boil. Skim any foam off the surface and stir in the lemon juice. Let cool to room temperature.

Preparing the *kunefe*

Melt the butter and let it cool to lukewarm.

Untangle the *kadayif* and, using scissors, cut it into approximately ¾-in. (2-cm) lengths. Scatter over a baking dish, pour in the melted butter, and gently toss until the pastry is evenly coated.

Spread half the buttered *kadayif* over the base of a medium skillet and scatter the mozzarella pieces over the top. Cover with the remaining pastry. Cook for about 10 minutes over medium heat, until the bottom is golden. To flip the *kunefe* over, place a large plate over the skillet and turn the skillet and plate over together. Slide the *kunefe* from the plate back into the pan, uncooked side down. Continue to cook for an additional 10 minutes, until the second side is golden. Carefully turn out of the pan onto a serving plate.

Serve hot, drizzled with the cooled syrup and sprinkled with finely chopped pistachios.

SERVES 4

Active time **20 minutes**
Cooking time **20 minutes**

INGREDIENTS

Syrup
· ½ cup (120 ml) water
· 1¼ cups (9 oz./250 g) sugar
· 1 tbsp lemon juice

Kunefe
· 1 stick + 2 tsp (4½ oz./125 g) butter
· 9 oz. (250 g) *kadayif* or kataifi (shredded phyllo dough)
· 9 oz. (250 g) mozzarella (or künefe peyniri), torn into small pieces

To serve
· Finely chopped pistachios

Fresh Tome Brioche

Brioche à la tome fraîche

Place a Bundt pan on a rack in the center of the oven and preheat the oven to 275°F (135°C/Gas Mark 1) with the pan inside (see Notes).

Grate the cheese on the large holes of a box grater into a large bowl. Add the eggs, flour, baking powder, and sugar, then mix together using your hands until well combined. The dough will be firm and sticky. If the cheese is quite hard and the dough seems dry, mix in the 3½ tablespoons (50 ml) milk.

Carefully transfer the dough to the hot Bundt pan. Bake for 50 minutes–1 hour, until the brioche is deeply golden, and a skewer inserted into the center comes out clean.

Let the brioche cool for several minutes in the pan, then turn it out onto a rack and let cool completely.

Cut into slices and serve with a fruit coulis or jam of your choice.

SERVES 8

Active time **20 minutes**
Cooking time **50 minutes–1 hour**

INGREDIENTS

· 1 lb. 2 oz. (500 g) tome fraîche, preferably Saint-Nectaire (or mozzarella)
· 3 eggs
· 2 cups (9 oz./250 g) all-purpose flour
· 2 tsp (8 g) baking powder
· 1¼ cups (9 oz./250 g) sugar
· 3½ tbsp (50 ml) whole milk, if necessary

To serve
· Fruit coulis or jam of your choice

NOTES If you do not have a Bundt pan, you can shape the dough into a ring on a silicone baking mat, although the shape will be less even.

Beaufort, Pear, and Ginger Crumble

Preheat the oven to 400°F (200°C/Gas Mark 6).

Place the butter, flour, and Parmesan in a large bowl. Using your fingertips, work the ingredients together to obtain a coarse, crumbly mixture.

Toss in the walnuts and Beaufort.

Peel, core, and quarter the pears. Place in a saucepan with the lemon juice and simmer over low heat for about 10 minutes, until just tender.

Transfer the pears to a baking dish. Finely grate the ginger over them.

Sprinkle the crumble topping over the top. Bake for about 15 minutes, or until golden brown and crisp.

SERVES 4

Active time **15 minutes**
Cooking time **25 minutes**

INGREDIENTS

· 3 tbsp (1½ oz./40 g) butter, diced and softened
· ½ cup (2 oz./60 g) all-purpose flour
· Scant ½ cup (1½ oz./40 g) grated Parmesan
· 6 walnuts, roughly chopped
· 1¾ oz. (50 g) Beaufort, diced
· 2 large pears
· Juice of 1 lemon
· ¾-in. (2-cm) piece fresh ginger, peeled

Ricotta Pancakes

Whisk together the ricotta, buttermilk, and egg yolks in a large bowl. Whisking gently, gradually add the flour, baking powder, and salt. Continue whisking on low speed until the mixture is smooth, although it is fine if there are a few small lumps of ricotta remaining.

Whisk the egg whites until they hold soft peaks. Gently fold them into the batter just until no streaks remain.

Preheat the oven to the lowest temperature and place a large heatproof plate inside.

Warm the oil or butter in a large skillet over medium heat. Pour in small ladlefuls of batter and cook the pancakes for a few minutes, until the undersides are golden and bubbles appear in the center. Using a spatula, flip them over and cook for 1–2 minutes, or until golden on the second side.

Transfer the pancakes to the plate in the oven to keep them warm while you cook the rest.

Serve immediately, with fruit coulis or another topping of your choice.

MAKES ABOUT 10

Active time **15 minutes**
Cooking time **20 minutes**

INGREDIENTS

· 1 cup (9 oz./250 g) ricotta
· ⅔ cup (150 ml) buttermilk
· 2 large eggs, separated
· 1½ cups (6¼ oz./180 g) all-purpose flour
· 1 tsp baking powder
· 1 large pinch salt
· 2 tsp peanut oil or butter

To serve
· Fruit coulis, jam, maple syrup, fresh seasonal fruit, or confectioners' sugar

Crémet d'Anjou

Pour the cream into a large bowl, then add the sugar. Split the vanilla bean lengthwise and scrape in the seeds. Whisk until the cream holds medium to firm peaks.

In a separate bowl, whisk the egg white and salt to firm peaks.

Place the fromage blanc in another large bowl. Using a flexible spatula, gently and gradually fold in the whipped cream and egg white.

Line the 4 molds with cheesecloth and place them in a rimmed dish to catch escaping liquid. Divide the cheese mixture between them.

Chill for at least 3 hours before serving.

SERVES 4

Active time **15 minutes**
Chilling time **3 hours**

EQUIPMENT

4 individual crémet,
cœur à la crème, or other
fresh cheese molds

INGREDIENTS

· ⅔ cup (150 ml) heavy cream
(min. 35% fat), well chilled
· 2 tsp (5 g) superfine sugar
· 1 vanilla bean
· 1 egg white
· 1 pinch salt
· 10½ oz. (300 g) fromage blanc
(or ricotta or quark)

Swiss Chard Tart

Tourte aux blettes

Preparing the rum-soaked raisins

Put the raisins and golden raisins in a small saucepan with the rum and bring to a simmer. Let simmer until the raisins are softened and plump. Let cool completely and drain if necessary before using.

Preparing the pastry dough

Pour the flour onto a work surface, make a well in the center, and place the eggs, butter, sugar, and salt into the well. Using your fingertips, work the ingredients together just until combined, without overworking the dough. Add a few drops of water if the mixture seems too dry and does not hold together. Let rest while you prepare the filling.

Preparing the filling

Remove the chard stems (save them for another recipe), keeping the green leaves only. Thinly slice the leaves and wash them in several changes of cold water, until the water is clear; this tempers the bitterness. Squeeze the leaves between your hands to remove as much water as possible.

In a large bowl, combine the chard leaves with the sugar, eggs, grated cheese, pine nuts, rum-soaked raisins, eau-de-vie, olive oil, anisette, salt, and pepper.

Assembling and baking the tart

Preheat the oven to 350°F (180°C/Gas Mark 4). Grease a 9½-in. (24-cm) tart pan with oil and dust it with flour. Divide the dough into two equal pieces. Roll one to a thickness of about ⅛ in. (3–4 mm), line the tart pan with it, and pierce all over with a fork. Spread the filling over the dough; it should be about ¾ in. (2 cm) thick. Roll out the second piece of dough to the same thickness as the first and lay it over the filling. Crimp the edges together using the tines of a fork and cut a cross-shaped hole in the center to allow steam to escape.

Bake for about 40 minutes, until the crust is golden and begins to pull away from the sides of the pan. Remove from the oven, sprinkle with superfine sugar, and let cool completely. Before serving, scatter toasted anise seeds and pine nuts over the top, and dust with confectioners' sugar, if you wish.

SERVES 6

Active time **40 minutes**
Cooking time **40 minutes**

INGREDIENTS

Rum-soaked raisins
- Scant ¼ cup (1 oz./30 g) raisins
- Scant ¼ cup (1 oz./30 g) golden raisins (sultanas)
- ⅔ cup (150 ml) rum

Pastry dough
- 4 cups (1 lb. 2 oz./500 g) all-purpose flour
- 2 eggs
- 2 sticks (9 oz./250 g) butter, diced and softened
- 1 cup (7 oz./200 g) superfine sugar
- 1 pinch salt
- Water, if needed

Filling
- 4½ lb. (2 kg) thin-ribbed Swiss chard leaves

- ¾ cup (5 oz./150 g) granulated or turbinado sugar
- 2 eggs
- 2 oz. (60 g) hard alpine cow's milk cheese, such as Sbrinz, grated
- Scant ¾ cup (3½ oz./100 g) pine nuts
- Rum-soaked raisins (see left)
- 3½ tbsp (50 ml) eau-de-vie or brandy
- 2 tbsp olive oil

- 2 tbsp anisette
- 1 pinch salt
- 1 pinch pepper
- Oil and flour, for greasing and dusting

To finish
- Superfine sugar
- Toasted anise seeds (optional)
- Toasted pine nuts (optional)
- Confectioners' sugar (optional)

Appendixes

Glossary

affinage
The final stage in the cheesemaking process, also known as **ripening, aging,** or **maturing.** In this step, fresh young cheese is refined and matured to reach its maximum potential in terms of aroma, flavor, and texture. Cheese-aging specialists are known as *affineurs.*

alpage
The high-mountain pastures in the Alps where animals graze in the summer and the style of cheese made there. Those who still make traditional seasonal Alpine cheeses are known as *alpagistes.*

annatto
A carotenoid-rich natural pigment obtained from the seeds of the achiote plant (*Bixa orellana*), native to South America and the Caribbean islands. It is responsible for the characteristic orange color of cheeses like mimolette, Gouda, and Cheddar.

AOC (Appellation d'Origine Contrôlée).
See **AOP.**

AOP (Appellation d'Origine Protégée)
A certification that protects cheeses and other agricultural products from fraudulent manufacture and ensures that they are produced traditionally within a specific geographical region. Established in 1996, AOP is the EU-level equivalent of the older French **AOC** certification. The English equivalent is **PDO** (Protected Denomination of Origin), while Italian and Spanish use **DOP**, for Denominazione di Origine Protetta and Denominación de Origen Protegida, respectively.

artisanal
Refers to cheeses made in small batches by a small team of artisans (usually ten or less), using traditional methods and milk from one or more local producers.

cave
A cool, humid environment—either natural or manmade—where cheese is aged. Also known as a **cellar** or **ripening/aging room.**

cheddaring
The process of stacking blocks of curd on top of one another and leaving them to mature for a few hours in the open air. The curd is then milled and placed in molds. This process is crucial in developing the distinctive flavors of "cheddared" cheeses.

chèvre
The French word for "goat," which is also used to describe all types of goat's milk cheese, from fresh to aged. It is typically used in English to refer to soft, fresh, French-style goat cheeses.

curd
The mass of solid matter produced when milk is coagulated or transformed from a liquid to a solid state, also known as the **coagulum** or **gel.** Technically speaking, coagulum and gel refer to curd that has not yet been cut.

DOP (Denominazione di Origine Protetta or Denominación de Origen Protegida).
See **AOP.**

estive, estivage
The summer period when animals are moved to graze in high-mountain pastures, especially in the Pyrenees, and the style of cheese made there (*d'estive*). In the Alps, this is known as *alpage.*

eyes
The technical term for the characteristic round holes found in some cheeses such as Gouda and Emmental that are caused by natural gases.

farmstead or **farmhouse** (*fermier*)
Refers to cheeses made by cheesemakers on their own farms using traditional techniques and milk solely from their own herds.

forage
Plants that serve as food for livestock, including grass, wildflowers, and herbs, either grazed fresh or eaten dried as hay.

fruitière
A traditional cooperative dairy in the Jura and Savoie regions that collects milk from several nearby farms to produce large wheels of cheese, such as Gruyère and Comté.

gerle
A large wooden vat used to make Salers cheese. Native microbes present in the wood naturally coagulate the milk.

IGP (Indication Géographique Protégée)
A certification that protects products at EU level but is less stringent than **AOP/PDO**, with more flexible criteria regarding geographical boundaries, production methods, history, and other factors. Known in English as **PGI** (Protected Geographic Indication).

laitier
Refers to cheeses produced on a slightly larger scale than artisanal cheeses, using milk sourced from several farms, which may or may not be local. The cheesemaking process is more automated but not as large-scale as in industrial factories.

mites (*cirons*)
Tiny insects that bore into rinds and feed on the cheese inside, contributing texture and flavor. Cheesemakers encourage mites in some cheeses, such as mimolette, but actively strive to prevent them in others, including some tommes.

morge
A solution of brine and surface cultures used to wash the rinds of some cheeses during the ripening process. It keeps the rind moist and encourages the growth of beneficial bacteria that contribute to texture and flavor.

natural cheese
Cheese made exclusively with raw milk—often from indigenous or rare breeds—and native microbes present in the milk and the cheesemaking environment, with no added starter cultures or rennet. These cheeses are characterized by remarkable typicity and aromatic complexity.

pasta filata
An Italian cheesemaking technique that involves melting the curd, then stretching and pulling it into a range of shapes. It is used to produce cheeses in the mozzarella and provolone families, also known as **stretched-curd** cheeses.

pasture
Open or enclosed land on which wild or cultivated grasses and other plants grow for direct consumption by livestock. It is sometimes referred to as a meadow or prairie. Pastured animals are allowed to graze and forage in pastures as opposed to being confined in feedlots.

PGI (Protected Geographic Indication).
See **IGP**.

PDO (Protected Denomination of Origin).
See **AOP**.

Penicillium
A genus of fungi with two species widely used in cheese production: *Penicillium candidum* (*camemberti*), which produces bloomy rinds, and *Penicillium roqueforti*, responsible for the molds found in many blue cheeses.

proteolysis
The breakdown of cheese proteins by enzymes during the ripening phase, altering the texture and contributing aromas and flavors.

raw milk (*lait cru*)
Milk from farm animals' mammary glands that has not been heated to more than 104°F (40°C) or subjected to any treatment producing an equivalent effect, according to Regulation (EC) No. 853/2004 of the European Parliament and of the Council (Annex I, Section 4.1).

rennet (*présure*)
A substance extracted from the abomasum—or fourth stomach—of young ruminants slaughtered before weaning (calves, kids, and lambs). It contains enzymes that aid in the digestion of milk. Most rennet used today is industrially produced from fungi or genetically modified organisms. There are also vegetable rennets extracted from plants such as fig trees or thistles. When added to milk, rennet causes the milk proteins to coagulate and form curd.

rind
The exterior of aged cheeses, also known as the **crust**. Rinds vary greatly depending on the ripening techniques used and whether they are intended to be eaten or cut off and discarded. There are three main categories: **bloomy rinds** (the downy white exteriors typical of Camembert and Brie); **natural rinds** (the thin, dry rinds found on French-style tommes, Cheddar, Parmigiano Reggiano, etc.); and **washed rinds** (the moist, sticky exteriors on cheeses like Époisses and Maroilles).

seasonal/seasonality
Related to or depending on the seasons. Industrial cheeses, which are made with standardized milk, are similar year-round, while farmstead and artisanal cheeses vary seasonally based on milk availability and the animals' diet.

silage
A method of preserving fresh, finely chopped forage via lactic fermentation. The forage is placed in a silo or in heaps and compacted to eliminate any air, which could contaminate the batch. Commonly used in intensive dairy farming, silage can pose health risks and affect the taste of the cheese.

standardization
The adjustment of the fat content in milk to make it more consistent throughout the year. Some manufacturers also standardize the milk's protein content, although this varies less.

Stresa Convention
Also known as the International Convention for the Use of Appellations of Origin and Denominations of Cheeses, this 1951 event, held in Italy, was the first multinational effort to define and legally protect cheese names and styles. The agreement was signed by eight European nations that vowed to respect the protected names and enforce their proper use.

syneresis
The natural contraction of the curd or gel and gradual expulsion of the constituent liquid—i.e., the whey. This key process in cheesemaking may be accelerated by cutting the curd into smaller pieces or pressing it at the draining stage.

turnout (*mise à l'herbe*)
The first time livestock leave the barn after the winter, when the grass begins to grow again. This is a welcome moment for the animals but more critical for the farmer, as the change in diet must be gradual.

turophile
A cheese lover or connoisseur.

typicity
This refers to the signature characteristics that make cheeses—especially natural, farmstead, or artisanal ones—unique. It is rooted in the raw materials, traditional tools and techniques, terroir, and even the native microbes found on individual farms.

tyrosine
An amino acid that crystallizes with age. The small crunchy bits in some dry, mature cheeses are often mistaken for salt crystals, but are in fact made of tyrosine.

whey
The liquid that separates from the curd when milk is coagulated. Primarily composed of water, it also contains a portion of the milk's dry matter, including protein (albumin and globulin), sugar (lactose), and minerals.

Bibliography

Books

— Andrieu, Julie. *Mes accords de goûts*. Paris: Agnès Viénot, 2009.

— Androuet, Pierre, and Yves Chabot. *Le Brie*. Étrépilly: Presses du Village, 1985.

— Androuet, Pierre. *Guide du fromage*. In collaboration with Gilles Lambert and Narcisse Roche. Paris: Stock, 1983.

— Beau, Maurice, and Ch. Bourgain. *L'Industrie fromagère*. Paris: J.B. Baillière et Fils, 1926.

— Boisard, Pierre. *Camembert: A National Myth*. Translated by Richard Miller. Berkeley: University of California Press, 2003.

— Brocart, Eric, Erick Casalta, Jean Chiorboli, and Paul Franceschi. *Corse, les fromages: Casgi, furmagli è brocci*. Ajaccio: Albiana, 2015.

— Carroll, Ricki. *Fromages maison: La petite Crémerie Home made*. Vanves: Marabout, 2012.

— Chancrin, Ernest, ed. *Larousse ménager: Dictionnaire illustré de la vie domestique*. In collaboration with Ferdinand Faideau. Paris: Larousse, 1926.

— Coulon, Pierre. *Le bon savoir du fromage*. Illustrated by Justine Saint-Lo. Paris: First, 2022.

— Dahan, Colette, and Emmanuel Mingasson. *Voix lactées: Sur la route du lait*. Self-published, 2016.

— Darlington, Tanaya. *Madame Fromage's Adventures in Cheese: How to Explore It, Pair It, and Love It, from the Creamiest Bries to the Funkiest Blues*. New York: Workman Publishing, 2023.

— Delfosse, Claire. *Le métier de crémier-fromager: De 1850 à nos jours*. Rinxent: Éditions Mer du Nord, 2014.

— Desjardins, Gustave. *Cartulaire de L'Abbaye de Conques en Rouergue*. 1879th edition. Vanves: Hachette Livre BnF, 2012.

— Donnelly, Catherine, ed. *The Oxford Companion to Cheese*. With a foreword by Mateo Kehler. New York: Oxford University Press, 2016.

— Fumey, Gilles, and Pierre Raffard. *Atlas de l'alimentation*. Paris: CNRS Éditions, 2018.

— Joigneaux, Pierre. *Le livre de la ferme et des maisons de campagne*. Paris: Victor Masson et fils, 1865.

— Palmer, Ned. *A Cheesemonger's History of the British Isles*. London: Profile Books, 2021.

— Pierini, Alessandra. *Petit Précis de gastronomie italienne: Parmigiano*. Paris: Editions du Pétrin, 2014.

— Pierre, Élisabeth, Anne-Laure Pham, and Mélody Denturck. *Bierographie: En 100 schémas et dessins*. Paris: Hachette Pratique, 2021.

— Robin, François. *Le fromage pour les nuls*. Paris: Pour les Nuls, 2019.

— Saxelby, Anne. *The New Rules of Cheese: A Freewheeling & Informative Guide*. California: Ten Speed Press, 2020.

— Segnit, Niki. *The Flavor Thesaurus: Pairings, Recipes, and Ideas for the Creative Cook*. New York: Bloomsbury Publishing, 2012.

— Stengel, Kilien, ed. *Des fromages et des hommes: Ethnographie pratique, culturelle et sociale du fromage*. Paris: Éditions L'Harmattan, 2015.

— Tyckaert, Maud, and Anne-Laure Pham. *Tour de France des saveurs*. Paris: Belles Balades Éditions, 2019.

— Villeroy, Félix. *Laiterie, beurre et fromages*. Paris: Librairie Agricole de la Maison Rustique, 1863.

— Zubillaga, Mayalen. *Brousse du Rove: L'appel des collines*. Paris: Les Éditions de l'Épure, 2018.

Other Sources

— Anquez, Michel. "Le froid en fromagerie." *Le Lait* 537 (July–August 1974): 422–431. https://doi.org/10.1051/lait:197453722

— ANSES. "Avis de l'Agence nationale de securite sanitaire de l'alimentation, de l'environnement et du travail relatif aux modalites de maitrise du risque lie a la presence de dangers microbiologiques dans les fromages et autres produits laitiers fabriques a partir de lait cru." January 19, 2022. https://www.anses.fr/fr/system/files/BIORISK2019SA0033.pdf

—Bengoumi, Mohammed, and Bernard Faye. "Production laitière cameline au Maghreb." *CIHEAM Watch Letter 35: Milk and Dairy Products in the Mediterranean* (December 2015). https://www.iamm.ciheam.org/ress_doc/opac_css/doc_num.php?explnum_id=14009

— Bertozzi, Leo, and G. Panari, "Cheeses with Appellation d'Origine Contrôlée (AOC): Factors that Affect Quality." *International Dairy Journal* 3, no. 4–6 (January 1993): 297–312. https://doi.org/10.1016/0958-6946(93)90019-v

— Bourgeat, Serge, and Catherine Bras. "Entre ancrage local, mondialisation culturelle et patrimonialisation: Une geographie de la tartiflette." *Géoconfluences*, December 14, 2021. https://geoconfluences.ens-lyon.fr/informations-scientifiques/dossiers-thematiques/patrimoine/articles/geographie-de-la-tartiflette

— Brisville, Marianne. "Les produits laitiers dans l'Occident islamique medieval." *Revue des mondes musulmans et de la Méditerranée* 150 (2021). https://doi.org/10.4000/remmm.15545

— Bruegel, Martin. Review of *La France fromagère (1850-1990)*, by Claire Delfosse. *Revue d'histoire moderne et contemporaine* 55-4, no. 4 (2008): 212. https://doi.org/10.3917/rhmc.554.0212

— Buhnik, Sophie. "Image à la une: Acheter et consommer du fromage français au Japon." *Géoconfluences*, January 25, 2022. http://geoconfluences.ens-lyon.fr/informations-scientifiques/a-la-une/image-a-la-une/acheter-et-consommer-du-fromage-francais-au-japon

— Castle, Stephen. "Pandemic Gives S.O.S. a New Meaning for U.K. Cheesemakers: Save Our Stilton. *The New York Times*, June 19, 2020.
https://www.nytimes.com/2020/06/19/world/europe/stilton-coronavirus.html

— CGDAM. "Les chèvres de Grèce." January 25, 2023.
https://cgdam.org/2023/01/25/les-chevres-de-grece/

— The Cheese Professor.
https://www.cheeseprofessor.com

— Confédération Nationale de l'Élevage. *Économie de l'élevage. Dossier Ovins – Filière Lait de Brebis*, no. 532. (September 2022).
https://idele.fr/?eID=cmis_download&oID=workspace%3A%2F%2FSpacesStore%2F70a9d3ab-40ef-4e2a-83df-0685a4ca137b&cHash=55f44d6f864da50ce5badd29e7cea7c0

— Coste, Vincent. "Petite devinette: Quel est le plus grand producteur de fromage de l'UE?" *Euronews*, August 22, 2022.
https://fr.euronews.com/my-europe/2022/08/19/petite-devinette-quel-est-le-plus-grand-producteur-de-fromage-de-lue#:~:text=Un%20outsider%20comme%20la%20Grèce,tambour)%20%3A%20l'Allemagne%20!

— Delfosse, Claire. "La France fromagère." PhD diss., Université Paris 1 Panthéon-Sorbonne, 1993.
http://www.theses.fr/1993PA010528

——. "La localisation de la production fromagère: Évolutions des approches géographiques." *Géocarrefour* 81, no. 4 (2006): 311–318.
https://doi.org/10.4000/geocarrefour.1674

— Déniel, Patrick. "Les secrets de La Vache Qui Rit enfin percés!" *L'Usine Nouvelle*, April 13, 2011.
https://www.usinenouvelle.com/article/les-secrets-de-la-vache-qui-rit-enfinperces.N149960

— Djouhri, Khadra, and Sabrina Madani. "Étude microbiologique d'un produit laitier fermenté traditionnel (J'ben): Isolement et identification des bactéries lactiques." Master's thesis, Université Kasdi Merbah Ouargla, 2015.

— European Commission. "Feta AOP." Agriculture and Rural Development. https://agriculture.ec.europa.eu/farming/geographical-indications-and-quality-schemes/geographical-indications-food-and-drink/feta-pdo_fr

——. "Lait et produits laitiers." Agriculture and Rural Development. https://agriculture.ec.europa.eu/farming/animal-products/milk-and-dairy-products_fr

— FAO. "Passarelle sur la production laitière et les produits laitiers: Codex Alimentarius."
https://www.fao.org/dairy-production-products/products/codex-alimentarius/fr/

— Fondazione Slow Food. "Fondazione Slow Food: Salva la biodiversità, salva il pianeta."
https://www.fondazioneslowfood.com/it/

— Fox, Jeffrey, ed. *FAQ: Microbes Make the Cheese. Report on an American Academy of Microbiology Colloquium Held in Washington, D.C., in June 2014*. Washington, D.C: American Society for Microbiology, 2015.
https://www.ncbi.nlm.nih.gov/books/NBK562892/pdf/Bookshelf_NBK562892.pdf

— France Culture. "Le lait: tout un fromage!" February 24, 2019.
https://www.radiofrance.fr/franceculture/podcasts/les-bonnes-choses/le-lait-tout-un-fromage-5411521

— Fromageries Androuet. "Guide du fromage par Androuet."
https://androuet.com/. https://androuet.com/guide-fromage.html

— Gautier, Alban. "Charlemagne, le brie et le roquefort." *Kentron* 35: 167–182 (2019).
https://doi.org/10.4000/kentron.3509

— Gonzales, Hadrien. "Que se cache-t-il dans l'emmental râpé Président?" *Le Parisien*, March 19, 2021. Video, 6:38.
https://www.leparisien.fr/bien-manger/video-que-se-cache-t-il-dans-lemmental- rape-president-18-03-2021-8429011.php

— Guillaume, Lena. "Dans les coulisses de Lactalis: Les secrets de l'emmental." *Agri53*, December 4, 2020.
https://www.agri53.fr/dans-les-coulisses-de-lactalis-les-secrets-de-lemmental

— Hassid, Marc-Jérôme. "Le terroir, un territoire hybride. L'exemple des fromages des Alpes du Nord." *Géoconfluences*, July 18, 2005.
http://geoconfluences.ens-lyon.fr/doc/territ/FranceMut/FranceMutDoc5.htm

— Howard, Hannah. "Harbison Cheese Is Creamy, Rustic, and Perfect for Snacking." *Bon Appétit*, March 2, 2023.
https://www.bonappetit.com/story/jasper-hill-harbison

— International Dairy Foundation. *L'importance du sel dans la fabrication et l'affinage du fromage*, no. 1401 (March 24, 2014).
https://www.fil-idf.org/wp-content/uploads/woocommerce_uploads/2014/03/Salt-Special-Issue-1401-in-french_CAT-pm6g3u.pdf

— Jan, Gwénaël. "Les bactéries propioniques laitières: Une source de probiotiques encore inexplorée?" *Cholé-Doc*, no. 142 (November–December 2014).
https://www.cerin.org/wp-content/uploads/2014/11/142-bacteries-propioniques-laitieres.pdf

——. "Comment l'effet matrice protège notre microbiote." *Ça m'intéresse*, May 1, 2020.

— Jeune Montagne. "La Tome fraîche de l'Aubrac IGP."
https://www.jeune-montagne-aubrac.fr/produits/tome-fraiche/

— Krumnow, Pascale. "Peut-on parler d'un système productif fromager?" *Les Cafés Géographiques*, November 19, 2014.
https://cafe-geo.net/peut-on-parler-dun-systeme-productif-fromager/

— Lefèvre, J. H. "La race bovine normande et le Herd-Book normand." *Études Normandes* 16, no. 57 (1955): 402–408.
https://doi.org/10.3406/etnor.1955.3213

— Légasse, Périco. "Histoire de la mimolette: Et le vieux hollande devint orange pour rester français." *Marianne*, May 15, 2021.
https://www.marianne.net/art-de-vivre/le-gout-de-la-france/histoire-de-la-mimolette-et-le-vieux-hollande-devint-orange-pour-rester-francais

— Légifrance. "Décret du 25 mars 1924 relatif au lait et aux produits de la laiterie."
https://www.legifrance.gouv.fr/loda/id/LEGISCTA000006097535

— Ménadier, Lydie. "Paysages de fromages: sensibilités au paysage, pratiques des agriculteurs et ancrage territorial des AOC fromagères de moyennes montagnes d'Auvergne et de Franche-Comté." *Carnets de géographes*, no. 4 (2012).
https://doi.org/10.4000/cdg.1037

— Menat, Eric. (2019). "Les laitages, amis ou ennemis." *HEGEL*, no. 2 (2019): 99–113.
https://doi.org/10.4267/2042/70214

— Ministère de l'Agriculture et de la Souveraineté Alimentaire. "Le Mont d'Or AOP, Vacherin du Haut-Doubs." January 26, 2023.
https://agriculture.gouv.fr/le-mont-dor-aopvacherin-du-haut-doubs#:~:text=Aussi%20appel%C3%A9%20Vacherin%20du%20Haut,prot%C3%A9g%C3%A9e%20(AOP)%20en%201996

— Ministère de l'Économie, des Finances et de l'Emploi. "Avis de mise en consultation d'une demande de modification du cahier des charges d'une appellation d'origine protégée concernant la dénomination « Parmigiano Reggiano » (fromage)."*Bulletin Officiel de la Concurrence, de la Consommation et de la Répression des Fraudes*, no. 2003-01, January 31, 2003.
https://www.economie.gouv.fr/files/files/directions_services/dgccrf/boccrf/03_01/a0010012.htm

— Moreau, Claude. "Nomenclature des Penicillium utiles a la préparation du Camembert." *Le Lait* 59, no. 585–586 (1979): 219–233.
https://doi.org/10.1051/lait:1979585-58611

— Pergament, Danielle. "Going to the Source for a Sacred Italian Cheese." *New York Times*, January 3, 2018.
https://www.nytimes.com/2018/01/03/travel/pecorino-di-pienza-cheese-tuscany-italy.html

— Petridou, Elia. "Au pays de la feta." *Ethnologie française* 35, no. 2 (2005): 255.
https://doi.org/10.3917/ethn.052.0255

— Petroni, Agostino. "Burrata: The Surprising Origin of Italy's Creamy Cheese." *BBC Travel*, September 29, 2020.
https://www.bbc.com/travel/article/20200928-the-surprising-origin-of-burrata-cheese

— Pichler, Andreas, ed. *Planet Milk.* ARTE Eikon, Miramonte/Magnetfilm, 2017.
https://www.netflix.com/title/80234791

— Les Produits Laitiers. "Connaissez-vous... les fromages forts?" October 25, 2022.
https://www.produits-laitiers.com/connaissez-vous-les-fromages-forts/

——."Question (pas) bête: pourquoi y a-t-il un papier autour des petits suisses?" October 26, 2022.
https://www.produits-laitiers.com/question-pas-bete-pourquoi-ya-t-il-un-papier-autour-des-petits-suisses/

— Raim, Laura. "Faut-il libérer les animaux domestiques? Les idées larges avec Valérie Chansigaud." *ARTE*, 2023. Video, 21:59.
https://www.arte.tv/fr/videos/113629-001-A/faut-il-liberer-les-animaux-domestiques/

— Ramet, J. P., and Food and Agriculture Organization of the United Nations. "La fromagerie et les variétés de fromages du bassin Méditerranéen."
https://ftpmirror.your.org/pub/misc/cd3wd/1005/_ag_cheese_mediterranean_fr_unfao_lp_105090_.pdf

— Reseau Fromages de Terroirs. "Colloque Fromages au lait cru, entre risques et bénéfices: la diversité au cœur du débat." January 30, 2020.
https://www.rmtfromagesdeterroirs.com/colloque-fromages-au-lait-cru/

— Sélosse, Marc-André. "Les Aliments fermentés." Ver de Terre Production. Filmed February 2019 at the Rencontres Internationales de l'Agriculture du Vivant. Video, 27:00.
https://wiki.tripleperformance.fr/wiki/Les_Aliments_Fermentés_-_Marc-André_SÉLOSSE

— Seminel, Laurent. *Le livre blanc du Brie de Meaux & de Melun.* Fromages & Chefs, 2016.
https://www.hotellerie-restauration.ac-versailles.fr/IMG/pdf/fromages_et_chefs._livre_blanc._brie.pdf

— Siniscalchi, Valeria, and Franco Zecchin. "Conservation et production de la valeur du Fiore Sardo." *Techniques & Culture*, no. 69 (2018): 56–73.
https://doi.org/10.4000/tc.8807

— Slow Food International. "An ABC of Balkan Cheeses." September 23, 2013.
https://www.slowfood.com/an-abc-of-balkan-cheeses/

— Thieulin, Gustave. Review of *Technologie du lait (constitution, récolte et transformation)*, by Roger Veisseyre. *Bulletin de L'Académie Vétérinaire de France* 129, no. 2 (1976): 171–172.
https:// www.persee.fr/doc/bavf_0001-4192_1976_num_129_2_6730

— Vallerand, François, Jean-Paul Dubeuf, and Konstantinos Tsiboukas. "Le lait de brebis et de chevre en Méditerranée et dans les Balkans: diversité des situations locales et des perspectives sectorielles." *Cahiers Agricultures* 16, no. 4 (July 2007): 258–264.
https://doi.org/10.1684/agr.2007.0111

— Vuitton, D. A., A. Divaret-Chauveau, M. Dalphin, J. Laplante, E. Von Mutius, and J. Dalphin. "Protection contre l'allergie par l'environnement de la ferme: en 15 ans, qu'avons-nous appris de la cohorte européenne « PASTURE »?" *Bulletin de l'Académie Nationale de Médecine* 203, no. 7 (October 2019): 618–630.
https://doi.org/10.1016/j.banm.2019.05.020

— Warmedahl, Trevor (@milktrekker).
https://www.instagram.com/milk_trekker/

——. "Exploring the Wide World of Rennet." *Culture: The Word on Cheese*, June 7, 2023.
https://culturecheesemag.com/stories/research-into-the-wide-world-of-rennet/

— Yang, Yimin, Anna Shevchenko, Andrea Knaust, Idelisi Abuduresule, Wenying Li, Xingjun Hu, Changsui Wang, and Andrej Shevchenko. "Proteomics Evidence for Kefir Dairy in Early Bronze Age China." *Journal of Archaeological Science* 45, no. 1 (May 2014): 178–186.
https://doi.org/10.1016/j.jas.2014.02.005

Index

Page numbers in **bold** indicate recipes

——

AB (Agriculture Biologique), 165, 179
Abbaye de Citeaux, 110–14
Abondance, 23, 140–42
    Fondue Savoyarde, **247**
acetic acid, 30
Aligot, **202–3**
allergies, 179
Allgäuer Emmentaler, 143
alpage, 135–38, 281
annatto, 28, 30, 75, 84, 117, 281
AOC/AOP (Appellation d'Origine Contrôlée/ Protégée), 164, 179, 281
Appenzeller®, 141–42
artisanal, 281
Asiago, 141
Axridda di Escalaplano, 155

——

Baked Camembert, **188–89**
Baked Mont d'Or, **198–99**
baladi, 16
Banon, 12, 66, 67
Bargkass, 111
Beaufort, 11, 134–39
    Beaufort Chalet d'Alpage, 15, 136, 139
    Beaufort, Pear, and Ginger Crumble, **272–73**
    Fondue Savoyarde, **247**
bell peppers: Spinach and Bell Pepper Pastilla, **226–27**
Bengali Cheese Sweets, **260–61**
Beurre de Bresse, 101
Beyaz peynir, 16, 47
Bieno Sirenje, 16
Bijeni sir, 47
Bleu d'Auvergne, 95–98
Bleu de Gex, 26, 99
Bleu de Laqueuille, 76, 95–98
Bleu de Termignon, 93, 127–31
Bleu des Causses, 95–98
Bleu du Queyras, 99
Blintzes, Cheese, **262–63**
Boeren-Leidse met sleutels, 115
Bosson maceré, 102
Bouillon de ravioles, **204–5**
Branza de Burduf, 16
Brazilian Cheese Bread, **224–25**
bread
    Brazilian Cheese Bread, **224–25**
    Georgian Cheese-Filled Bread, **216–17**
    Grilled Cheese Sandwich, **214–15**
    Welsh Rarebit, **244–45**

Breaded Fresh Goat Cheese with Spiced Quince Paste, **222–23**
breuil, 57–58
Brie, 10, 11, 76–79
    Brie de Coulommiers, 76
    Brie de Meaux, 23, 76–79
    Brie de Melun, 76–78
Brillat-Savarin, 69–72
Brioche à la tome fraîche, **270–71**
brocciu, 57, 59, 60–61, 98
    Brocciu-Stuffed Sardines, **234–35**
    Corsican Cheesecake, **258–59**
Brousse du Rove, 13, 15, 24, 57
burrata, 23, 51–54
buying cheese, 164–65, 179

——

Cabrales, 127–30
caciocavallo, 159–62
    Caciocavallo Silano, 161
Cacioricotta, 57
Caerphilly, 123–26
caillebotte, 45–46
    Caillebottes à la Chardonnette, **28**
calcium carbonate, 30
calcium chloride, 29
Calenzana, 83, 84
Camembert, 10, 11, 23, 76–81
    Baked Camembert, **188–89**
    Camembert de Normandie, 33, 76–81
cancoillotte, 100–103
Cantal, 23, 119–22
    Red Kuri Squash Stuffed with Spelt and Cantal, **250–51**
Castelmagno, 127–30
cave, 38–39, 97–98, 281
Cervelle de canut, **184–85**
Chabichou du Poitou, 12, 65, 66
Chaource, 69–72
Charolais, 65, 66
Chavignol, 65, 66
Cheddar, 15, 17, 23, 123–26
    Cheddar Crackers, **190–91**
    Grilled Cheese Sandwich, **214–15**
    Mac and Cheese, **220–21**
    Puff Pastry Cheese Straws, **252–53**
    Quesadillas, **232–33**
    Welsh Rarebit, **244–45**
cheddaring, 37, 281
Cheese Blintzes, **262–63**
cheese boards, 166–68
Cheese Sauce, **236–37**
Cheese Straws, **252–53**
Cheese-Filled Ravioli in Broth, **204–5**
Cheesy Mashed Potatoes, **202–3**
cheese spread, 100–103
    Lyon-Style Herbed Cheese Spread, **184–85**

Cheesecake, **256–57**
    Corsican Cheesecake, **258–59**
cheesemaking, 7–17, 20–29, 33–39
    acidification, 35
    affinage, 38–39, 281
    coagulation (curdling), 35–36
    curds, 36–37, 281
    draining, 36
    molding, 37
    pressing, 37
    salting, 38
    thermization, 34
Cheshire, 123–25
chèvre, 64–68, 281
    Breaded Fresh Goat Cheese with Spiced Quince Paste, **222–23**
    Four-Cheese Pizza, **230–31**
    fresh, 45
    Marinated Goat Cheese, **194–95**
    Quesadillas, **232–33**
Chevrotin, 90
Chimay, 113
citric acid, 29
coatings, 30
colorings, 30
Comté, 23, 136
    Fondue Savoyarde, **247**
Corsican Cheesecake, **258–59**
Crackers, Cheddar, **190–91**
cream cheese, 44–46
    Cheese Blintzes, **262–63**
    Cheesecake, **256–57**
    Smoked Mackerel and Fresh Cheese Dip, **192–93**
Crème de Bresse, 101
Crème de fromage. *See* cheese spread
Crémet d'Anjou, **276–77**
Crottin de Chavignol, 66
Crumble, Beaufort, Pear, and Ginger, **272–73**
cultures, 25–27, 34
cutting cheese, 165–66

——

Dangke, 17
Domiati, 47–49
    Fresh Cheese with Chili-Tahini Sauce, **196–97**
DOP. *See* AOC/AOP
Double Gloucester, 125
Dumplings, Georgian Cheese and Herb-Stuffed, **218–19**

——

Edam, 115–17
    Quesadillas, **232–33**
Emmental, 11, 136, 143–46, 178
    Allgäuer Emmentaler, 143
    Brazilian Cheese Bread, **224–25**
    Cheese Sauce, **236–37**

Emmental de Savoie, 143–44
Emmental Français Est-Central, 143–44
    Fondue, **246–47**
    Fondue Savoyarde, **247**
    Georgian Cheese-Filled Bread, **216–17**
    Grilled Cheese Sandwich, **214–15**
    Puff Pastry Cheese Straws, **252–53**
    Spinach and Bell Pepper Pastilla, **226–27**
    Veal Cordon Bleu, **208–9**
Époisses, 12, 23, 73–75
Escalopes cordon bleu, **208–9**
estive, *estivage*, 281
"eyes," 26, 115, 135, 141–47, 281

——

faisselle, 45–46
farmstead/farmhouse (*fermier*), 13, 281
fats, 176–77
feta, 47–50, 98
    feta martini, 50
    Fresh Cheese with Chili-Tahini Sauce, **196–97**
    Georgian Cheese-Filled Bread, **216–17**
Feuilletés au fromage, **252–53**
Fiadone, **258–59**
Fior di latte, 51
Fiore Sardo, 11, 37, 107, 155, 157
fish
    Brocciu-Stuffed Sardines, **234–35**
    Smoked Mackerel and Fresh Cheese Dip, **192–93**
Flamiche au maroilles, **210–11**
flavored fresh cheeses, 44–46
flavorings, 30
Fondue, **246–47**
Fontina, 11, 141–42
forage, 281
fort de Bethune, 102
fort de Ventoux, 102
foudjou, 102
Four-Cheese Pizza, **230–31**
Fourme d'Ambert, 95–98, 130
Fourme de Montbrison, 127
Fourme de Rochefort, 119–21
Fresh Cheese with Chili-Tahini Sauce, **196–97**
Fresh Sheep's Milk Cheese Balls, **186–87**
Fresh Tome Brioche, **270–71**
Frittata, Smoked Scamorza, **212–13**
Fromage à la pie, 45
fromage blanc, 44–46

Cheesecake, **256–57**
Crémet d'Anjou, **276–77**
Lyon-Style Herbed
    Cheese Spread, **184–85**
Smoked Mackerel and
    Fresh Cheese Dip,
    192–93
Fromage de chèvre mariné,
    194–95
fromage fort, 101–103
fromage fort de la Croix
    Rousse, 102
fruitière, 9–10, 89, 136, 281

Gebnah, **196–97**
Geitost, 57
Georgian Cheese and
    Herb-Stuffed
    Dumplings, **218–19**
Georgian Cheese-Filled
    Bread, **216–17**
gerle, 26, 121–22, 281
goat cheese, 64–68
    Breaded Fresh Goat
        Cheese with Spiced
        Quince Paste, **222–23**
    Marinated Goat Cheese,
        194–95
    See also chèvre
Gorgonzola, 15, 23, 91–94
Gouda, 15, 17, 115–18
    Gouda Nougat, **266–67**
Grana Padano, 93, 147–52
greuil, 57–58
Grilled Cheese Sandwich,
    214–15
Gris de Lille, 83
Gruyère, 23, 101, 134–38, 144
    Fondue, **246–47**
    Fondue "*moitié-moitié*,"
        247
    Fondue Savoyarde, **247**
    Four-Cheese Pizza,
        230–31
    Gruyère de France, 135
Gwell, 13, 34

halloumi, 16, 51–55
health benefits of cheese,
    175–79
Herve, 83–84

IGP (Indication
    Géographique
    Protégée), 165, 281
Imeruli, 17

Jben, 16
Jibneh arabieh, 16
jonchée, 28, 46

kashkaval, 160
khachapuri, **216–17**
Khinkali qvelit, **218–19**
Kostromskoy, 17
Kunefe, **268–69**

L'Etivaz, 134–39
"La Manigodine," 87
La Trappe, 113
La Vache Qui Rit (The
    Laughing Cow), 11,
    101–102, 146

Label Rouge, 165
Laguiole, 11, 23, 119–22
    Laguiole "Buron," 122
laitier, 112, 281
Lancashire, 123–26
Langres, 10, 23, 73–75
Leerdamer, 143
Limburger, 83
Livarot, 10, 23, 83–84
Lyon-Style Herbed Cheese
    Spread, **184–85**
lysozyme, 30

Maasdam, 115
Mac and Cheese, **220–21**
Macônnais, 65–66
Mahón-Menorca, 111
Manchego, 15, 23, 107
Manouri, 57–58
maquée, 58
Marinated Goat Cheese,
    194–95
Maroilles, 76, 83–84
    Maroilles Tart, **210–11**
mascarpone, 59
    Tiramisu, **264–65**
Masdaam, 143
microbes, 34, 178–79
milk, 19–25, 33–34
    fat, 33
    preparing, 33
    ultrafiltered, 34
mimolette, 115–17
Minas, 17
Mishavin, 16
mites, 39, 117, 281
Mizithra, 58
Mont d'Or, 23, 87–90
    Baked Mont d'Or,
        198–99
    Fondue au Vacherin
        Mont-d'Or, **247**
Mont des Cats, 113
Monterey Jack, 17
Morbier, 23, 110–14
morge, 29, 137, 281
mozzarella, 51–54
    Four-Cheese Pizza,
        230–31
    Turkish Sweet Cheese
        Pastry, **268–69**
Munster, 23, 82–86
    Munster made with
        Vosgian cow's milk, 85

Nangis, 76
natural cheese, 26–27, 281
Neufchâtel, 23, 69–71
Niolo, 83, 84
Noord-Hollandse
    Edammer, 115
Noord-Hollandse Gouda,
    115
Nougat, Gouda, **266–67**

Orval, 111, 113, 114
Ossau-Iraty, 98, 107, 109

Pallone di Gravina, 159
Pancakes, Ricotta, **274–75**
paneer, 17
panir, 16
Pão de queijo, **224–25**

Parmesan (Parmigiano
    Reggiano), 23, 93,
    147–52
    Beaufort, Pear, and
        Ginger Crumble,
        272–73
    Brazilian Cheese Bread,
        224–25
    Parmesan Soufflé,
        238–39
    Parmesan Tuiles, **242–43**
    Pesto, **228–29**
    Puff Pastry Cheese
        Straws, **252–53**
    Spaghetti Carbonara,
        206–7
    Veal Cordon Bleu, **208–9**
    See also Grana Padano
pasta
    Cheese-Filled Ravioli in
        Broth, **204–5**
    Mac and Cheese, **220–21**
    Spaghetti Carbonara,
        206–7
pasta filata, 15, 51–54, 160,
    282
pasteurization, 10, 34
Pastilla, Spinach and Bell
    Pepper, **226–27**
pasture, 282
PDO. *See* AOC/AOP
pears: Beaufort, Pear, and
    Ginger Crumble,
    272–73
pecorino, 153–57
    Pecorino Balze
        Volterrane, 153
    Pecorino Crotonese, 155
    Pecorino del Monte Poro,
        155
    Pecorino di Filiano, 155
    Pecorino di Picinisco, 155
    Pecorino Romano, 11, 23,
        153–57
    Pecorino Sardo, 153–55
    Pecorino Siciliano,
        153–55
    Pecorino Toscano,
        153–55
    Pesto, **228–29**
pélardon, 65, 66
Penicillium, 26, 84, 282
pérail, 65
Pesto, **228–29**
pétafine, 102
Petit Suisse, 45–46
PGI. *See* IGP
picodon, 11, 65–66
Pizza, Four-Cheese, **230–31**
Pont-l'Évêque, 10, 23, 83, 84
Port Salut, 11, 112
Poshekhonsky, 17
potassium chloride, 30
potatoes
    Cheesy Mashed Potatoes,
        202–3
    Raclette, **248–49**
    Smoked Scamorza
        Frittata, **212–13**
    Tartiflette, **240–41**
Pouligny-Saint-Pierre, 65,
    66
pourri bressan, 102

preservatives, 30
processing aids, 29–31
proteins, 177
proteolysis, 39, 69, 75, 89,
    93, 282
provola, 158–62
    provolone, 11, 159
    Provolone Valpadena,
        160
    Puff Pastry Cheese Straws,
        252–53

Quesadillas, **232–33**
Queso Manchego.
    See Manchego
Quince Paste, Spiced,
    222–23

raclette, 112, 142, 167
    Four-Cheese Pizza,
        230–31
    Raclette, **248–49**
    Raclette de Savoie, 111–13
    Raclette du Valais, 141–42
Ragusano, 159–61
Ravioli in Broth, Cheese-
    Filled, **204–5**
raw milk, 12, 25, 33–35, 179,
    282
reblochon, 23, 90
    Tartiflette, **240–41**
Recuite, 58
Red Kuri Squash Stuffed
    with Spelt and Cantal,
    250–51
Red Leicester, 123–25
rennet, 27–28, 35–37, 49, 282
ricotta, 56–59
    Cheese Blintzes, **262–63**
    Georgian Cheese and
        Herb-Stuffed
        Dumplings, **218–19**
    ricotta infornata, 162
    Ricotta Pancakes, **274–75**
    ricotta salata, 162
Rigotte de Condrieu, 65, 66
rigouta, 59
rind, 282
Rocamadour, 65, 66
Roquefort, 10–11, 23, 95–99
rubing, 17
rushan, 17

Saint Paulin, 11
Saint-Marcellin, 65
Saint-Nectaire, 23, 107–109
    Fresh Tome Brioche,
        270–71
Sainte Maure de Touraine,
    65–66
Salers, 13, 23, 119–22
salt, 29, 38, 178
Sandesh, **260–61**
Sardines farcies au brocciu,
    234–35
Sassenage, 99
Sauce, Cheese, **236–37**
Sbrinz, 11, 147, 148
    Swiss Chard Tart, **278–79**
scamorza, 30, 51, 54
    Smoked Scamorza
        Frittata, **212–13**
seasonal/seasonality, 282

Selles-sur-Cher, 65, 66
sérac, 57, 58, 59
Serra da Estrela, 23
serving cheese, 168–69
    choosing breads, 170
    pairing drinks, 172–74
Sheep's milk cheese, 19,
    47–50, 109, 153–57
    Fresh Sheep's Milk
        Cheese Balls, **186–87**
Shepherd's Fiore Sardo.
    See Fiore Sardo
silage, 24, 25, 30, 175, 282
Sirene, 47
Slovenská Parenica, 161
Smoked Mackerel and
    Fresh Cheese Dip,
    192–93
Smoked Scamorza Frittata,
    212–13
Soufflé, Parmesan, **238–39**
Soumaintrain, 73–75
Spaghetti Carbonara, **206–7**
Spinach and Bell Pepper
    Pastilla, **226–27**
Squash, Red Kuri, Stuffed
    with Spelt and Cantal,
    250–51

standardization, 12, 282
Stilton, 127–30
Stinking Bishop, 23, 83, 86
Storico Ribelle, 135
storing cheese, 175
stracchino, 91–94
    Stracchino all'antica
        delle valli orobiche, 91
strachitunt, 91–94
Stresa Convention, 11, 136,
    144, 148, 282
sugars, 176
Sulguni, 14, 17
Sweets, Bengali Cheese,
    260–61
Swiss Chard Tart, **278–79**
syneresis, 36, 155, 282
—
Taleggio, 91–94
Tartiflette, **240–41**
tarts
    Maroilles Tart, **210–11**
    Swiss Chard Tart, **278–79**
tasting cheese, 168–70
Tête de Moine, 141–42
Timanoix, 113
Tiramisu, **264–65**
Tome de la Brigue, 108

Tome de la Vésubie, 108
Tome des Bauges, 107, 108
Tome Fraîche de l'Aubrac,
    122
    Cheesy Mashed Potatoes,
        202–3
Tomme de Savoie, 106–9
tomme fort de Savoie, 102
tommes "*d'estive*," 13, 109
Torta del Casar, 23
Tourte aux blettes, **278–79**
Traditional Welsh
    Caerphilly/Caerffili,
    126
Trappe d'Echourgnac, 113
Trentingrana, 147, 151
Tulum, 16
Tuiles, Parmesan, **242–43**
Turkish Sweet Cheese
    Pastry, **268–69**
turnout, 282
turophile, 282
typicity, 26, 67, 282
tyrosine, 39, 115, 143, 147,
    282
—
Uglichsky, 17
Urdă, 57, 58

vacherin, 87–90
    Fondue Fribourgeois, **247**
    Fondue "*moitié-moitié*,"
        247
    Vacherin d'Abondance,
        87
    Vacherin des Aillons, 87
    Vacherin des Aravis, 87
    Vacherin du Haut-Doubs,
        87
    Vacherin Mont d'Or,
        87–90
Valençay, 65, 66
Veal Cordon Bleu, **208–9**
venachese, 83, 84
Vieux-Lille, 83
vitamins and minerals, 178
—
Welsh Rarebit, **244–45**
West Country Farmhouse
    Cheddar, 126
Westmalle, 113
whey, 36–37, 58–59, 282

Acknowledgments

MERCI!

Mathieu would like to thank Anne-Laure, his wife, for being a constant source of support and inspiration. Without her, he would never have had the courage to write so many pages.

Anne-Laure would like to thank Mathieu for his sunny disposition, his energy, his passion for cheese, and his "lactic" love.

The authors wish to extend their heartfelt thanks to:

Timothé, for his patience and understanding, despite the fact that he doesn't yet fully appreciate all of the cheeses his dad sells.

Their dear parents and families, who have given them invaluable help.

Nico, for his technical revisions and for their cheese projects together.

Estérelle, for helping them to get started and for her reassuring encouragement.

Clélia, for her constant good cheer and kind feedback.

The cheesemakers who work wonders every day: Nico, Marika, Laëtitia, Aloïse, Elsa, Mireille, Jean-André, Jean-Bernard, Cécile, Cédric, Lionel, David, Jean-François and Bertrand, Émilie, Catherine, Lucie and Gallien, Anneke, Marieke, and many more, as well as all those they have forgotten and everyone who champions these exceptional cheeses.

All of their friends, who they haven't seen much of in recent months (except at their wedding). They can't wait to get together again for a giant karaoke extravaganza.

Jonathan Cohen, who penned the song that they listened to as they finished this book. As he croons, "*Nous ne regrettons rien*"—we regret nothing. "*Pas du tout*"—not in the very least.